I, CROWLEY

Almost The BEAST's Last Will, and Testament.
666
by Snoo Wilson.

The Further & even more Abominable Confessions
of Edward Alexander Crowley, Gentleman.
Unexpurgated.

Copyright © 1997 and 1999
by Snoo Wilson and Mandrake of Oxford
second edition

All rights reserved. No part of this work may be reproduced or utilized in any form by any means electronic or mechanical, including *xerography, photocopying, microfilm*, and *recording,* or by any information storage system without permission in writing from the author.

Published by
Mandrake of Oxford
PO Box 250
OXFORD
OX1 1AP (UK)

A CIP catalogue record for this book is available from the British Library and the US Library of Congress.

ISBN 1 869928 457

Also by Snoo Wilson and published by Mandrake of Oxford
More Light - a play about the heretic Giordano Bruno.

Contents

0	The Fool.	5
1	The Magus	32
II	The Priestess	36
III	The Empress.	44
IV	The Emperor	60
V	The Hierophant	82
VI.	The Lovers	95
VII.	The Chariot	109
VIII.	Justice	121
IX	The Hermit	137
X	Fortune	146
XI	Lust	156
XII.	The Hanged Man	167
XIII	Death	176
XIV	Art, or Temperance	189
XV	The Devil	201
XVI	The Blasted Tower	213
XVII	The Star	223
XVIII	The Moon	230
XIX	The Sun	234
XX	The Last Judgement	239
XXI	The Universe	245

'And yet The Beast goes always masked:
it cannot be his face that looks like mine'

Angela Carter, *The Tiger's Bride*

0 The Fool.

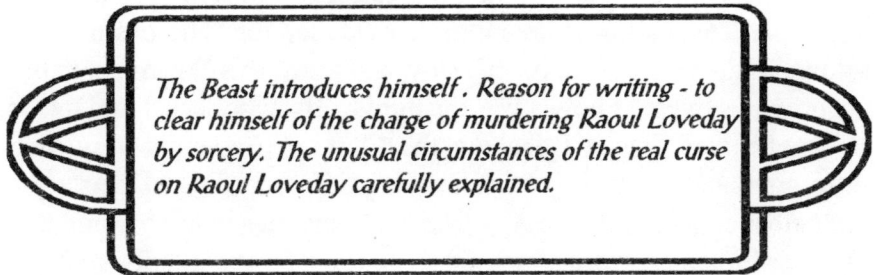

The Beast introduces himself. Reason for writing - to clear himself of the charge of murdering Raoul Loveday by sorcery. The unusual circumstances of the real curse on Raoul Loveday carefully explained.

Dearly Beloved-
A reputation is the very devil of a thing to keep puffed and permanently pumped up: likewise, a Jade Stem has the same tendency to go away to almost nothing just as one's partner is warming to a dialogue with their Holy Guardian Angel.

The antique wisdom of China professes two qualities of jade. The white jade is the highest, for it is from the outpourings of the mystical dragons whose energies arise from earth and are plunged into her again. The excitement of this caress in the earth produces the best white jade.

The Chinese, when they wish to seek out this precious semen of the gods, send barefoot virgins into the mountainous spring waters in springtime, when the snows melt and the torrent fiercely turns over rocks and stones. The white jade, naturally, is attracted to the virgins' feet.

It is unfortunate that the rulers of that great land are currently undone, by veniality and lechery. Shrouded in the fug in their opium dens, they are unable to comprehend the energies which their ascetic sages have located, within the earth. It is left to me to bring the wisdom of the East, which comprehends it not, to the West.

6 Snoo Wilson

White Jade.

What the Americans call jiss'm, from the primal forces that created time, space and our puny planet, one among a million million stars. White-Jade-as-Jissum is the tangible evidence for 'The Eternal Unfolding of the Universe to Itself'. How do I know this? I can remember my previous lives[1], is how. I was the thief Kelly, who scried for Doctor Dee, who was Queen Elizabeth the First of England's very own astrologer, and set the day for her coronation according to the stars. I remember conversing with Angels using a chequer-board of numbers, spelling Enochian words backwards so their power did not split the universe. Dee had great regard for my Word. Kelly (or I) laid his cropped ears upon his master's pillow and tupped Dee's wife, while at the same instance, the scholarly Dee took Mistress Kelly; for Kelly (or I) had passed on to my Master instructions from Angels that our wives should be held in common. O Life! O, Ages! I feel my manhood shuggle under my sporran, as I contemplate all my former lives, under the slowly stirring, ever-awakening milky dream of the heavens.

But back to the classroom, to slow the detumescence of the unlovely minute. The shaven headed Instructor, Number 666 patiently awaits the Moment, when each Jade Stem will be grasped by its owner; yea, even by the most sluggish self-manipulators at the back of the class. But the night cometh when no man will work. I am old as I write this tonight. Soon I may be called to the Other Side, taking any residual wisdom with me. What I have to say is - Live, my pupils! All I have to say to you is - Live!

I explained the workings of jade in detail to a mistress of mine, who went (and for all I know, still goes) under the name of Roddie Minor. Roddie was my sexual amplifier, to the higher realms of existence. We 'made love'- to use popular parlance - in New York. Head down, Roddie Minor, and concentrate on what you are doing, or you will stay

---

1 *The skill required takes some years practice, but is well worth it. A.C.*

behind until you have produced enough White Jade. It was during the 1914-1918 conflict. Roddie herself later fell in the trenches of her own ignorance and baseness. In spite of her claims to be a Thelemite, that is, to be above sexual jealousy, she could never suppress her own feelings in that regard, and we parted.

My honeymoon with my first wife, Rose coincided with the bringing of the *Book of the Law* to an ungrateful humanity. It was in 1904. It was ten years before the Arch-Duke Ferdinand took it like a man from an assassin, close to a wrought iron bridge in Sarajevo, an act which started the Great War. That turgid war proved to me the rightness beyond a shadow of a doubt of the writings of the *Book of the Law*. I had 'taken down' the *Book of the Law* when I was in Egypt, newly married. Aiwass dictated and I wrote it down. Dictation suits his style, too. *The Book of the Law*! I do not insist that you purchase a copy, you may steal one if you are moved to. But remember the cautionary proverb which goes:-

Buy the egg of a black hen without haggling.[2]

I am sometimes astonished at the strength and wisdom of these ancient occult *grimoires*. Another ancient tradition has it, that the more you know, the more you know *nothing*. Not even the price of a black hen. I'd go along with that, most nights. There appears to be some internal contradiction here in the wisdom of the Ancients that will have to be resolved another time.

Back to the sad case of Roddie Minor, Scarlet Woman (failed):- In New York, during the Great War (as we called it then) Roddie accompanied me on many of my mystical searchings, and rarely misbehaved. To say she was a companion of the highest order would

---

2 Nowadays, with so many people buying eggs from shops without the least idea where eggs come from, it may be necessary to buy the whole chicken first, in order to make sure that the egg you are purchasing comes from a truly black hen.

however be misleading. Her appetites were vigorous, her turn of phrase loud and repetitious when in coition. She was a Scarlet Woman, of sorts. That from me, is a compliment. But frequently Roddie forgot what we were meant to be doing and simply indulged herself in 'a good pump' at my expense. I noticed more and more that her attention to spirituality was in decline, though she denied it vehemently. Finally I had to call a halt to our sessions. The reason I gave her was correct. I cannot allow liars to associate with me, once they have been found out. The phlebitis in my leg was made worse in these sessions, and still throbs a little, to this day.

But I don't blame Roddie. On the contrary, all feuds are anathema to me, and I have not a malicious bone in my body. I would never micturate, sneeringly on those literary giants of the yellow press who have in the past entangled their well-licked indelible pencils with the silver thread of my existence. The comic contradictions of denigrators' various 'takes' on my character and actions are simply the price paid for individuality, and can be safely ignored by seekers after truth: Christ, after all had four biographers at the outset, and none of them could even agree how many loaves and fishes there were, let alone whether his foreskin went to heaven along with the rest of him.

In Chinese whispers, lips are blistered.
All I want - you buy my sister.

I do, however, want to set the record straight about one calumny that has been imputed to me. Set it up in 24 point Roman Bold, if you please, to lord it over the text.

I *never* killed Raoul Loveday with a magic spell. Never, never, never!

This wicked rumour was started because I had drawn up his astrological birth chart. I spotted that Raoul, who was weak with enteritis, was about to have what astrologers call a 'malefic transit'. I was asked when he might be in greatest danger of death by his wife.

Betty May was a Chelsea 'model' some years his senior. I told Betty, and it came to pass that on the hour and the day I had specified, at four in the afternoon, he embraced his Will to die.

Betty went back to England alone. When Beaverbrook serialised her autobiography, which was full of accounts of cocaine-fuelled orgies with soldiers on leave, the editors ignored all that. They took the account she had written of me, which was hostile, while still respectful of my powers, and turned it into the most atrocious sensationalist tosh.

They even suggested that Leah, who was my Scarlet Woman during our stay at the Abbey above Cefalu, had been forced, by me, to have sexual intercourse with a goat. This is simply not true - it is like saying I murdered babies.[3]

It is true Raoul's death was not the only one to visit my fledgling community. Little Poupée died at the Abbey too. Strangely, thirty years on, I've absolutely no idea what became of her mother.

My life has been peppered with the cases of people who were unable to cope with the heightened sensibility that Love Under Law placed on their nervous system. The same is true of the stimulants I used to rise to the astral plane.[4] For my Scarlet Woman Leah, an eighth of a grain of heroin, far from preparing her for the Great Work, would simply render her comatose.[5]

The teeth with which I bestowed on her my Serpent's Kiss, drawing

---

3   A misunderstanding that arose when I made a joke about the loss of male semen in an operation of the XI°. The unjust smear has clung to me, like ivy to the wall of Trinity College Cambridge, where I once was an undergraduate. The college refused to have me back to lecture them, as a direct result of calumnies like these. Yes, I hear you say, but Socrates was also held guilty of corrupting Athenian youth, was he not? A.C.

4   Anhanolium Lewinii, a peyote extract that I introduced to a number of people in the so called 'literary set' was wasted on Katherine Mansfield, a pox-ridden New Zealander and self-confessed short story writer. She said it made her sick. A.C.

5   It is a sad business when drugs are redeemed solely for their properties as vulgar anaesthetics, the basest function of them all, where the questing soul is concerned. A.C.

blood, are long gone. I hope for her own sake Leah took herself back to America. I should probably spit at her today, if our paths crossed in the Wandering Waste.

I refute the charges against my constraint of Leah, thus:

1. I would never force someone to do something against their Will. That is against the Law of Thelema. There are few laws, but that is one of them.
2. If Leah, a mature woman, chose to enact a symbolic coupling with the animal known throughout history as an emblem of lust, this was entirely in line with her own Will, and her own self-appointed position as Scarlet Woman.[6]

In any case, the squeamish can breathe again. There was a goat at the Abbey, but it was unwilling to perform its duties. Its Will, if you like, lay elsewhere. I wonder what they would have said if they had found out what Raoul and I really were up to together before that? There are no names for these deeds in what are called 'Family newspapers', and I do not know if the reader is 'gentle', in the spirit of nineteenth century parlour fiction, or properly Nietzschean. Do you dare to soar, dare to understand me?

I invited Raoul Loveday and his wife Betty May to visit my community in Cefalù, for the greater enrichment of their souls. Sometimes, death arrives as the price of that enrichment. I will not lie simply because I wish to protect my reputation.

As for my writings on *Magick* - there are many, too many, perhaps, and this last voice is designed to introduce them, even if it does not (my

---

[6] The role of the Scarlet Woman, in case you were wondering, was to 'be loud and adulterous, and wear finery'. Leah, I recall was wearing her magnificent Abbey cloak, and some very striking earrings at the time. The goat appeared to be unimpressed. AC

greatest wish) *supersede* them altogether. How is that possible? It is very possible, if not very likely that it should happen in a lifetime. I will demonstrate.

¶ A writer might, by an act of *will* summarise everything that had gone before in his life in a simple sentence.

¶ This condensation occurs by a process akin to the reductive sigils produced by the likes of Austin O. Spare.[7]

¶ When the correct mental preparation has been undergone, success at summarising the procedure will be assured. Here endeth the lesson.

You want more, or you don't believe me. Why are you reading this? Why? Ask me, have I had one or more reductive trances myself, in which I saw my own birth and death, its part in the great cosmic system?

I should have to answer, a myriad. Every day is a tribute to the brimming cosmology of the Filled Cup of Life, from which we all flow, and into which we must all, regardless of unusual practices, return; —What Victor Neuberg (A poor poet, but a poet nonetheless) was shocked to hear me refer humorously to our arrangements to contact the Great Unnameable as 'The Oneness of All Buggers'.[8]

Victor was never able to admit that once he laid himself open to being possessed by Pan. The pain to him caused by Victor's varicose testicles flapping on my rump are probably the cause, in him at any rate, of the reluctance to admit the fierce joy that was available to us both, under the African moon, in the sun or on the burning sands. His

---

7 *Immeasurably inferior to my work, but worth mentioning as an example in this, which whether I or the reader likes it or not, will have to serve as another general introduction to the Magickal process. A.C.*

8 *The poet Victor Neuberg was once a close companion of A.C. [A Certain Magus], who he later abjured with great horror. There are a number of accounts of the quarrel, including one where Frater Perdurabo convinced the younger man that he had turned him into a camel. A.C.*

hitherto unadventurous and ritually circumcised Stem nosing comically into glory *per vas nefandum*. Spinning the wheel of my lowest chakra till it sparked. What a dance we did that day!

And then, some malicious ninny starts the story that what really happened was that I had waved my wand, and turned Victor into a camel. Well, really. There are deeds without names, some of which are clearly impossible.

My frame is small. I am inclined to plumpness, with small hands and am not much above medium height, or dilation. I could never have physically allowed a giant beast of a camel such intimacies, even the chimerical Neuberg-καμιλοσ. ☞

DROMEDARY ARRESTED

Camel In Court.

I hear the publishers shriek :-
'Take it out! Take it out! Zoophilia is forbidden by law.'
Can't these people take a joke? I was mentioning something impossible. 'Accusations of sodomy against persons living are legal dynamite. If proven, you could both go down.' I say:-
'Either arrest the camel, or like Victor's own stem, let it rise free!' I do not care myself, if the League of Stinking Purity is paddling their smegmatic canoes towards us, laden to the gunwales with lawyers already defecating *fasces* of writs in this direction. What the League, and the law can do to me, they have already done. What boots it? I have writ *The Book Of The Law*.

It should be relatively easy to clear oneself of the charge of Wickedest Man in The World, in theory. Let us start at the beginning, that is to say, in the time of the 1920's in the vulgar Christian Annals, which is to say the Jazz Age, when the beat from Africa arrived in

Europe by way of St Louis. In that Beginning, when I was a mere sapling of less than fifty summers, I came into my title in the public eye. I was undone by the newspapers. I was marred, tarred-and-feathered, and barred. 'Hideous Orgies Impossible Of [sic] Description.' Give the man who wrote that headline a raise! How does it happen in this green and pleasant land? I shall tell you.

Lord Beaverbrook is a colonial whose newspapers have done much harm to the common literary level in England. Few today can read, let alone understand, words of more than one syllable. Lord Beaverbrook's scummy editors heard his song, which was of circulation, and so they bestowed the title 'Wickedest Man' on me. Or who knows, since history is written by the last fellow at the typesetter, the Night Editor did it.

Does it matter? My reputation was filleted, dehumanised, and demonised. I sued, but was made bankrupt. Is this sounding familiar? And where Beaverbrook made his waves of ordure, the smaller smut merchants followed. In particular, Horatio Bottomley (well he deserved his name), the owner of a magazine called 'John Bull' felt free to join in too and pillory me.

When Raoul died at my Abbey, they had a crime ready to fit me. It was called 'Murder By Black Magic.' My reflections went as follows:

Should I have claimed in court that I could not perform magic? That would be a lie to save my skin. Aiwass would have seen to it that I was punished. I would never have performed a spell on Raoul. I loved him. Love between men is a 'sin'. It cannot be confessed in public.

Ergo -

My innocence is unprovable in this life, in the present hypocrisy about sexual mores. My tormentors, morally naked, are draped in the only garment that conceals true filth, the folds of British Justice.

My come-uppance was organised by the press machine driven by a man who is a complete sexual hypocrite. Beaverbrook is a promiscuous spanker, a man who has had too many mistresses to count, and yet no one dares name them. Here is a man who enjoys the crack of leather on female flesh, to the hilt. He is in charge of informing the masses, his sway is indisputable: but his twisted passions have run riot, corrupted by his absolute power.

I give you an example.

Beaverbrook got it into his head that the country was going to run out of aluminium for aeroplanes, in the Second World war, and organised the virtual confiscation of every piece of aluminium kitchenware in the land. It was completely unnecessary. But for years, because of him, people have had to cook the family dinner in fire buckets. As for his stable mates, the other Yellow Paper salesmen and horsemen of my private apocalypse, they are no better.

Horatio Bottomley, magazine owner, was by general consent, a 'pillar of society and family values'. If that wasn't bad enough, he was also a Member for Parliament and fund raiser for Our Boys in the Battle against the Bosch.

During the Great War, when I was generally credited with running away to America, Bottomley went up and down England, in no great personal danger, selling War Bonds in vast rallies, so that Our Boys could be machine-gunned by Kaiser Bill in even larger numbers.

Or at any rate, that was what he told the crowds he was doing with their money. In fact, when the police caught up with him, he had trousered the dosh himself, and spent it on hotels and 'love-nests'.

Off he went to chokey.

Always, the greatest struggle is with the self, but I think I deserve a better class of antagonist than I have been pitted against, in this world.

I have suffered, and not just from slander or the lingering pain of not being believed. I have undergone the anguish of oxygen deprivation through asthma, rendered critical over 20,000 feet on

Kangchenjunga. (I don't want anyone in the class to ask who was it who forced me to go up K2, the Five Sacred Peaks, in the first place.) I have undergone the misery of frequently withdrawing from opiates. Nowadays, I find that a quiet life and a regulated dose is probably the best way to a tranquil old age. Friend, I have been there, between the rock and the hard place. I have suffered blows, and harsh words! Loved ones and infants who depart to Eternity unexpectedly! Looking back, I have seen it was their Will to do such a thing. I have lost all my teeth, but what of it? It means I can do things with my tongue now that would make Betty May's organ look like a poor weak thing. Pain has, on occasion awoken levels of perception in me that I would never have reached otherwise. Indeed, without intense suffering I would never have been allowed to achieve the rank of *Ipsissimus*.[9] Like Napoleon, I crowned myself, in mystical communion with the college of Secret Chiefs.

My Spanking Lord Beaverbrook, being immensely wealthy and owning large numbers of newspapers, was able to indulge his 'little vices' without anything being printed against him, in his or indeed anyone else's newspapers. I am not saying that there was anything necessarily wrong in the drunken weekend sessions in hotels where he tied prostitutes up and was permitted to whip their posteriors with a buckled belt till they bled. After all, the tarts got paid. What is very deeply 'wrong' in this picture of traditional depravity is that none of the participants were getting any *spiritual advancement* from the undertaking. Till the Fates sever them from the web of existence, their suffering will be blind.

It might be useful for those who are considering full initiation into

---

9 *A Magickal grade, dearly beloved, absolutely the highest, which I was able to bestow on myself, after being purged by the bereavement of my own child. Allow the smoke from the pipe in Uncle Alec's mouth to wreathe upwards when he talks, and simply listen to the words. All will become clear, in due course. A.C.*

Crowleyanity to break off at this point, and perform a short meditation. I suggest one on Death, XIII in the Tarot sequence. I have had the Tarot pack revised, and it was about time too. Clear of all that medieval mumble-jumble! One day, there will be a little shop near to you, no doubt, which will hold the cards and their esoteric symbols in my new, powerful form. If I am remembered for little else, this will be one of the more important Acts of my life. Few have been able to combine the esoteric knowledge as well as the passion and have succeeded in redefining the Tarot pack. Besides mine, all other packs will slowly fade into insignificance. The cards are also an extremely important artistic record, and I predict that the originals will be worth a great deal of money a hundred years hence. As for the original MS of the *Book of the Law* -

To consider what it is worth on the 'open market' is of course, the trick of the nation of shopkeepers. It steers the text safely past any real consideration of worth. What are the Holy Gospels worth?

To categorise by monetary worth is not, in the end, to think clearly at all.

The Book of the Law: Literature, religion or dogshit?

If a publisher was to be asked for an opinion about The Book as a work of literature, he would have said, perhaps,

'There are too many exclamation marks. The author is an obsessional cryptoid-copraphiliac, suffering from an injured *amour propre*, and an excess of zeal to impress.' Looking at what I have just written, I am inclined to agree, one day out of five. The Book is, to say the least, unusually dense and terse.[10]

But then again, this judgement on its stylistic merits may be the

---

10 *I should say in my defence that the A. Crowley school of Fine Writing has a number of other magnificent examples under its belt - even the 'potboilers' that I wrote to keep the Abbey harridans in wine, henna, opium and cigarettes will have their place one day in literature.*

most frightful *lèse-majestie*, inviting thunder and lightning on my pate, and scrofula upon my balls, like Job.

Who am I, a mere mortal, to dispute style with the Ancients?

Who is to say that the future will not be just as alarming as the Book says, as the world? There are indeed passages in it which I still do not understand. But history has confounded my puny critical standards already. It was when the Zeppelins bombed Yarmouth in the Great War that I realised with a shock that in spite of my own misgivings, I had described the future.

The Book, in short, leaves the puffed-up writings of other social 'prophets' - lower class persons with small heads[11] - standing in the sidelines of history, as well as literature and poetry.

Drugs and Crowleyanity. The unvarnished facts.

Those who desire to take the road to hell do so with the best intentions possible, and I shall not waste ink warning youth about the dangers of addiction. Everyone has assumed D and C go together. I am frequently asked questions about the effects of heroin on potency.

It might be better, at this juncture, to openly admit this drawback to addiction, but then add, 'But is erection, and indeed priapism, the be-all and end-all of life?' I find it leaves the anti-drugs lobby writhing on the floor as it were, clutching their crutches in the painful throes of argument-withdrawal.

Long term, I would say that the effect of heroin, *et al.* on one's Jade Stem is possibly debilitating. But that may be from the greater release of Essence at the inception.

One formula for freedom from narcotic dependency goes: whenever dependency on heroin threatens, switch to cocaine.

Do likewise, when heroin appears to be gaining the upper hand.

---

11 I have not mentioned H.G.Wells yet, and I suggest the editor follows my discretion. A.C.

Over the years I have employed it frequently, and now, in my eightieth decade, I only have the occasional bout of asthma, which one or the other can speedily efface.

In the past, my intake of laudanum, brandy, heroin and cocaine has been, to put it mildly, heroic. Enough to kill a horse, in the words of a Hastings doctor. Nowadays, my regime is of a modesty and regularity which you might expect of a literary gentleman in the prime of his middle age. But - Do What Thou Wilt shall be the whole of The Law.

A retired senior pathologist in Stockport wrote the following enquiry to me, a while back:- 'If Coleridge had been able to follow your drug reduction regime, would we have had a longer 'Kubla Khan'? I think it is the most beautiful poem in the English Language and I am tormented by its brevity.'

I told him, on the back of a dull postcard of the Hastings seafront—'In brief, as for Coleridge: the truth is that the poor fellow could never decide on a final form for 'Kubla Khan'. The story of the Person from Porlock interrupting him is a smokescreen for his own lack of Will, and I am afraid his drugs intake had a great deal to do with it. Yours in haste, A.C.'

Poor Sam! Sleepless, awash with opium, he would stand transfixed by the sight of his own urine in a white chamberpot, as red worms writhed dully in his peripheral vision. In his nightgown, at the window, in the moonlight, realising he was in for a second-rate eternity. And for all that, not as good a poet as

I.

I am not parading my own poetic works for comparison here. That much, at least, has been agreed with those fat, idle fiends, my Publishers; (Yet to come up with an advance, by the look of yesterday afternoon's post). And as for my Tarot pack: the reconstituted fourfold personal Predictor, the Devil's new picture book? No helpful illustrations allowed here - either - The Aeon is open! Go and get yourself one, throw the cards on the floor, and see what you come up with, you silly girl!

Product warning

¶ The Tarot is a powerfully seductive magickal force and you might not be ready for it. It may not 'censor' the forces of death and creation which constantly test us. Death could well tear a hole, not perhaps in the page as such, but in your life, reader.

¶ Yea! He will Scythe for himself, throughout frail flesh, the uttermost Exit Arsehole, and you will creep hence...

....Not yet though, if you're still reading this. The publishers - devious unprincipled scoundrels, to a man, say they cannot afford illustrations, in any case. A likely story. Thus we return to the text; words, words, whence we only depart, in fancy.

I have also undertaken not to 'essay any noxious spells' in this work. The snivelling, cockcheese-paring cretins no doubt fear the actions of lawyers upon their corporate profits - viz.
'My client read that distillation of evil, *I, Crowley*, and immediately slipped on a banana skin. Give me £10,000 by return of post or we will sue you for twice the amount.'

I may be unusual, but I am innocent of the crimes imputed to me. My dear sirs, how can this Evil sit in me? On the contrary, I propose to show that I am fallible, but that my intentions were always good. I hope to show, further, as we go on, that the public are more superstitious than they will ever admit.
I will put it down now, in black and white. There is no straightforward black magic in this book. Mr Dennis Wheatley, a scribbler, confessed he used to appropriate my rituals for his dreary horror stories, and change a few details in order to smudge the 'secrets of Satanism', and thus, in his mind, keep the instruction book for evoking

the horned god out of the suburban potting shed.[12]

I shall, in general, but not invariably, follow his example, and have deliberately corrupted the text. I am not above throwing in a few crackers of my own to liven things up, so if you are scanning this, gentle reader, in an effort to find your True Will, it is best to believe it is not Holy Writ.

In any case, I am buggered if I am letting out any more secrets.[13] But the devil has the best tunes, the biggest battalions, and like me, he is a gentleman who only desires your unending *pleasure*. Perhaps you should conclude that what you hold in your hands now is an Entertainment. *Do not* open this book and place your finger upon a chosen passage at random, like persons do with Virgil, and derive advice from your life thereby. Particularly not the following heading.

A LOAD OF COCK

In order to discourage such superstitious practices, which would, in any case place the unworthy author on a par with the Ancients, further 'new' material has been introduced, which could not possibly have been written by blind Homer or Abra-Merlin, viz.,

---

12 *Those students who have detected a striking similarity of style and ritual between a certain book on witchcraft by a certain 'Gardener' may be able to work out what I am getting at. The truth is that the author found himself unequal to the task, and after feebly attempting to plagiarise my work, gave up the struggle. I completed the handbook without credit on which modern Wicca is based, and most of the ideas in it are based on the Thelemic ideal.*

13 *Note to browsers, which can be safely ignored by the poor mutts who started patiently at page 1. This would be true, if existence itself was not the best-kept Secret of them all. An example of a sentence which means diametrically the opposite of what it says, whichever way you take it. A.C.*

You'll wonder where the Yellow went, when you clean your teeth with Pepsodent.[14]

Introducing this base element *proves* this book cannot be wholly Satanic. Though I am told, more and more, that modern advertising is actually a ploy where audience's attention is increasingly drawn to **Vice**! Under the subliminal spell hidden in the slogans, their arms will grow heavy, their eyes roll up into their heads, their fingers wander to their genitals for a spot of Operation VIII°.

I would never encourage such behaviour. But in order to understand yourself, you must first misunderstand me.[15]

How To Misunderstand The Author's Intent.

Firstly, enjoy the screaming headlines in the trashy paper which you read, oh Suburban Man, as the train leaves Waterloo for Clapham Junction,[16] tiddly bum, tiddly bum. It will have no scrap of relationship to reality, so anything will do - **SHAVEN HEADED BRIT IN TURKISH BATH ROMP.** As you rock back and forth on your journey, turn the pages, salivating, and devour, if you will, the details

---

14 *Self evidently nonsense. I have lost my teeth in any case. A.C.*

15 *If you read this offer and do not immediately understand its cabalistic meaning, you should run, rather than walk to the nearest canal and fling this from you, before the contraption you are holding goes off in your hands. A.C.*

16 *Clapham Junction is the place where Oscar Wilde was pilloried in transit to Reading Gaol, left in shackles for an hour, his crime the penning of farces that exposed the hypocrisies of the upper classes. Not even Oscar, twenty years before my own Martyrdom, could think of quips to take the mind of the public away from the endless, dreary parading of the evidence of his damnation: rent boys and their fecal stains. The Junction will be for ever, a place of hypocritical prurience. A.C.*

of my fictive life - not a word of it is true, but has that ever mattered? Come, inky fingers, prise me open and dabble me grey, before I sere, to yellow leaf -

> *Aluster Crowley was surprised last night in the midst of a Satanic homosexual romp in a New York Bathhouse on 42nd Street. Asked to explain was he was doing, he replied, 'I am pursuing my True Will. Satanism is merely the worship of Satan or Sha'itan, the Hebrew word for adversary.' The New York Chief of Police, flexing his nightstick, confirmed that Crowley's catchphrase 'Do What thou Wilt shall be the whole of the Law', is indeed a parody of St Augustine's 'Love and do what thou wilt', and that a copyright case is in the pipeline. He added, 'St Augustine was from Numibia, and repented his excesses. Crowley is from Leamington in Warwickshire and, sadly, regrets very little.' An investigation for medical fraud, when AC rolled pills containing his own semen and passed them off on the gullible as medicine, is ongoing. (Further report, Page 6)*

The Weekly Filth. P. 6.

'The man in the gold cloak was looking at me strangely that morning. But he had promised he would cure my impotence and I was prepared to accept his course of medicine. He settled himself in his comfortable leather chair, behind his desk, and rearranged the Tam O'Shanter which perched precariously on his curly black wig. The wig was covering an entirely bald head. His stare was nevertheless hypnotic and I began to feel uncomfortable. "I have had a breakthrough.. I have here something especially for you." he finally said. He pushed a small pill-box over towards me. In it were seven whitish pills, irregular in shape. "Take these if you ever feel

poorly." His high nasal tones had a subdued hint of excitement. "That will be seven guineas," he added, with a smirk. I noticed that he was wearing the largest ruby ring I have ever seen, except on a pantomime dame, on his right hand.'

The Beaverbrook newspapers christened me 'The Wickedest Man in the World'. Perhaps they should have confined me to the theatrical revues, the 'Wickedest Pantomime Dame'.
    I once resented my title of 'Wickedest Man '. More recently I have come to feel that since Byron passed into the mysts around the ramparts of gothic hokum, *someone* has had to do it. Byron's cloak of deception, (beneath which he sodomised his besotted sister) has fallen to me. Sisters have I none! I may be Tristan, but where is my Iseult? *Chinese whispers missed his sister.*
    Roll up, roll up. Let's brew some trouble. Shake the dust of Clapham Junction and Transylvania together, dollop the outfall from an Operation VIII° onto some *menses*, purée and bake at Gas Mark 5 for thirty minutes. Consume your Cakes of Light without using a knife or fork, within spitting distance of a writer for the newspapers. You will, I solemnly promise, instantly become 'The Wickedest Man in the World'. If not, write to me, Beast 666, c/o Diss, and you'll instantly get your money back.[17]

---

[17] *I'm joking, of course, about the address. Netherwood, Hastings, England, will find me. A.C.*

Through my researches into occultism I am able to assure you of the immortality of the soul. But a magus should always have his wits about him - the pranksome goetia like nothing better than to trick and trap the very stuff of consciousness into an overblown state in which each hoodwinked seer believes that He or She is an Ipsissimus, the Magickal version of the Real McCoy. When I was first initiated into my first magickal order - a ramshackle affair hosted by the likes of Willy Yeats and other halfbaked nitwits - I was stopped in my tracks by one genuine initiate, who could see spirits. He told me that my earlier researches had resulted in a psychic infestation. Frankly I would rather have had the goetia around me than the pallid, ivory tower poetasting of the professional Irishman.

What should I care, in any case? I have written, or rather taken down at Aiwass' behest, the slim volume that will guide the human race, when it has struck off the fetters of the twentieth century from its suppurating limbs. Through me, sexual repression will be a thing of pre-history, and Humanity will step out into the noontide sun of Crowleyanity.

The price of my future vindication is that in this life, I have had to publish my poetry at my own expense. It has not been well circulated, and it is alas, Yeats' pirated regurgitations of the mental inscapes of the Order of the Golden Dawn that make simpering sophomores from Calgary to Timbuctu[18] affect to swoon.

Like my Lord Beaverbrook's whores, the simpering sophomores will never be in a position to profit spiritually from the predicament they are in. If only they had met me, *I* would have cast a cold eye on them that would have been unforgettable. But the duties of Prophecy for the present time stand before the delights of Poesy.

Though I declare; that in the coming Age
Old Baldilocks shall smirk, from ev'ry Page.

---

18 *I know what I am talking about. I have been to Timbuctu. A.C.*

(Footnote 19)

It is time to meet Raoul Loveday.

He who was once my beloved, my Man. The year is 1918. We go inside the British Museum. The room is resplendent, a magnificent invocation of the age of the Pharoahs. You may hear my whispered voice but I shall only be 'directing traffic', as it were, a friendly astral presence.

Before we meet Raoul I should explain. In reality, at this moment, I was astride a fat black whore, very sensuous, three thousand miles away in New York in the heat of summer. If we stuck strictly with Greenwich Mean Time, she would be squealing delightedly as I slipped a cornucopia of products from the local ice house into her *vas nefandum*. But; - by virtue of my Parker pen, I am hovering here in the British Museum, in the Egyptian room, a ghostly Virgil, to guide you towards your meeting.

Come with me, oh sensation-seeking novitiates, past Babylonian lions, and giant relics of vast statues of the Pharoahs of Egypt. Let me

---

19 [Editor's note.] Not since William Blake composed the Songs of Innocence and Experience has an important English poet offered a testament as this of his life and beliefs illustrated with his own graphic skills.. Unfortunately almost all Crowley's original illustrations which were pasted into the main body of the handwritten manuscript are lost forever since Crowley had a belief in the efficacy of his own semen [?] as glue, that is sadly not supported by history. For this edition, the editors have created a computer-generated sequence of 'Crowleyanic' punctuations using the gaps in the original MS as guidelines. We have made no attempt to attempt to recreate the no doubt unique and characteristic frenzy of the original visions, in an unknown medium, whose power and Inspiration which we can now only guess at.

move you past the mummies in their bitumen-soaked linen wraps, the golden scarabs and riddling sphinxes. Here a giant arm, there a huge disembodied head. Shelley caught fallen greatness in his web here over a hundred years ago.[20] And yet, what is a hundred years to Ra and Osiris?

Sunlight shines through the boards, shafting into the exotic gloom. Peace has arrived at last, but the windows are still boarded up after Zeppelin damage. The atmosphere in here is of dark, brooding intensity. Footsteps on stone echo round the high ceilings. Sounds of hackney horse-drawn cabs filter through from outside, and an infrequent intrusive motor car.

A young couple are examining the exhibits. They have the glow of youth upon them. The young man is tale, pale and excitable, with flopping dark hair, his movements feline and attractive, the woman, short, older than him, brassy and self-assured. Yes! It is Raoul Loveday and his wife. This way, dear boy. Come and claim your dread destiny. The Museum is where your die will be cast.

Raoul is so overcome by the atmosphere breathed out by the relics, he cannot understand how anyone can not be equally moved. But Betty does not, cannot ever share his sublime thoughts.

Raoul's head is ablaze with the laws of numbers that underpin the firmament. Betty is thinking about the impression she made on his parents at their wedding. The age difference, do you see, must have been mentioned. Her being so much older than him, already tweaking and bleaching her tiny moustache, pulling in her flaccid stomach as she tummocks in the altogether for boys from the Slade Art School, who are all wearing berets and green corduroy smocks, and worrying whether they have, or do not have, the clap -

Betty and Raoul. Alone in the British Museum. With me, Like Raoul's Holy Guardian Angel, hovering above.

---

20 *'Oyymandias' was written after a visit. A.C.*

How did Raoul find me? In search of a mentor, he had written to me about the laws of magic in mathematics before the war, and I courteously returned his schoolboy enquiries by outlining some paths of exploration her could pursue relating to the numeric structure of the 'Qabal, and the relationship of π to the Sephiroth. We met, after the war, which I am not afraid to say, I spent in America. I was almost too old to fight, certainly too wise to drown like a dog in Flanders mud. In any case, my services as a secret agent[21] for the British Government having been refused, I had a mind to take America by storm.[22]

When I came back to England, Raoul had grown into a man. But he had taken ether under my supervision. When he married Betty, she made him swear he would not touch me, or drugs again. Betty came from Soho, in London, and the prevailing 'wisdom' of artists models and tarts alike (Indistinguishable categories around the likes of Augustus John[23]) was that boys like Raoul had to be kept on the straight and narrow, or, in shopgirl parlance, they went 'to the bad'.

I will say one thing for Betty. She was never backward about supporting the pair of them, using her body. She was close to being that impossibility, an honest whore. Her cocaine intake had been stupendous, but she had pulled away from it.

---

21 Since I have signed the Official Secrets Act, I regret I am not at liberty to disclose what passed between me and the War Office, and what my actual role became. A.C.

22 I should admit a soft impeachment here. I wanted to found a spiritual empire in America. If the Mormons had walked into Utah, why could not I walk into California? The Secret Chiefs, who have overseen all my actions, saw to it that I failed. I suspect I simply was not experienced enough at that stage to begin a proper Movement, and this is why, in turn, I have had to endure such universal calumny at home. A.C.

23 Augustus John the so-called 'free love' painter did a number of portraits of me. He begged to be initiated into the mysteries, but I could not help him, his lusts were many, but casual. His spirit burned, but burned with an impure flame. If there is one thing I cannot stand it is loose morality under the guise of artistic genius. A.C.

'There was once a religion which could have united mankind. We have to rediscover the source of inspiration.' Raoul's whisper to her in that echoing room falls on stony ground. Betty's scornful rasp would have come back something like -

'I thought Mister Crowley had the secret already and went to America to keep it safe.' Never mind I was in two minds about getting involved in the stupidest epidemic of hostilities in history. By the end of the conflict, The War Office in England had been bullied into conscripting anyone under forty-five. In Betty's view if I had joined the Clerkenwell cattle on their way to the slaughterhouse, it would at least have got rid of me.

Raoul had told her that I wanted to work in Europe, and that I had plans for an idealistic community which he wanted to join. She of course sneered.

Raoul related to me how the tragedy snowballed after that.

Betty had sneered first at me, then at Anubis. Anubis is the jackal-headed god, with a human body, who ferries the souls of the dead to the underworld. Anubis sees both life and death. There was a fine statue of him there. He is a kindly psychopomp, unlikely to take offence.

Betty's third slight, which wound up destiny irrevocably, was to a priestess of Amon Ra, a most powerful lord of life and death, and unable, if you wish for my opinion, to take such a thing lightly.

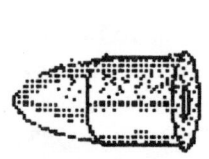  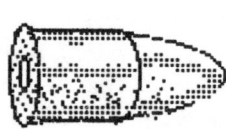

According to Raoul, they were standing before the imposing mummy of the handmaiden to Amon Ra. Betty began making flippant remarks, while poor Raoul was stuttering that he wanted the priestess to bless their wedding. Not even the high god, the priestess. Raoul was always humble.

Then Betty did this foolish thing. Her insult was to thumb her nose at the mummy, in a deliberate fashion.

Raoul begged her not to do it, to apologise. Naturally, Amon-Ra could not overlook this insult to his handmaiden.

'What's wrong?' Betty said. The words dried in his mouth, he told me. He could not speak, and all he could think of was numbers. Behind her, Raoul could see a boarded up door with a message on it, which boded ill. It read **NO ENTRY. ZEPPELIN DAMAGE**. Just then Betty, undaunted by her new husband, to cap her insolence, stuck her tongue out as far as it would go, at the handmaiden of Amon Ra.

Sometimes it is necessary to arrest insolent ignorance at the point of issue, or it breeds pestilence. If I had been in Raoul's shoes, wed to Betty, I would have fetched her a smack in the chops that would have carried her across the room, and put her out of modelling work for a week. Raoul, of course, being Raoul, kept his hands to himself.

'Betty! Stop!' Raoul whimpered.

The tongue, stuck out like Betty stuck it out is a particular insult to the Egyptian Eternals. For the old Egyptian language - (lost to us now, alas, we only have debased hieroglyphics) - is the closest we may ever get to the Words of the Creator.

The Tongue shares the blame for The Fall. Sometimes I believe I will meet one of the Secret Chiefs[24] who will address me in that divine language. I speak prayers in Enochian,[25] but the Highest Angelic discourse has not yet been reclaimed.

---

24 *There are a small number of Secret Chiefs, they are wise and ancient, and they appear when needed to guide the policies of the human race. McGregor Mathers, who founded the Order of the Golden Dawn, met not one, but three at once on the street in Paris. The sheer numbers makes this an important even - provided it happened. Mathers was also not above exaggerating, to impress neophyte magicians who had equal powers to his. No names, no packdrill! A.C.*

25 *Angelic language used by Elisabeth I's astrologer, Doctor John Dee, who, less illustriously, is increasingly credited with the foundation of the British Empire. A.C.*

- To return to our thickened plot -

Betty, having offended the gods with her tongue, (Hers went out a particularly long way, I noticed when they came to Cefalù) turned on one polished heel, like the slut she was, and walked smartly away. Her footsteps echoed. Raoul cried -

'Betty - come back and apologise - *please*.' Of course she did nothing of the sort, but continued titupping out of the room.

Raoul turned, full of foreboding, to the statue of Amon Ra himself. He sank to his knees to the stone god. The foolish boy tried to bargain, to protect The Model, his slatternly new bride. So much charcoal had been crushed by so many 'artists' depicting Betty's plumply endowed bush it is surprising the area had any mystery left in it. But Raoul was young. Like the doomed youths who went 'over the top' for Horatio Bottomley and the rest of the war profiteers, he took it upon himself to expiate others' crime with his own blood-offering. Raoul bleated to Amon-Ra -

'Don't take it out on her. If there must be a judgement, great Lord, let it be on me - on me!'

Naturally, Amon Ra took him at his word.

Later, Raoul answered my summons to the Abbey, Betty reluctantly accompanying him.

London, Dover, Calais, Paris, Palermo. Betty was spared but Raoul was called, and was buried by me outside the cemetery of Cefalu, with a huge crowd of Sicilians ogling the goings-on.

Subsequently there was a great brouhaha in the Beaverbrook press about a 'Satanic' burial by the light of babies being burned, in unconsecrated ground. The same old lies that Christians have told about Jews for two thousand years.

The truth is, Raoul could not possibly have been buried inside the cemetery, he was not a Catholic.

In fact, Raoul's soul had a fine send-off. We danced and sang and threw libations. The robes of the Abbey came in for applause from the crowds, who were openly disappointed when the magnificent show came to an end. It was the frankness and sexual openness of the community women which really touched the imaginations of the crowds of short, greasy Sicilian men. Even Betty had to admit that the funeral touched the heartstrings. If I had not been expelled from Italy immediately after, I would have been able to staff any number of Abbeys from amongst the local population. I sent Raoul off with my very best poem, one we used to recite almost daily in our rituals together, my 'Hymn to Pan'. If you cannot find a copy in your local library, do feel free to make your own Hymn.

I'm sure Pan will not mind.

Your fond uncle,

Aleister Crowley

1 The Magus

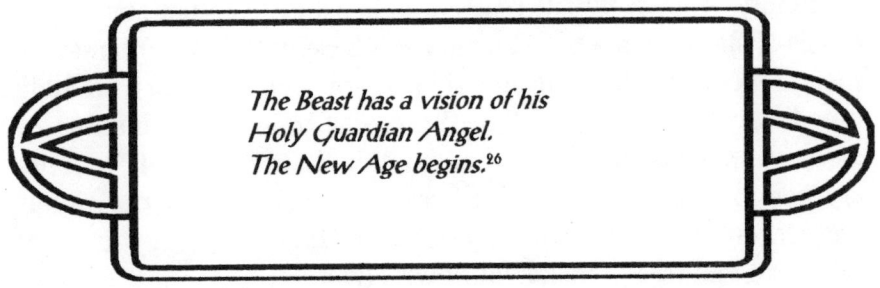

The Beast has a vision of his Holy Guardian Angel. The New Age begins.[26]

My Angel comes to me, on waves of ether, gliding low over the moonlit wasteland,[27] a desert of dunes and rocks with dried up rivercourses without signs of human habitation. But before she has descended fully to encounter me, I have already gone to her, I am clinging to her breast.

I look out sideways from the rushing wind of her descent to see the leading edge of a huge bird's wing, with golden feathers gleaming dully in the moonlight. The pinion feathers stiff against the air; the smaller feathers occasionally rippling in an eddy. Looking up, I am not surprised to find human features on this creature I find myself riding. The face is the face of the priestess of Amon-Ra. She is alive: airborne; immortal.

The outstretched, mighty wings of my celestial votaress etch their sharp shadow in moonlight on the ground below her. The black silhouette flows ever onwards, passing effortlessly over rocks, sliding over precipices without pause, and slipping through the thorn thickets.

---

26 *That should be more than enough for one chapter!*
27 *There is a poem of no consequence which openly plagiarises this name. I understand its author is a young American from Mississippi who took leave of his wits, and then committed his wife to an asylum for the insane and converted to Anglo-Catholicism. Enough said! A.C.*

And now, a small oasis town, alone in the desert comes into view, white-walled, with a number of gates. In the middle of the huddle of buildings, there is a mighty ziggurat. She heads straight for the vast, seven-tiered pyramid, and circling slows down for a turn about it, as if looking for an entrance. There is a hissing, as of a thousand serpents. The air round the half closed hands of the claws seems to sigh -

'The sands! The soughing, riddling sands!' In the distance, the three-quarter moon is picked up in the distant glint of a mighty river.

'The Tigris -' the pinion feathers seem to whisper: 'The Euphrates' the smaller feathers correct, mockingly. I am drunk with sensation. Then the river's brightness closes, like the eye of a dying lizard, and then as we circle closer, the Ziggurat's dark imposing bulk wipes out the horizon.

The sheer walls give no hint of a door or an entrance. My angelic bearer hovers on the dark side of the mighty ziggurat, slower and slower. Every time the great wings go up, I fear we will fall. Every time they sweep down, and we rise again.

And then I can no longer hear the wind through the feathers. My feet are on the ground. She has given me the slip, shed me, sloughed me off, and I am now somehow imprisoned, on the topmost level, inside the Ziggurat. I have to get out again, and seize my salvation, which is Her. Like Jacob, I know I have to wrestle my guardian angel, or lose a blessing.

Inside the top room of the Ziggurat, at the end of an ancient narrow stone passage, I contest my imprisonment. I throw back the sleeves on my sun-yellow priest's robes and wrestle with an ancient green bronze bolt on a sloping door to the outside. This bolt is wrought like a serpent. It is stiff with verdigris. No one has opened it for centuries. I can hear the fluffing of wings outside as She prepares to go. I struggle with desperation to slide the snake bolt open before my angel disappears.

The jewelled eye of the bronze serpent starts to glow uncannily. The door is bewitched. I renew my struggles. The eyes of the serpent on the bolt dim, and die. Finally with a crash and a cloud of dust, the bolt slides to the side. I fall out onto the dark terrace. Clouds obscure the night sky.

My guardian angel is nowhere to be seen.

I awake, though I do not wish to awake.

The above is an exact as possible account of a dream. I was thrust back into the world from the dream in the late afternoon of Armistice Day, November 11th 1918, where, or perhaps I should say 'when' the narrative continues.

I woke to find myself lying on the floor, alone, surrounded by my paintings, in coldwater walk up apartment, which had a view of the head of the Statue of Liberty if you stood on tiptoe, in one of the poorer Manhattan neighbourhoods. Outside, dusk was coming on and there were enough fireworks being detonated to wake the dead. The air is bright and dense, with explosions from on high.

There was no time to invoke Choronzon's terrible anathema on the *feu d'artificiers* for interrupting my Congress with my Holy Guardian Angel. If I was to eat and drink that night, I had to move. There was a payment which had been promised me for writing for a powerful and influential magazine. A few minutes later and they would be closed, and I would have a dollar-less weekend, in New York, which was about to throw the party of the century - not that the century was that old, yet - in recognition of having beaten Kaiser Bill back over the trenches of the Marne, and back across the Siegfried Line. There was no time to lose.

I shaved, dressed, and throwing my purple cloak on, ducked out of the window and ran down the fire escape as if I was a panting ten yards ahead of the descending wall of an avalanche in the Himalayas, with half a mile of ridge to go to safety.

The skies redoubled their orgastic, bursting shapes of flames and exploding nebulae as I flew down the steel web.

By the light of the man-made stars, I could see that the tops of the fire escapes of every tall tenement that I passed were clotted with insect-like piles of heaving, copulating couples. They were celebrating the cessation of hostilities. The New Age, as I prophesied, had begun.

II The Priestess

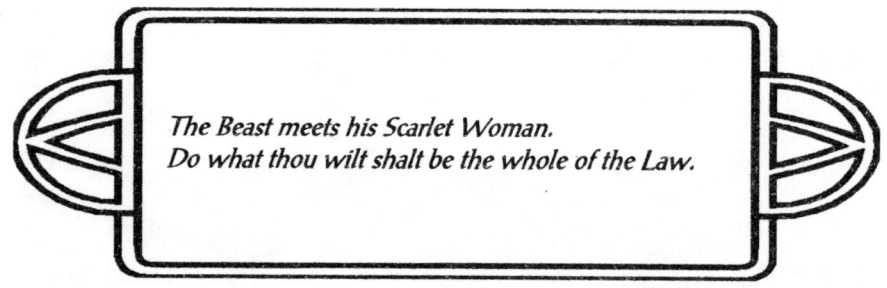

The Beast meets his Scarlet Woman.
Do what thou wilt shalt be the whole of the Law.

As I contemplated the happy couples in the streets and on the fire escapes, their frenzied gyrations started to move to a tune that had lodged in my head. Preparing to go out a few moments before, I had just finished shaving my cranium, as I do for photographers and other special occasions, and I was trying on a large orange beret with a thistle brooch at the front, in the mirror when I caught sight of a garish poster on the wall.

It was to the effect that Aleister Crowley proudly presented his Dancing Troupe, the Diabolical Dancing Dervishes, The Ragged Ragtime Girls - fresh from their success in London at the New Theatre, Pushkin Street, Moscow.

Although the poster was six years old, the opening chorus of the Ragged Ragtime girls, played as ever to a tinkling accompaniment, by the simpering pianist, burst in and maddeningly went around and around my head.

I'll go with you, you've got the knack
Of giving me my laughter back
You are the joker of the pack
So come and dance with me
Oh ha ha hee hee.

I finished my toilet, took up my Wand of the hour, a brass casting, which I had had shortened, heavy enough to see off muggers who wanted my fake diamond ring, and rejected the beret for a collapsible opera hat, which I slipped into the lining of my cloak. But the Ragged Ragtime Girls would not go away. I cursed my own lack of mental training, that they could stay with me. It was only when I threw myself down the fire escape that their voices started to fade.

I have only got one card
If I am trumped I find it hard
You catch me when I'm off guard
ho ho ho ho hee
Shuffle me and see
Which one is it to be

Perhaps I should not have been so harsh on them. The Ragged Ragtime Girls, while being trite and ephemeral, brought me to my first meeting with an aspect of my Holy Guardian Angel.[28]

As a troupe they were a cheap-violin line-up, with a mule-like reluctance to rehearse anything but the most banal of end of the pier routines. There was an endless bickering, and an eternal failure to agree the hotels that I found for any of them were satisfactory. Worst, were the chippy ripostes and the cheap sexual stinginess of those born within spitting distance of the Hackney Empire -

'You can put it away. I'm not doing anything with that, I've got to save my throat for tomorrow night!'

I had been a little overhung when I awoke to the firework barrage. My indulgence had been due to a disappointment in love the previous evening with my partner of choice, a usually agreeable whore from the

---

28 *This had nothing to do with their spiritual awareness. My H.G.A had decided to make herself known to me by purchasing a ticket and sitting in the audience like an ordinary mortal. More of which, anon. A.C.*

bar across the street, who called herself 'Helen'. Helen had passed out from opiates ignorantly administered - morphine, I believe, before she had been able to make it up the stairs. I whacked her heartily, but to no avail, she did not stir. So I left her at the bottom of the stairs in a stupor.

Neptune the planet of illusion is placed opposite Venus in my natal chart, and my idealism extending to 'unconscious' or otherwise unavailable partners has been a recurring pattern in my life. My first wife, Rose Kelly, sister of a famous painter, became a dipsomaniac after she had married me. She had an unparalleled facility to empty a bottle of Scotch while apparently engaged in an innocent search for a missing chess piece. I had indeed been critical to her face, of Helen's little weaknesses, and likewise I had tried, but failed to control Rose's drinking. In the end, I gave up preaching to either of them, as they seemed hell-bent on self destruction.

The revellers shouted, and thronged bars and side alleys with their agitated bodies. On street corners were the last editions and newspaper sellers trying to cash in with yet another Armistice Day Special. Manhattan was abandoning itself to what it does best - the mindless orgy, which meant that Canal Street was all but impassible.

I knocked out my folding opera hat, and put it on, to strike an appearance of authority which would allow me passage through, but the way was blocked with copulating sailors, who formed a barricade, and insultingly, paid me not the slightest bit of notice.

As the daylight failed and the street lamps came on, the only people who looked at me with any interest were a couple of detectives who wore the regulation snap-brim hats and raincoats of their trade. I was familiar to them already in all my guises: ever since I had been earning a perilous living writing for a magazine, which I was now trying to reach, I had been assigned two po-faced 'tecs, who on warm days shadowed the building and followed me when I went out.

I suppose they must have had instructions to find out what other dangerous anarchists I was meeting with. I was surprised to find that on Armistice Night my 'tecs were still on duty. Both of them looked the worse for wear for drink. I raised my opera hat to them. 'You must be on overtime, gentlemen!' They failed as ever to return my salute.

The noise of revelry, bands from the cafés, with the continuous barrage of the fireworks above made for a glorious assault on the senses. The culmination of it all was seeing a young girl, lean, rather fetchingly Asiatic in feature, with cat-like eyes but a great slash of a mouth, helping herself to a salami, which hung outside an Italian grocery shop. She was wearing a plum coloured, crushed velvet dress.

I remembered now that I'd seen her before, and we had exchanged what Falstaff calls 'judicious oeillades' when I was giving a lecture on astrology. The lecture was on Neptune, the planet of deception's entry into Leo.[29]

Her name was Leah, she was a 'student' on some eternal course, in New York.[30] At our first encounter we did not speak to each other. Leah had sat ogling me. Next to her was her fat sister, Renata who had eyebrows which met in the middle.

My cape of choice was that of Abra-Merlin the Mage. When I am wearing it, while I know people are looking at me for *that* reason, I can generally tell what their True Will is towards me. It was clear what was going on in Leah's mind as she beheld me. And now I stood under a street lamp, and let its light fall on me, so she could be in no doubt.

Leah, having palmed the salami, had a good long look at me. I

---

29   Leo is my ascendant, and I should have been prepared for Leah's own eventual abandonment of The Work. Her final tergiversation occurred, naturally, when Neptune, the planet of ether, delusion and hunger for the impossibly infinite left the boyish fires of Leo after ten years for the cool virginity of the great goddess of corn, immortal Virgo. I carried on with The Work. I am not Frater Perdurabo for nothing. A.C.

30   It is unbelievable how Americans can spend their lives at university. As a Trinity man myself, who left when Cambridge had nothing more to teach me, I would urge students everywhere to throw over the traces, to defy authority, step out into the world, otherwise you will never find your True Will. A.C.

pretended not to mind if anybody noticed me. Then I heard the cry. Recognition.

'*Look! There's Aleister Crowley!*' Her great mouth opened.

Her sister Renata tugged at her sleeve. A mute warning. Drugs. Sexual depravity. Delusion. Madness. Infant sacrifices.[31] Black magic. She shook her sister off.

'*No Renata, no. This time, I wanna meeeet him.*'

Suddenly it seemed she was in another dimension, moving towards me effortlessly through a bacchanalian sea of dark faces and groping hands. The ritual greeting of the day was not 'Do What Thou Wilt' but 'The War is over'. When you had said that to someone, it seemed that you were both at liberty to take intimacy as far as it went. Leah called to me -

'*The war is over!*' Then she hopped over a drunk in the gutter, and kissed me full on the lips.

I tried to subdue the priapic idea that I might be interested in an immediate consummation, like the rest of the couples in Canal Street who were wafting their scents of love around us. I had bigger fish to fry, than a moment's orgiastic pleasure, at Kaiser Bill's expense. I suggested we met later, in a more private venue. She shyly concurred. I invited her over for the evening. She said she would come, but that her sister might have to come too, as a chaperone.

That was how people behaved in the dark days, before Crowleyanity. They could think of nothing else but sex.

I told Leah she could bring her sister, but not to forget the salami, and set off to collect my rightful wages from the offices of 'The Internationalist'.

'The Internationalist' had been notable in New York for putting the pro-German case of the war. They had failed to create any ripples of

---

31   I shall make a clean breast of any sacrifices. If I had driven a motor car over the same period the death toll would have been higher. It goes, one cat, circa 1888, one toad, circa 1916, one cat circa 1922. A.C.

opinion and America had weighed in against the Kaiser in the final two years. Their offices were down on the Hudson. I had been engaged to write articles, as a prominent Englishman in New York, who understood and was sympathetic to the German position. I had been recruited by a man on top of a bus, who approached me and asked me if I was in favour of a 'fair deal' for Germany. Since in hindsight, the failure of the world to abide by commonsense at Versailles has led to the Second World war, this would seem to be an eminently sensible position. My lack of traditional 'patriotism' is the result of an independent eye, and I believe that eventually I will be vindicated.

'The old familiar lie, *Dulce et decorum est pro Patria Mori*'

Wilfred Owen could write that, but, as a noncombatant, accepting German silver for journalism I was judged guilty of treason to my country.[32] In order to assure readers that I was not as serious about my assignments as my editors wished, I would put in little teases, showing that the articles could not be taken seriously by intelligent persons.

I wrote for instance, that the German Zeppelin raids on London were not going far enough, and included my aunt's address, as a marker for them. 'The Internationalist' solemnly printed the street directions for finding my aunt's house, from ten thousand feet in the air.

Although Zeppelin damage anywhere in the Great War was minimal, I have to say I could not make the same joke again today. The ruins of Coventry, Dresden, London, Berlin, Nagasaki and Hiroshima stare up from our picture newspapers. The Warrior Lords of the forties, prefigured in the *Book of the Law* have indeed been busy fellows.

---

32   For the record I do not consider that the land of Beethoven, Mozart, Steiner, Nietzsche, and so forth is much inferior to the land of Shakespeare, Marlowe, Rochester, and Crowley. A.C.

Nothing directly to do with me, of course.

Shops were being rapidly boarded up against the crowds as I went below Bleeker Street. I turned the corner, away from the crowds, and saw here and there, a few lights where people were still working. The street lamps were becoming more and more infrequent. Realising I might be a target, I fell into a rapid mode of progress, used by Tibetan yogis. Mexican brujos call it 'The Gait of Power'. The 'tecs had the greatest trouble keeping up.

The fireworks had exhausted themselves. The office of the paper had been on a waterside street, and there was no one about, and only the sound of dark slapping water. Still with my hopes fatuously high on my coming payment, but now with the possibility of being deprived of the fruits of my labour (Perfidious Neptune again, in the tenth house) having ceased the Gait of Power, I began to practice defensive strokes in the dark, with my wand, against urban brigands, till I arrived at the newspaper office.

I found I had arrived at a freshly created ruin. The doors had been stoved in and the offices of 'The Internationalist' had been gutted. There was no one about. Internal walls had been demolished, and there was not a pane of glass in the building. There was blood at head height, on some damaged plaster by the door, as if someone had been thrown at the wall, very hard, earlier. I remember reflecting out loud on seeing this, that there is nothing comparable in violence to the American scorn for a loser.

Outside, pages of print were blowing up and down from the murdered paper. Some sodden pieces stuck to kerbs. Others, still light and dry, scurried over the cobbles to commit suicide off the chilly wharfs protruding into the black river. My final article had been a tongue in cheek appreciation of Field Marshall Haig's less than uncanny ability to foresee the future. I had foolishly failed to keep a

---

33 *After losing thirty thousand men before lunch, the great man presciently wrote, in 1918, 'We will die with our backs to the wall, believing in the justice of our cause.'* A.C.

copy. Only words! Lost now, to literature, as well as history. *Venite, Oblivium*.

The two 'tecs finally caught up with me, panting. I first frightened them by throwing my staff in the air, then caught it expertly, wheeled around and headed for my apartment at a speed they could manage. The 'tecs followed sullenly, two sulky curs uncomprehending trotting behind the Lion Ascendant, Of Leamington.

III The Empress.

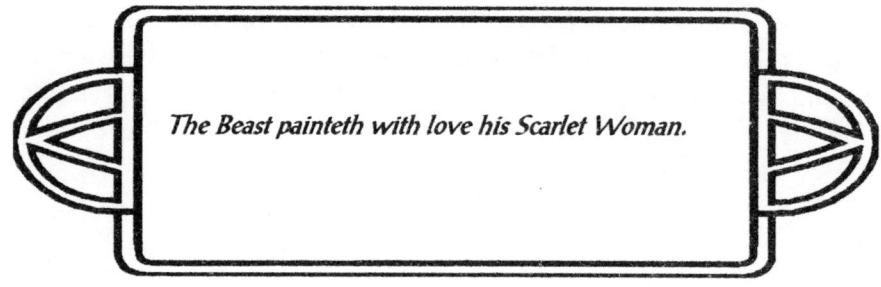

The Beast painteth with love his Scarlet Woman.

At the apartment, the landlord still allowed me to receive mail but it arrived with the ink having run, because the 'tecs always steamed it open first. One letter, somewhat foxed in this fashion, was from Raoul Loveday in England. I was as ever immediately impressed by the vigour of his mind coupled with innocence and youthful enthusiasm. Sadly, he had been unable so far to raise money for my passage to London, and his parents had refused to help. Raoul said they had been indignant when asked, and his father had described me as 'that vile man.' Oh well. Go ahead. Heap on the insults. Not for nothing is this poor Beast *Frater Perdurabo quid tollet peccata mundi.*[34]

The rest of Raoul's letter was taken up with his proposed marriage - the fond boy was In Love, with an eager undertaking to bring his bride out whenever I should summon him, for them both to join me in an idealistic commune: he would come if I set up shop in Antarctica; if I founded a colony on the moon he would arrange for them both to be fired there by a large cannon. I could not suppress a smile as I read his affectionate and humorous undertaking.

There was a knock on the door, which I had left open in my haste. Two faces peered round the door jamb, one in a cloche hat. I beckoned them in without speaking, and finished reading Raoul's letter as they

---

34   *Who takes upon himself the sins of the World. A.C.*

inspected my artist's studio. I did not wish too appear too eager for Leah to drop into my lap. Renata said loudly,

'What a dump!' Something dripped from a cardboard box she was carrying carefully onto an oil painting of mine, which was drying on the floor. 'Oh s*oorrry* about the icecream' she said, meaning the exact opposite. She peered at the painting, which was an idealised self portrait I had been working on, and removed the food, as well as some of the oil paint, from a corner.

The apartment suited my needs at the time admirably, and there was even a small antechamber which had room for an altar. Renata's attack on the self portrait, TO MEGA THERION,[35] had done little to reduce its magnificence. I courteously waved Renata and Leah to a chesterfield, suggesting that if they took off the piled books they would be comfortable there. I continued reading Raoul's letter. After a few minutes Renata said.

'My name's Renata.' Leah shushed her but she continued 'You won't remember us. This is my kid sister Leah.' I judged it suitable to put the letter away and make eye-contact with Leah. I bowed low over her hand. No lovebites, just a kiss. I didn't want to risk frightening her. Renata was peeved I didn't do the same for her.

'We're taking law at New York University. Don't mess with us, or we'll sue.' Charming.

Leah said suddenly, 'Don't be stupid, Renata.' Her face was very still, especially round the cheekbones. Her voice was quiet but deep.

'How do you do. My name is Aleister Crowley.' Renata's icecream dripped faster. She held it fastidiously aloft, as if its siftings were nothing to do with her.

'Are you busy tonight?' Renata asked me.

'I'm looking for a model' I said. Renata stood up and said to Leah.

'Okay, that's enough. We're going to dinner. We'll call by again, someday.'

'Someday may be too late. I have to leave for England in a little while. I've been summoned.' I waved the letter from Raoul, beguil-

---

35   *The Great Beast, or The Master Therion.* A.C

ingly. 'My people need me.'

'Who are your people?' snarled Renata.

'Thelemites.' I replied. 'Those who believe in the Law of Thelema.' Renata's eyes glazed over in the way that many in America had in the past four years, when I had tried to obtain converts. Neptune's entry into Leo had not in any way reduced a certain aggressive scepticism in the population. I seem to have come over to them as often as not as a 'snake-oil' salesman. The country was full of successful snake oil salesmen who had ended up believing their own sales talk. Whereas I, who was extremely diffident about the *Book of the Law*, not least about my own ability to interpret it, had found so few converts that it was laughable.

'Come on. Leah..... The icecream's melting' Renata added, superfluously. I gave Leah my deepest and most compelling stare. She said later that she felt it pierce her like a unicorn's horn, straight through her breastbone.

'Would you be able to stay and model for me, now?' I asked. Leah stood up but remained rooted to the spot, even though her big sister was tugging at her.

'C'mon baby, let's go eat' said Renata. She scratched at her thigh coarsely, as if there were no one else in the room.

'I'm sorry I have no flea powder to offer you.' I said, hoping to get a smile from Leah. Renata realised that she was on the outside, looking in. Suddenly it was as if an invisible bond between the sisters broke. Renata pulled her hand away from Leah.

'OK, be like that' she said to Leah. Ignoring me, she marched through the door, and tried to slam it. The effect was muffled by a copy of the New York Times which I had cleaned some brushes with and which had stuck to the bottom of the door. After the third try, she gave up and we could hear her heavy footsteps going away down the hallway.

'Big sister likes to think she's in charge of me. But I'm free' Leah said. She reached into her slip and produced the salami. 'Are you hungry? I am.' She put the salami in my hand. 'I guess I shouldn't have stolen this but it's so wild out there.' I ignored the invitation to censure. I always do.

'Do you like being free?' I asked.

'I guess so. I want to be.' As Renata descend the third set of stairs, the tack tack of her shoes faded, and Leah moved again. She shuffled her feet and arched her back like a cat's. I could not tell what she was doing for a moment. It was like watching a statue come to life. Then suddenly her dress came off and dropped to her ankles.

'You said you were looking for a model' she said.

For too long had I lain with the Roddy Minors of this world and suffered the chill banality of a third rate Magical Current. I knew I would become properly intoxicated with Leah's spirit as I feasted on her lotus. Unafraid in return, she would taste Neptune's triple spear, and dare do every deed with the Logos of the Aeon.

I painted Leah's picture that night, as she posed naked for me. It was an exhilarating, awesome experience as she bared her soul for the brush: our first act of love together. After an eternity, I had broken through the Wall of Self to find a fellow being.

Leah's eyelids narrowed slightly, but no more, when I pierced the skin on the back of her hand with my Serpent's Kiss for the first time. I felt I had met my match, the most extraordinary, exhilarating, mysterious, fearless Scarlet Woman that the Secret Chiefs had ever sent me.

I put a purple candle on a packing case and lit it ceremoniously, praying that the φαλλοσ would start to work its way wordlessly into her soul. She watched impassively as I lit joss sticks, and made an invocation to Anubis, the dogheaded Egyptian psychopomp, who carries souls over to the other side, where they are prepared to be reborn. At the conclusion I held out my hand to her, and she kissed it. I had rather hoped she would bite it, but her teeth were too regular. She held my hand with what would in due course turn to adoration. It was time to start instructing her.

'This ring belonged to Akhnaten, the monarch who united Upper and Lower Egypt.' She touched the ring with a sort of innocent interest.

'Did you know him? Akna...?.'

How much did she know about reincarnation?

'He died five thousand years ago.' How much did she know about anything, this flat-breasted Swiss-American bitch?

'Yes, I knew him.' Leah's wide brow corrugated for a moment.

'I don't understand.'

'In a previous life.' Leah nodded.

'Do you think we met in a previous life?' I asked, testing her. She smiled dazzlingly.

'Maybe if we don't meet in this one, we'll never meet. So we'd better get on with it.'

She always looked as though she was about to cry, my Scarlet Woman. I was not to blame - she said she had felt like that since she was born. But since my sadistic and erotic impulses are close-coupled,[36] goading each other on when I am aroused in either state, Leah and I always ended up falling in and out of fighting and fucking. There was no *via media* in our love.

But love it was. I defy you to say that the Beast had a heart too cold for love. I loved my Leah with the most scarlet intensity. Sometimes I wished she had killed me before we parted. Later, under my direction, she was the most accomplished astral traveller, like Rose, even though she had little or no experience, and less understanding of the realms visited.

Forgive me Leah. You loved me, but in the end, I only am able to

---

36 *Should I confess reader, or should you guess? Introspection is not my forte. What is the etiquette of this pretended intimacy? Will you tell me your problems, anon? Never mind. Read on. A.C.*

love Aiwass, Aiwaz, Eyewash, my more-than-I-am, my Superior being, my cruel God. He seems to have left me at the end of my life to wither on the vine, in Hastings, the Elba of the south coast. *My god, my god, why hast thou forsaken me?*

It's only because I am too old to care what anyone thinks that I can possibly write this stuff down.

Leah and I began by sharing a bottle of Californian brandy, and soon made short work of the salami.
'Are you reeelly a....magus?' she asked finally.
'For my sins.' I said, mock-repentant, hoping Aiwass wasn't listening.
'What is.... a magus?' Leah's cat-like eyes had a minute candle flame at the centre of each. She was divine, unreadable. I could either win her or leave America with my tail between my legs.
'This is what this magus does. I took down the *Book of the Law* in Cairo, in April 1904.'
'Cairo, New York?'
'Egypt' I said.
'I was twenty two, then.' Leah said. She was seven younger than me.
'I didn't realise that it was important at the time. I was really just the mouthpiece.' I asked her what she wanted to be painted as. She must have read my thoughts. It happened so frequently in those early days I am surprised we bothered with conversation. She replied,
'A dead soul.' Leah pulled a circle of salami skin out through her thick, wide lips. They looked whitish, and curiously unwrinkled.
'So is the *Book of the Law* all done, now?'
'I am forbidden to alter a single punctuation mark. I would not dare.'
'So what's next?'
'You mean for the rest of the evening?' Steady, Beast, steady.
'No I mean, for the rest of your life. Do you have any other

projects?'

'The knowledge of what is occult, or hidden, must be made over to everybody. Then the world will change. To that end I write, I preach, and I await further instruction.'

'Instruction from who? Aiwass?'

'If Aiwass wants to contact me. It could be someone else.' One of Leah's legs was in contact with some of Renata's icecream. She took her forefinger and ran it over her flesh. I wanted to stop her doing it, so I could lick it off. She put her finger into her wide mouth and slowly sucked it.

'Are those guys who were on the stairs onto you?' I guessed that the flatfoot 'tecs, keen to discover if I had a German Dreadnought hidden in the bath, had quizzed my visitors on the way up.

'They think I'm a spy, but they don't have a clue who I am.' I said.

'Neither do I, exactly' said Leah. Her wide flat mouth parted for a moment as it accepted another fingerful of Renata's cinnamon-flavoured emissions. Then, catlike, she got up and started to explore. I was fascinated to see what would attract her.

She curiously picked up the top one of a pile of small black books, an edition of *The Book of the Law*, then laid it on one side. Not ready for that? I could wait. I said nothing and pretended not to notice. Next she flicked through some copies of *The Equinox*. Should I tell her it was a publication which I had created and supported with numerous learnéd articles? No. Should I take her into the small room and show her the pentagram and the altar, only to hear her compare the eye of Horus painted on it with 'That weird stuff you see on a dollar bill'? She went into the altar room, and emerged a moment later. Silence.

Leah's attention finally homed onto two canvases stacked against the walls.

'So you paint.'

'Sometimes I am so inspired I do four or five a night.' I said.

'Have you studied painting?'

'A little..... What I am trying to do is grasp the essence.' I tried to sound offhand. Should I tell her that none of the arts would be the same after I had touched on them? No, save the best wine till last.

Leah's basilisk eyes opened wide. She was impressed with the contrast between my gifts and my obvious modesty. She came and sat down again, and I selflessly gave her the last of the brandy.

'What does TO MEGA THERION mean?' she asked.

'It has many meanings. You could say it meant 'The Great Beast'' I replied modestly.

'Is Aleister Crowley the Great Beast, as well?' I nodded.

Normally, when courting - and when is one not? - I rub a little ointment including civet into the base of the hairs. Having closely barbered myself that day, I had been obliged to smear a little of my heavenly jar of come-to-me behind each ear.

I got up and bowed formally, standing as close to my new goddess as my magus-hood allowed. As I did so, I noticed that my left foot was squirting out a strange bowel-coloured, wormlike emanation from underneath the sole. It was a relief to discover that this was not an apport of excrement, a calling card of malicious Goetia determined to spoil my fun. I had simply been standing carelessly on an opened tube of yellow oil paint.

I moved my sandal to one side, and then I bowed again. Down, down, phallotropic head! The candle flickered and I stood back again. With a wave of the sleeves of my robe, my essence was finally wafted over. I saw her nostrils flare, slightly. She was hooked, mine. She would give herself willingly to the service of The Work. 'At your service, madam.' We would raise each other to the heights of passionate happiness, and then -

(More Next Week)

It was Leah who suggested I go to purchase another bottle of brandy. I arrived at the bar across the street to witness an extraordinary sight. Both my 'tecs, filled to their snap-brims with likker, were paying court to the enormous Renata in a very small booth next to the bar. Presumably they thought there was enough of her to go round for both of them. In order that they could file their bar chits as expenses, the 'tecs were still quizzing - insofar as their sozzled condition allowed - Renata, on my credentials. I was standing directly in her eyeline, when she turned round looking for me, and reader, *she never saw me*.

BEAST DISAPPEARS

Those of you who are thinking that she must have left her spectacles at home are barking up completely the wrong tree. If she had been that blind, she would not have bothered looking. What was happening, was that I had *made myself invisible*. The conversation shows the sort of oppression that I had had to endure in my days as a magus in America, but invisibility enabled me to effortlessly eavesdrop.

'To obtain credit...has Herr Crowley ever used any of these aliases?...' Vern was passed a piece of paper by his identical chum. 'Here, Vern.' Vern One bent to read the list under the oil lamp on the barrel head table. Vern Two now had his hand covertly on Renata's generous dimpled thigh, the scoundrel.
'Compte de Belstrae.' Renata shook her head.
'Nope' Vern tried again.
'Baron Svaroff? The Laird of Boleskine?'
'Yeah' said Renata, clearly distracted. 'That's what he calls himself. Baron Sure-nuff, the Lord of....' Then Renata, in stage parlance, 'dried', as the hands upon her grew bolder. I was tempted to smack her. I had all my aliases posted prominently on my doorbell but as soon as some drunken gumshoe put his Saturn finger up her, the stupid slut couldn't remember even one of them.
'Relax honey, we got all night. We know he's a German spy. We're just waiting to see who else he contacts before we turn him in.'
'I didn't know he was a German spy!' Renata squealed. ' My sister is in there with him right now! He could be murdering her!' She tried to get up, but the two Verns now jointly held her down.
'Sit down, honey. He won't be **able** to hurt her.'
'How can I know she's safe?' **Renata** sniffed.

Renata peered round the brightly lit bar to check I had not escaped. A completely naked negro, who had been balancing on a barrel behind us lost his balance and fell backwards through the window, to jeers from his friends. A second later he reappeared in the window, covered in his own blood, vaulted through and stepped up to the bar. Renata's eyes almost popped out of her head as he ordered a beer. But she still did not notice me.

'That's right honey, relax. We got a man in the hall. Germany may have surrendered but Herr Crowley's not going anywhere.'

The 'tecs then invited Renata to a 'swell party uptown'. As I left they were pooling their cash for a cabriolet, to make a night of it. Dionysus had called to the Righteous Sister, and away went her devotion to her sister, her dinner party and I have not doubt, as the evening wore on, her pink satin girdle with whalebone stays.

EXPLANATION OF INVISIBILITY

A true Adept should always be able to make himself invisible. The Adept who murdered six prostitutes in London in 1888 and eviscerated them - popularly known as Jack The Ripper - had the highest mastery of that Art. The murders gave him all the necromantic powers he needed so at the end, 'Jack' could disappear from people actively seeking him.

I had myself mastered the simple basics of the technique and-without directly murdering anyone - could by my Will reduce my impression on people to a negligible one. When undergoing a test via a Kirlean photograph, which measures the energies of the etheric body, I have, when my Will is imposed to reduce my presence made no impression on the negative of the Ether at all. This is a proven fact. Seven Professors at the Sorbonne have attested to my abilities in this field.

In the bar I had carefully repeated this state of reduced emanation, to avoid being drawn into the conversation. In fact I had been so successful in self diminution that in spite of the fact I was wearing a kilt of the McGregor tartan, it took some time to obtain the attention of the young barkeep. Eventually, by exuding the etheric selectively in his direction, then using my hypnotic stare, I was able to persuade the boy, new to the neighbourhood, to give me two bottles on credit. Confirmation that my powers of invisibility were still at their zenith was vouchsafed when both 'tecs stared straight through me as I left.

This all shows that I would have made a very good German Agent indeed, if I had been minded to place occult powers in the service of the Reich, instead of writing tongue-in-cheek articles, published because Germans have no sense of humour. During the Second World War, my occult skills were finally recognised and put to use for my country during the crucial Battle of Britain. I could explain how, in due course. It is literally, an astonishing story, and would leave you in no doubt as to my genuine patriotism. That, however is another story.

Back in the apartment, with my Subtle Bodies reflating slowly to their previous dimensions, I went to work painting, with a kitchen knife, ochre, burnt Siena and umber, mixed on an old dinner plate, while Leah lay naked, smelling faintly of damp bedlinen, on the ottoman at the side of the main room of my apartment, an oil lamp by her side. I slashed at any canvases that resisted my genius.

By dawn, on my fifth canvas, I had something satisfactory. Its raw power astonished even Leah. At eight in the following morning, we went out for coffee and bagels before returning to the flat for our next, and most pertinent assignation with the Eternal. For the sex instinct is the only Eternal, is the only god - did you not know that?

I surreptitiously refreshed myself with stimulants that enhanced the god of love's visitations, and then for the next twentyfour hours we made endless love.

In the ensuing weeks, until it got too cold, Leah would sit around naked in my apartment with the Mark of The Beast, four concentric rings with a maltese cross in the middle, drawn between her breasts. Some Scarlet Women have been tattooed, some branded with the Mark, but Leah's Will was indifferent on permanent markings. I cannot say I understood why, but after one or two tries on my part, with her tears flowing, and the magical current clearly not induced, I encouraged her, as a sign of my continuing favour, to simply use henna or mascara on herself, and 'mark' me for her own instead.

I gave her the same Chinese dagger which I had wanted to use on her. She heated it in a candle flame, and then, having made an invocation to Aiwass I had penned, she pressed the smoking blade upon my rump, which sizzled satisfyingly for a second.

The pain was excruciating. The greasy smoke from my barbequed behind wreathed and coiled at waist level around us both. I bit into a pillow to stop myself screaming. Later I remembered a cryptic, non-canonical saying of Christ: He that is near me is near the Flame.

However stoical I was, I could feel my Angel's heart was not in the task. I yearned for a cruel, indomitable woman to perform atrocities on me without further ado, and Leah had a natural modesty at that time which inhibited her from more than one or two sadistic excursions. Later on, of course, her real beastliness came out, till she finally renounced all contact with me.

For the most part, during this period our relationship was innocently cordial, our cupid - strewn path very much in the public eye. I would paint the naked Leah while chatting to visitors in a friendly fashion, sometimes wearing a painter's smock, sometimes simply my birthday suit. It all would seem the most natural thing in the world. I have never bettered the artistic effort that I put into those first canvases.

The door was seldom locked. So every weekend her fat sister would appear and try to drag her away. Leah's mother had no objections to us living together and the sister's visits became hilarious examples of staged indignation at the natural course of affection. Leah wrote the final visit out as a playlet. Since I triumph in it, it must display some aspect of poetic truth, however much it carries the stains of melodrama of its day-

NOVA SPECCIA DE LA BESTIA TRIONFANTE[37]
OR
HIS SCARLET WOMAN

[The studio of The Beast, a prominent Necromancer, painter, and - in spite of himself - Philanthropist, in Lower Manhattan. Bohemian ambience. Paintings of Leah, his mistress are strewn everywhere, finished in the careless yet powerful style of the Logos. Leah herself, a slim young woman with a large mouth, is sitting next to a sickly oil stove, re-filling a henna pattern of the Mark of The Beast, between her breasts. ~~She thinks her breasts are too small. The Beast thinks they are adorable.~~[38] *She is looking critically at her work in a mirror as Renata, Leah's sister, bursts through the door. Renata is clothed all in grey wool, and like a mad sheep, begins screaming right away. This goes on for ten minutes and is the high point of the tragedy.]*

Finally-

Renata [Gasping] Leah - come. You poor darling. You are in Danger, you do not Realise. I have heard the most DREADFUL things about this man. Not only is he is a black magician, he visits Turkish baths. He will betray you with Another if he has not done so already. (*Renata sees henna marks*) Oh, what has he

---

37   With sincere apologies to Fr G. Bruno. A.C.
38   *Scratched out in Leah's original version, after a disagreement with the cunning little bitch over how the Mark of the Beast should be applied. Henna is a temporary decoration. Trying to instruct her by example, I allowed her to pierce my earlobes with a cobbler's hole punch using the altar as a rest for my head. A.C.*

done to you now?! [*Weeps. Leah, in contrast to her sister, is calm and untroubled. She smiles, pityingly.*]

Leah   I don't need rescuing, Renata. It's alright. He says that every man and every woman is a Star. Isn't that beautiful?

Renata   It's insane!

Leah   He is a Good Man. He tells me my Soul is a Star.

[*Hubbub in the body of the house. Cries of 'hear, hear' from the packed audience. Leah holds up a little black book.*]

Leah   He has been chosen to bring in the New Age. You can read all it in the Book of the Law.

Renata   Horses' ass!

[*Hisses from the audience, Thelemites all, to their sandal-thongs.*]

Leah   Don't be afraid for me, sister. He has revived my soul and given me an awakening through love!

Renata   Oh, this will end badly, mark my words!

Leah   You're just jealous. [*Violins strike up. Lighting change. Rose petals fall from the flies.*] I'm going to be his Scarlet Woman for ever now. My Name shall be Alostrael!

Renata   And what is THAT supposed to mean??

[*Music. To Mega Therion, The Great Beast arrives on a golden throne carried by naked male Slaves of the Bathhouse. He acknowledges the applause of the crowd. Renata points to the smirking, towel-draped Slaves.*]

Renata   How are you going to keep him at home, anyhow? In the last week alone, this guy you're going with has been buggered in every Turkish Bath in Manhattan!

Leah   [*To the gods*] You don't understand! We both are votaries of the god of Ecstasy! For my part, I'm going to be loud, and adulterous. I'm going to dare to do every deed! Now, leave, and never darken our doorway again!

[*Renata starts screaming again as rotten tomatoes and dead cats are thrown at her from the audience of Thelemites. Rapturous applause for the Triumphant Beast as he takes Alostrael onto his throne, to sit beside him. Curtain torn down, to triumphant music as universal Satyriasis breaks out between audience and performers.*[39]]

In fact I was not there at all at the last visit of Renata. I was uptown, arranging an exhibition of my canvases.[40] Unveiled, their raw power literally staggered the gallery owners. However as soon as they heard I intended shortly to return to England, they stifled their earlier admiration, and pretended a lack of interest.

One example will suffice of the treatment I received. I brought my canvases through to an office in the rear of one gallery. The owner, an effeminate young bachelor with monocle, blazer and spotted bow tie

---

39   In Theatre, as in everything else, it is clear that Thelemic practices are years ahead of their time. A.C.

40   I was let down at the last moment. The American art market is as closely guarded a phalanx of interests as I have ever come across, apart from the smut peddling news fraternity, and the Bank of England. Outsiders who try to 'break in' to any of those 'gentlemens' clubs are coldshouldered with the steely-eyed determination that only money can provide. A.C.

and affecting a 'phoney' English accent had the cheek to ask me if I had ever studied painting 'properly'.

'No' I replied. 'I have studied rock climbing. Is that good enough for you?' Young master Monocle excused himself and went away to fawn upon a poodle-carrying customer who want to buy a seascape.

I decided to teach him a lesson. I took down the visitor's book from its podium, deposited one of the Logos' own distinctive calling cards in the middle pages, replaced the open book on its podium, and left, after petting the poodle and smiling to all and sundry.[41]

A less fun-filled magus than myself would have simply set Aiwass loose to take the place apart, in the same way that Elisha set she-bears upon the children who mocked his baldness. But why destroy the gallery system when one day it will show my vision to an astonished world?

I was determined to take Leah home with me, as soon as we had enough money for two tickets. Leah liked the idea of going back to her birthplace, to heal its bleeding wounds. She also now became pregnant, to her surprise, as well as mine. The three tortoiseshell sticks that I used for consulting the *I King*[42] kept coming up with the same trigrams indicating that the child should be born in Europe. We began a series of exercises designed to attract sufficient capital. By Exercises, I refer of course to the discipline, central to Crowleyanity, known vulgarly as 'Sex Magic.'

Hold on to your hats at the back there. The roller coaster you are now sitting on is going to take some unusual turns.

---

41 *The Dalai Lama's excrement is sacred, and mine, wherever it is left, is a sacred, Magickal Act. Amen. A.C.*

42 *In the first two decades of this century, Oriental wisdom was largely confined to the Orient. I had to drag it, kicking and screaming, to London. Today, in the shadow of the second Great Conflict, I note that no less an authority than Professor Carl Jung of Zurich has endorsed the use of the book of the I King. It is a perfect example of the syncretic effects of Crowleyanity, outwardly denied but in fact today permeating the world, its forbidden perfumes wafting through every conscious barrier erected against them. A.C.*

IV The Emperor

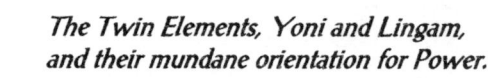

The Twin Elements, Yoni and Lingam, and their mundane orientation for Power.

A Short Disquisition on
SEX MAGICK

THEORETICAL BASIS OF SEX MAGICK FROM THE TANTRIC TRADITION

The *Book of the Law* instructs me personally - there you go again, I had nothing to do with it - to be a teacher of men, and although this is not, and never will be a handbook of Magick, I shall set down a little of wandsmanship - since half of you out there already have a Wand and you might as well know how to use it on the other half - in as simple a form as possible. Those in possession of a Yoni, known in occult lore as The Mouth Of Isis, may be aware that to lift the veil of Isis is to penetrate a great mystery: and this is what we are going to do.

Naturally I am fully aware as an Adept, that a little knowledge is a dangerous thing, and that at a certain stage in your Adeptship, before you are fully qualified, you will have a Little Knowledge. But you cannot make an omelette without breaking eggs. My advice is to avoid the danger period by reading the following, then putting it into action as quickly as possible, preferably while holding the book in one hand, as a crib.

¶ Both halves of humanity are assured of possessing an arsehole, 'asshole', a *vas nefandum* whose outward and visible Sign is like to an Asterisk.[43]

DO NOT GO TO SLEEP, AT THE BACK OF THE CLASS!

Depending on where it is placed, you may need a mirror to find yours. Check it is yours, by touching it lightly with a lingam.[44] Put your name upon it using a special sub-Enochian language, but your Mirror will be able to magically decode it-

Aleister Crowley (Dirty Bugger)

¶ The Wands, asterisks, Yonis etc., all are Sites Of Pleasure, useful in any combination for raising the Ecstatic Current. The ancient Greeks were told by Tieresias, who changed sex, that Woman *could* have more pleasure than Man. One of Woman's Sites of Pleasure, called by the Greeks, χλιτορισ, the 'key', is particularly important in this respect. (Girls, all together, don't look so bored, try finding each others' for a change.)

---

43   A mouse's arsehole, and the Star of Bethlehem both suffer the same designation in this wretched two dimensional world. Tell me, do they 'mean' the same thing, then??.   **** !   Four mice to you, too. A.C.
44   Adepts may use their own, but this is not *recommended for beginners. A.C*

¶ When enough current has been raised, a wish may be made, preferably at the point of orgasm.

¶ Remember to hold the desired object as strongly as possible in your mind at the crucial moment.

¶ If you are greedy in your Wants for sex magic, you will not get everything you ask for.[45]

¶ The ecstatic current raised on its own in a solitary Act may also have considerable consequences, if the instructions are followed through. But as in most Yogic practices, a minimum of twenty years training is required for the best results.

One of the ignorant slanders raised against my name in the Yellow Papers was that I sponged off those gullible people who followed me.

In the first place, I rebut firmly the idea of slavish 'followers'. The job of life is to find your own True Will, not someone else's. Besides, in America it was slim pickings all the way. The reader will have already understood already that during my stay in America I was regularly handicapped by a shortage of funds. Does this accord with the idea of 'cashing in'? No, someone else will do that, for the country welcomes frauds, fake fakirs and hucksters with open arms. It is the genuine article that they cannot stand. It is an oriental tradition that the Magus is supported by his disciples or followers, but in America, if

---

45 A Scarlet Woman of mine put it succinctly. 'You will get what you need, with sex magic, which is not necessarily what you think you want.'

you actually have something to impart they have no time for you, and will not bother to try to understand you.

I am sure that this will all change as the New Aeon gets under way.

I arrived back at the apartment after the fiasco of the gallery, and attempted to raise the ecstatic current with Leah. We were in dire straits, financially. I banished all thoughts during the Act relating to Mercury's ongoing retrograde, unhappily aspected to Saturn. I was rewarded - within two days - with a letter from Raoul, but only containing a very small cheque.

Raoul's cheque was not enough for even the meanest passage. I told Leah that we would have to work night and day to raise more money, and she should put away all thoughts of scepticism about the process until we had achieved the desired objective, explaining that when her morning sickness was upon her, I would have to find other partners in order to make an unbroken sequence of supplications.

Understanding it was for a greater purpose, and rapidly learning that the Law of Thelema meant that the True Will was never thwarted, she concurred, and I sought out the services of Helen. Since she had failed to mount the stairs when she was paid to do so, she owed me one, but I never found her again.

People have frequently asked me what proof I have that Sex Magic works. I think it might be a good idea to include at this stage the testimony of someone else, who is a sober and diligent witness. Fortunately I have an excellent, almost eidetic recall of speech patterns, so I only have to muse for a moment before an example comes to me.

G***** was once a youthful disciple of mine, and had been able to regulate the troublesome business of my funding, after I was declared bankrupt over ten years ago. His family, were appalled by his association with me and young G***** has begged me that his name not be coupled with anything which might be a blot upon the family escutcheon.⁴⁶

G***** was fascinated by my tales of China and when his family were trying to separate us, he went to China as Reuters correspondent. G*****'s idea of reporting was to get hold of a Chinaman who spoke English and keep him on a string. Heaven knows what nonsense they told him. It is probably why China is in such a mess now. Hither, G*****.

Imagine G***** today in his chair, tall with an aquiline profile, his eyes twinkling, his hands round the bowl of his pipe as he knocks out the ash which falls on his carpet slippers. As he speaks, he shows a pair of prominent canine teeth, rather yellow. In Bulgaria, he was taken for a vampire and several persons he tells me, tried to avert the Evil Eye when they saw him. Let me as a domestic touch put his wife, a tall, giraffe like woman, on the opposite side of the fire in their comfortable country house in ——shire. Giraffe pours the tea for you. You bend forward so as not to miss a syllable of G*****'s sonorous, patrician testimony.

'I was interested in all kinds of Eastern philosophies, when I was up at university. Then I met Mr Crowley, who had been at Trinity Cambridge at the height of the university's infatuation with Oscar Wilde. I was present at an invocation of his, and had definitely felt a presence which I located at one corner of the room. However, when I spoke to others it was clear that although they felt it too, they had placed it elsewhere. But I was hooked. At any rate, I decided to test out Mr Crowley's system of 'sex magic' for myself. Since I was attracted to the opposite sex, that seemed to be the way forward.'

A log falls in, sending up a shower of sparks in the large baronial hall. G***** pushes it back with his foot. 'Can't have the carpet burning up, it's an original William Morris. I know it needs replacing, but cost a fortune to have it all redone.' Come, we have not summoned

---

46   *G*****'s brother even changed his name to become a second rate novelist, trying to distance himself from the family, who manufacture ceramic lavatories. The family escutcheon which gave such trouble, presumably included a picture of their product. A.C.*

G***** to have him talk of his recarpeting his fourteenth century hall, although as supplier of closets to the Empire, he could do it twenty times. The light is dying outside. Soon he will have to go and balance the accounts books for his farms- 'And that's a bloody boring job too.' Oh, the burden of inherited wealth! He should have followed my example and run through it. Get on with it, G*****.

'Where were we?'

'Sex magic.'

'Ah yes. Well I had this flat in Paddington at the time. It was not difficult to find someone. I went out and I found a prostitute.' The wife demurely pours milk into your tea, at a nod. G***** is wed, for many years now, amused at his flagrant former self, reformed. You refuse the sugar bowl with its menacing tongs.

' I took her back to my flat and fucked her.' There is a little silence, and G***** chuckles, in the silence, to fill it up. 'At the moment of orgasm, I wished for a teacher. Someone from whom I could learn about the *Egyptian Book of The Dead.*'

You will of course see from the direction that the anecdote is taking, that G****** was not above referring to other sources of mysticism than my writings to explore his Will. If he had asked me, in the first place I would of course have been able to tell him anything he wished to know about the *Egyptian Book of the Dead.*

'Did you tell the prostitute what you were doing?'

'No. I walked to Paddington railway station afterwards, and got on a train. I stayed on the train as far as it went. When the train finally stopped I got off and started walking. I walked until it started to grow dark, when I found shelter in a cave. I spent the night in the cave. In the morning, feeling hungry, I went into the local village to buy some breakfast. In the greengrocers' I went into, the man behind the counter was reading *The Egyptian Book of the Dead.* Oh yes, and the grocer later told me that the cave I had stayed the night in was the same cave that Merlin's teacher lived in.'

Q.E.D.

(This is a putrid adolescent little sketch that Leah did after I told her of my vision of Anubis coming for Raoul. I told her he was wearing a tail coat and I notice now the stupid cow has put him in a white dinner jacket. I think I can almost detect a smirk on his face, as well. But I include it as an example of canonical errors in the vision of Crowleyanity within these pages.)

In order to explain Raoul's absolute fascination with Crowleyanity, we do not need to look into Greek Love, potions, cats or crucified toads accused of being Christ and other slimy maledictions. It was his Will, just as it was his Will to follow me. The Will is the sacred path of each individual. It cannot be guessed at by scrutinising the fathers of remarkable men. My father, for instance, was a brewer, albeit a teetotal one. Peter Brook, a promising young theatre director who recently has solicited my help in correctly interpreting the occult invocations in Marlowe's 'Doctor Faustus'[47] had a father who manufactured laxatives.

Raoul's father was a nobody, a lower class man of timid views, whose only ambitions in life were vested in his brilliant son, whose mind he could never understand. See him at Raoul's wedding with his head cocked, standing uncertainly at the side, in his shabby suit. Betty the bride laughs out loud, in a cocktail dress studded with mother of pearl, a red hat with a red veil on her head: Betty drinks, and thinks fondly of high old times in the Café Royal, with salt cellars full of

---

47 *Faustus you will remember has Helen brought to him, and tries to achieve immortality by intimacy, 'Sweet Helen, make me immortal with a kiss!' Just as Milton was of the devil's party without knowing it, Marlowe was a Thelemite, before time.*

cocaine. Raoul drinks and his liquid eyes open. His capacity for vision and ecstasy stirs, ready to take flight. But the father's eyes glaze over with anxiety at what Youth is getting into. He looks away for an instant at his mousey wife, and then when he looks back again at Raoul, he starts at a flash of white light. The photographer has started. He presses his bulb again. Too late. The wedding cake has already begun to fall.

When the dancers have been helped down from the table and sent home, the honeymoon begins - at home. The Father tries desperately to show Betty the serious side of life. At one end of the chintz- covered drawing room hanging on the wall is a little shrine made of black crepe, around a black framed photograph of a private, recently killed in action, with his medal below.
This is Raoul's cousin, who died in the War. Raoul used to worship him, when he was a boy. When he died it left a gap. I'm afraid that dreadful man is filling it. Hero worship. I would like to show you something I have been collecting, newspaper items about Mr Crowley, ever since my son began corresponding with this animal. Mr Crowley is vermin. He is filth. He is the lowest of the low. Depraved and corrupt. If you read between the lines - excuse my language - bugger. And worse. He has been refused permission to speak at Cambridge, for fear of corrupting the undergraduates. I would like you to swear upon this bible, if you please, that now you are married you will keep Raoul from him. He says he will go and join Crowley wherever and whenever he is bid. You should tell him, now he is married to you, he should support you, and not go gallivanting around.
And Betty would laugh her special Café Royale laugh, when all the heads of the tables round would turn to see what Tiger Woman would get up to next. She would light a cigarette, - *does anyone mind if I fume?* - and puffing a fat ball of smoke at the photograph of the dead cousin, would say;
'Don't worry, Mr Loveday. I've lived well in the past. Just because I'm married again doesn't mean I have to stop taking my clothes off. I can support us both now by modelling.' And Raoul's mother would

say that he son would never live off his wife's earnings, particularly when he was so well qualified, and Raoul and Betty would smile a secret laugh at each other. And Raoul would repeat his creed, the creed of eternal optimism and youth,

'I know I've got a degree now father, from Cambridge, but what is the point, tell me, of spending a lifetime miserably calculating the trajectory of falling bombs, or some such new science, when with the right spiritual guidance I could be tapping into the real secrets of the universe?'

And the mother's little eyes would moisten in her small, floury face, and her hands would start scrimping round for the apron corner to wipe all evidence of emotion away as soon as it arrived. And the father would fold his cuttings again, and put the rubber band round them, and put them reverently back in the drawer, all the time shaking his venerable grey and empty head, as if they, not *Liber Legis*, were the true Holy Writ.

KING OF DEPRAVITY ESCAPES

In the end, Leah's mother was persuaded to give us the money for the passage to England. The night I was looking for her, Helen had disappeared from the bar to get some 'dope'; morphine in her case (she had become addicted when a nurse). I found that I was alone at the counter with Vern the 'tec: on his own. I decided to see if he could understand the rudiments of Thelemic Law. I explained what I was planning to do with Helen was for a specific result. At the same time, I was beginning to suspect that a mercenary or unconscious partner made the successful achievement of aims in Sex Magic that much more difficult.

'Ya mean, it's no good screwin' wid Helen? Like a dead battery?'

'Precisely. It may be why I have not got the money to leave yet'

'You're plum nuts. You're still here because we haven't busted you yet, buddy. Just you wait.' Vern drank up, and left, importantly.

Vern's warning was timely. I realised that several members of a secret group who I had been in contact with during the War would be visiting me next week. They had written to me accusing me of plagiarism of one of their secret rites. While I was more than willing to defend myself against the charge, it was not worth persuading Verns One and Two that the governing body of the O.T.O.[48] were not German spies, but maguses. The last thing I needed at that moment was an arrest, and a foolish court case. I decided to concentrate my Will into a rapid resolution of the situation, without Helen.

Back at the flat I performed a very detailed and vigorous Operation VIII°, imagining myself taken by Pan, who arrived in a shower of gold. It kept turning to silver, and threatened to go to copper, but I won through by willpower. At the end, my Ecstasy was so great I must have passed out. Sheer exhaustion had made me forget to re-ingest the fluids[49] but even so, when I opened my eyes I was lying on the floor, lingam in hand while Leah was making water upon my face. It had been something I had asked her to do a number of days ago, to invoke money, and Leah had obviously been turning it over in her mind.

When she had emptied herself on me, she got up and slowly started plastering my head with dollar bills, first wetting them by dunking them on the floor.

'I've got the money' she said. It was then I realised I must have done better than I thought on the astral plane.

'Of course. Not for the first time, I've surpassed myself.' I re-

---

48 *Ordo Templi Orientis*, a German masonic order, who believed that I had stolen their secrets when I advocated the magician imbibing the sexual juices after IX°. In the end they realised that I had come across this important magickal conclusion independently. As for me, the increased reach of my tongue in recent years has been prodigiously helpful in this regard. I realise teeth were always overrated. A.C.

49 Essential for practitioners of serious sex-magic. If you remember to do it regularly, your supply of prana will be enhanced and you will live a long happy and healthy life. Look at me! A.C.

marked. We then had a foolish argument about who had done most to obtain the money. Leah claimed the credit, with her Golden Shower operation. Since she was holding the money in her hand at the time, I remarked I could not see how Cause could lead to Effect, even in magick. Time would have had to flow backward.

'Well then, you're stupid.' Leah said. 'I've been thinking about nothing else, right? And *that's* why it's worked.' The dying Henry says to his son,

'Thy wish is father, Harry to that thought.' Useless to quote the only poet of note[50] to Leah, at this moment. The Swiss/American axis of her education, or lack of it, did not include much culture till I arrived.

'I was holding on to it coming back here' says my Scarlet Woman. I went and wiped myself down.

Though the cause of our good fortune continued to be a bone of contention, we were able to book the last double berth on the *SS Sirius* (naturally), which was leaving at midnight the next night. We stole down the fire escape, my pregnant Scarlet Woman and I, hand in hand, giving the 'tecs, the landlord, and the O.T.O. the slip. I took my papers, but left most of the paintings on the walls, as in an Egyptian tomb: their eyes staring out forever at the abandoned six sided altar and its strange hues. I also left the pentagram on the floor, and in the air the insidious hint of of my own Perfume of Immortality, overlaid with incense mixed with old marijuana smoke.

I looked out of the stern of the boat as the lights of New York fell below the horizon, and remembered that Helen still owed me a fuck. I have never been back to claim it.

---

50   Apart from myself.. A.C.

I sometimes take walks, of an afternoon, upon the beach in Hastings, England, where I am writing[51] this account. With my moon in Pisces, it is hardly surprising that the sea brings on the thoughts of eternity. I do not climb the muddy cliffs. My Conversion of America (Failed) ended thirty years ago. My asthma has been bad and so I am confined to the shingle, and besides, my weight, I notice has been dropping. My muscles are slowly wasting away. I dwell here, alone in my boarding house, sometimes I think I am no better than a beggar. They are revered in India, I know.

I moved out of London when it started to get bombed. The problem with Age, and Hastings, and the War's End, is the awful and unending *boredom*. Hitler at least was a proper diabolic adversary. It would be better, if I had chess opponents, or mountains I could climb. Anything: More *cunt*.

Your end serves you right, you might say, after that nasty joke you made about your aunt, giving her address for the Zeppelin to drop a land mine on her. My aunt is dead. Where are my relatives, my loved ones? Nowhere. *My Name is Alastor, Wanderer of the Waste.*

I really don't like being old, at all. I think I shall pretend it is not happening. It's getting harder and harder to find a vein, I tell you. And that's no joke, particularly when you need a little something fast, to keep the asthma at bay.

Recently, storms tore at the shingle on the beach, and it yielded the carcase of a Dutch merchantman, filled with spirits and wine, which had been driven onto the beach in a storm, two hundred years ago. Instead of making for harbour when the storm broke and smashed the rudder, the crew had become drunk, mutinied and - perhaps hoping for a share in the wrecked vessels valuable cargo - had driven her hard onto the beach. The storm was so violent that the ship was immediately

---

51   *My landlord offered to act as secretary - in exchange for the treatment I was giving him for some little trouble with his wand however it is best for him, for the moment, not to discover what the components are of the pills I administer to him are, which I fear he would do if the MS was entrusted to him. Incidentally he reports excellent results. A. C.*

incarcerated in the stones and sand which the sea threw down.

Now there are a dozen retired colonels with plans for raiding the hulk, with the prospect of gold - there always has to be gold, and two hundred year old bottles of port as prizes.

Nothing will be done here of course. It is all just words. No one knows who has title to the wreck. The town is in a coma. The whole country is spiritually bankrupt, from the effort of winning a just war.

As for me, I suspect the end might be nigh. The wand is still operative, but the right hip joint is frankly, arthritic. I step over the blackened ridges of timber of the Dutchman, when the tide is out. Will my reputation be picked up, one day? Or will it be forgotten? I agree I have been bad, but not as bad as some. Do we tell the puffers of Reputation, on Fleet Street, that The Beast died a stalwart patriot?

'Come off it. We can't use that, guv!'

Not even if patriotism is revealed as the last refuge of a scoundrel? Come back, Rupert Brooke,[52] all is forgiven.

Perhaps I should have been worse. Eternity is a long time to wait, for recognition. Back to our tale.

MONSTER OF LUST ON HIGH SEAS

The cabin that Leah had secured was pokey, foul smelling and about as far below the waterline as passengers could get without actually stepping in bilgewater. Oddly, there were no corners. It was like living inside a decayed egg. The walls were bubbling with rust, and there was a box which ran down the middle of the floor that I suspect carried the propeller shaft. This suspicion was confirmed when a noisy grinding and thudding started emanating from it, as we got under way. I immediately protested to the purser that the inhuman conditions would bring on all sorts of illnesses, including the Scarlet Woman's termination, for which he would be permanently cursed anywhere he sailed through the seven seas.

---

52   *A minor poet who died of a mosquito bite.A.C.*

After weighing up the curse, he awarded us a slightly better cabin, with a porthole. I felt rather proud of myself. Back in New York, the crack regiments of the O.T.O., the vigilant 'tecs, Helen and even the rent hungry landlord would be milling slowly round a deepening mystery, trying to put together the story of my final hours, sifting through the apartment, half-expecting me to jump out of one of my pictures. *Whither did they vanish?* In order to pay for the better accommodation, I agreed to fill in as ship's lecturer, since their regular man had gone down with 'flu. I suggested I begin with a lecture on Freemasonry.

As soon as I repeated the word, 'Freemasonry', forked lightning broke out in the clouds above, and destroyed the radio mast and most of the ship's navigational equipment.

I should have known it was to be no regular voyage. In the four hours that it took to prepare my Masonic text, the *SS Sirius*, now with no compass or working radio sailed straight into one of the worst storms that the North Atlantic could provide. On board the reeling *SS Sirius*, unable to radio for help, the stewards puked, the fires in the galleys died and in the raging dark with its fluorescent spume, the New Era shyly introduced itself. Lo, the Logos of the Aeon was on board, and the Scarlet Woman was carrying their Beast Cub.

The captain's deluded belief was that we should head for the centre of the storm, so we did just that. Within six hours, the *SS Sirius* was blindly scaling the sides of greenish-black hundred foot waves, and carving timorously through their slathering crested peaks, before it dived queasily into the troughs. Leah wisely took to her bed, but I became exhilarated.

There was a blackboard in the empty stateroom with a chalked announcement on it, that due to heavy seas, the shipping company would accept no responsibility for any passengers that ventured on deck. I scrubbed that out, and wrote that Doctor Aleister Crowley would lecture on Freemasonry at 6 pm sharp. I ordered the rows of gilt chairs to be lashed together so that the audience would not slide about uncontrollably on the wooden floor. I wished to clear my head before the lecture, so I went outside, ignoring the stewards' foolish shrieked warnings.

In the main, the class of person attracted to shipboard service seem to be pernicious sodomites.

The difficulty I had opening the heavy doors to the deck reminded me of another door, in a Ziggurat, in a dream, when I had been granted a closeness to my Holy Guardian Angel. I had no idea, as I stepped through into the maëlstrom for a breath of fresh air, that I would encounter her in the flesh later that night.

I think I may go down and perform an operation VIII° over the wreck of the Dutchman, tonight. Up against one of the ribs, which stick out of the sand now, like a Spice Island native copulating with an unfruitful pepper tree. The difference of course is that the Spice Island natives have the support of an animist tradition, and will be cheered on, no doubt by the village. I would probably be arrested for exposure. Perhaps I should ignore the standing timbers, move inside the hull, lie down and simply fuck the mud.[53] It's a new moon in forty eight hours, a new spirit of emotional independence, free of all that nauseous and putrid regret-

It will be done at ☾'s eclipse after she has entered the First Degree of the First Decan of The Archer.[54]

Aiwass hath intoned!
Frater Perdurabo hath affirmed!

---

53 *Several accounts of how God created the first sentient creature include a similar rite. A.C.*
54 *5.30 PM GMT 24th November 1946.*

The worm will cringe, but obey the Will.
Oh, for the eternal service to Pan! *Vivat, vivat Vagina!*

INTENT OF OPERATION: To raise the energies of the past to the understanding of the present.[55] To bring to this flat, exhausted hinterland of postwar socialism all the manic, giggling glee with which the shrieking, drunken miscreants seized control of the rigging, cracked out more sail, gagged the master, and defying a hail of musket fire from the poopdeck, bayed to Satan to bring them to wreck on the shore.
A vision-
The ship's wheel spins uselessly as Satan's slaves impale the ship's goat and the Master's wife alike in god-like embraces. Monkey-like cabin boys ride on each other's backs in the driving spume, as the town lights wink and bob towards them over the writhing wavetops. Loose the topgallants! On! On to destruction!

Really Hitler put the wrong group in the camps. He should have rounded up anyone, regardless of creed or colour, who felt regret, in any form. It needs to be expunged from the human psyche, one way or another.

Passengers had been warned not to step onto the decks, but as a mountaineer, the conditions were no more than moderately challenging. A man who has survived the worst that K2 can throw at him can afford to take lesser threats to life and limb in his stride and there were enough handholds on the heaving, twisting superstructure of the boat for a novice, let alone an experienced Alpinist to feel quite safe. While I have smallish - and some say - feminine hands, with a deceptively slight frame about the shoulders, the same Tantric skills whereby I have gained understanding of my Holy Guardian Angel allowed me to use my body as a climbing instrument of endless subtlety and skill.
In fact it is a great pity that there is no film of me when I was in my

---

55   *Specifically, to find a typist for my manuscript. In this, it was immediately successful.. A.C.*

climbing prime. In the words of one expert, 'I was able to ascend underhangs with apparent ease which the professionals all judged impossible.' In other words, the disciples watched Christ ascending into heaven.

Climbing is all 'in the body'. The modern school of climbing, to propose to surmount K2 or Everest, by carrying as much oxygen as possible, is an insult to the experience, the mountain as well as one's own physique. I don't wish to meet god with a face mask on. (Some people don't wish to meet god by 'chasing the dragon', but the ecstatic component is structured differently in different persons. θελεμα does not preach.)

From the way the lifeboats swung widely in their stays, I judged the full roll of the ship to be in the nature of 75°. I crawled towards the front rail, using one of the port scuppers as a climbing chimney, as the mighty vessel threw itself crazily about, as if to toss me off its back. Fortunately I was wearing my climbing boots, as well as plus fours: if I had set out in my kilt, I would have lost the skin on my knees and more besides.

The salt water dashed at me from above, below, and beyond. I pulled myself upright at the forward railing. Fifty feet ahead of me was the bows. On either side of them, irregularly, huge swatches of water creamed out side ways, like angelic wings. Imagining Aiwass was in the lowering sky above me, I attempted to frig myself off, though both hands were needed to avoid being swept overboard. Before I retreated and left the elements to fight amongst themselves, I saw an eye, I cannot be sure if it was Aiwass', or Anubis, looking straight past me from the black clouds above.

I must have been in communion with the elements for longer than ordinary mortals. When I arrived in the state room for the lecture the gilt chairs were almost empty. The purser, a timorous English suburban type with a long face and sideburns as if he aspired to be something drawn by 'Boz', called naturally, Mr Whiskers, whispered unctuously that had been a few others half an hour before, but they had left, pleading sea sickness. He apologised. I said I did not care how many were there, as long as they listened and understood.

It was true that the room was pitching about in a most alarming way, if one was prone to take alarm at that sort of thing. I try to take it in my stride. With the right sort of mental training it is perfectly possible to keep the mind fixed on a objective no matter what mayhem is breaking out around you. Leah was sitting in the front row, green as a young lime, holding her stomach with her jaw half forward as if she was going pitch our last meal together into her own lap.[56] The purser banged with a duster on the podium for attention. He was barely audible above the continuous roaring of the storm outside, as he shuffled his hastily pencilled notes.

'In spite of the er, inclement weather, our lecturer bravely insists that he tells the few *heroic* souls who have made the dangerous pilgrimage here about Masonic Symbols in the Magic Flute.' I had proposed nothing of the kind, but that is the problem with letting others handle the announcements for one's public engagements. As for heroism, I had performed enough of that in the last half hour to make it a tale worth telling. Was no one even curious as to why I was standing in a widening puddle of salt water? Did they imagine I was magically creating water as I stood there?

One of the lessons of life is, that the stranger one appears, the fewer questions people will ask.

'Mr Crawley tells us (Oh, *dear*, no)... he is a distinguished poet and mountaineer.' (And?) 'He's walked across the Gobi Desert, - wherever that might be -' (Keep your humorous asides out of this, Whiskers.) - 'And he's now returning to England from New York, in order to propagate - (*Promulgate*, oaf.[57]) - 'the next World Religion which he tells us, and asks us not to be shocked, may well supercede Christianity.'

---

56   *It was just as well that I had not indeed paid for it, using my well cloak of invisibility to leave the restaurant after the rack of lamb, half a bottle of '88 brandy, and before the bill.*

57   *The incubation period for the New Age is concluded.*

'It will indeed' I said, in my most friendly and matter of fact voice. A whole row of the chairs which were not weighed down by being sat on made a sudden slide forward, as the *SS Sirius* recovered from a steeper wave than usual and nosed down into the next yawning trough.

'And there's a sign for you' I said. Whiskers looked round nervously, as if the demonic keening from the storm outside was specially for him.

Leah's chocolate gateau looked as if it was on the way back up, as well.[58] My first thought - uncharacteristic, I admit, but I do have a paterfamilias side - was a fear that she might give birth on the spot, and a fascination as to what might come out if she did -

HARLOT OF 'BEAST' DISCHARGES ANIMAL

The nausea and distress written on Leah's brow reminded me of my own mother's expression when she came upon me performing my first Creative Act. Some of you, reading 'John Bull' and other patriotic magazines owned by Horatio Bottomley, might be surprised to learn that I had a mother at all. My birth was of course my only sexual encounter with Mrs Crowley, Senior: Neither of us have had any desire to extend our forced intimacy by repetition -

My mother's doubts about her son were confirmed when she found me enjoying an early *empurplement* on the billiard table, with a parlour maid. We should have both been at prayers of a different kind. The maid was of course dismissed, but her own son was harder to get rid of.

My first fumblings were rapid, furtive and quite unremarkable, like other young men brought up in the squalid deprivation of the Exclu-

---

58 *The finest piece of American poetry - if that is not a contradiction in terms - I know was taught to me by a whore in New Orleans. It goes,*
   'There was a young girl called McNeil/Who went up on a large Ferris Wheel/ Halfway down, she looked down at the ground/and wasted a four dollar meal.'
   A.C.

sive Brethren, even more exclusive than the Plymouth Brethren, who consider themselves God's Chosen. I was born of the Elect, and my mother abhorred me, on instinct. When she discovered me and lusty Sally Lowe in the midst of sinfully staining the green baize, her mistrust hardened into the knowledge that I was a soul lost to Christ, born for the lakes of brimstone that quench not.

Of course, it was Sally who 'fell': the easiest employment open to her after having been dismissed from domestic service would have been to become a common prostitute.

When I was thirteen, and already doomed, in my mother's eye, the country was caught up in the mystery of the identity of the notorious 'Jack the Ripper' as a number of London women were murdered on the streets that they plied their trade on.

I became obsessed with the idea that I had caused the fall into prostitution of this woman, which had led to her paths crossing with The Ripper. As well as provoking guilty feelings in me, the notion provoked intense sexual excitement.

Later, photographs of the victims were in covert circulation amongst 'gentlemen' of all classes. By close inspection of the excisions, and taking into account my own earlier researches, I can confidently assert today that the perpetrator was an Adept of extraordinary skill, finally achieving the goal of invisibility by his magickal Acts. His Will was executed with skill and timing. He was able to disappear completely and this was why they never caught him.

'Why?' You enquire, with a hostile grimace. Let me finish, before you send off the telegram you have dashed off to the League Of Purity.

The 'gentlemen' are quite normal, if they felt a stirring in their Chakras. Human sacrifice been the way to contact the Godhead for far longer that the two thousand years which shall be known as Christ's aeons, before Crowley's. The adepts understood always that sacrifice has been the way to rapture, uniting even the lowest Chakras with Universal Consciousness. At some periods animals have been substituted- rams caught in thickets by their horns[59] - cats, toads -

While the Christian reader will - of course - pin all the blame for this repugnant custom on me, *quid tollet peccata mundi*, etc., sacrifice is what his religion is about too. The Jewish religion begins where Abraham, god-instructed, prepares to kill his son and then the 'New' Testament overcomes all of the deity's previous scruples and celebrates a full human sacrifice of an innocent victim.

I have not during this lifetime been able to confirm my thesis of my own complicity in the Jack the Ripper murders. But it has preoccupied me. I believe that one of the women he killed has been assigned an erroneous name and biography.[60] Her face is turned away in the photograph, but faces mean little. I know in my heart it was Sally Lowe, whose first mistake had been to give herself to me, for free. I feel that is my fault that damned her, and me to a squalid historical complicity with a maniac. At the same time, those feelings of shame, guilt and horror have an enabling potency which directs itself through my Wand. Should I be ashamed that shame itself and mutilation and degradation all excite me? Should Christians be ashamed that Christ's sacrifice shames and excites them in equal proportions? Should I say that Abraham's copulation with and subsequent execution of an innocent trapped ruminant brought him closer to his God? I may be able to lie on matters of no importance, but religion is not one of them.

My first awakening was when I was four, and in our garden. For some reason, I forget what, I was unable to find out where anyone else was. Since I was told, night and day, that we were always to be ready for the last judgement, where the Elect would be taken straight to heaven, I imagined that everyone else had been taken up into Abraham

---

59 *This is a clear reference to the month of Aries, which would have been at that time, [considering the precession of the Equinoxes,] the annual sacrifice of the blessed Easter Son. A.C.*

60 *Hardly surprising, when you think of the general competence of the police in the case, their complicity with all grades of sexual slavery, and the low, anonymous milieu in which the victims operated. A. C.*

the Sheep-fancier's Bosom, and I alone, wicked and shameless, had been left on the earth and I fell to the cold soil in a swoon. The die had been cast. I was The Beast, indeed.

When I opened my eyes, I could hear voices calling from the house. The bare branches of the trees above mocked me. I was not alone, after all. But something had changed forever in those vital moments of solitude. I realised later that I had experienced my vocation, (the Beast) and had enjoyed to confirm it, a spontaneous orgasm.

That's enough (more than enough, I hear you cry) about my early life. We have strayed from the Masonic lecture, to which we will return now, in the sonorously entitled next section.

V The Hierophant

The Beast encounters his Holy Guardian Angel, again.

Before I began my lecture, on board ship, I was able, by an act of extreme concentration, to slow down the movements of the gilt chairs up and down the polished parquet of the stateroom floor. I had injected an amount of heroin earlier, which always helps. Then the lighting in the room began to alter. I thought that I might be passing out from the effort of holding the chairs still, just as I was about to instruct my remaining audience of two men and a Purser: sustained magickal kinesis requires a huge amount of Will. But in fact I had misinterpreted the phenomena entirely. The main lights of the stateroom stayed on but it was as if they were on a different plane of illumination.

The room became suffused with what the Secret Chiefs call the *Soph Lura*,[61] similar to the light I experienced when Rose my first wife and I spent the night, vibrant with godhead, in the King's Chamber of the pyramid at Cheops.

A woman entered the room and stood for a moment in the aisle between the chairs, facing me. It was as if her body blazed, and in the cone of light that surrounded her, angelic wings flapped. In her hands, held in her long white gloved hands in front of her, she was holding a

---

61 'The Limitless Light' A.C.

reticule sewn with tiny pearls. All the sounds of the storm seem to have ceased, for a moment. Then there was a muffled thump as a larger wave than usual struck the ship, and the chandelier shuddered and dropped glass tears around her, as the woman sat down. Her eyes never left my face for a moment, and I knew I was speaking only to her.

How was I going to deal with my Holy Guardian Angel with Leah in the room? Since she had become pregnant, the stupid bitch had started more and more objections to any kind of sexual commerce outside monogamy.

'I can always tell what you're thinking' she would say. I had made no secret of my other encounter with my Holy Guardian Angel, which had taken place in Moscow. It had ended tamely, I had thought, although five years later, Russia was set ablaze in the fires of revolution.[62] If I had to choose between saving the world and saving Leah's feelings, the world always was going to come first.

'My Lords, Ladies, and Gentlemen, good evening.' Leah's gaze had been unwisely fixed on the swinging chandelier. Seeing the difficulty that I was in, my Holy Guardian Angel saw to it that Leah got up at that moment and bolted unsteadily from the room. The coast was clear. I felt myself grow in stature a full six inches as I addressed her.

'There will not be a Masonic lecture tonight. The audience has no need of one. I come before you, I, To Mega Therion 666, having been Aiwass' instrument in taking down the *Book of the Law*, I humbly beg my next instruction. I have spent years in the wilderness of America. I have been mocked and spat on. I know I have the Truth, but how shall I transmit it to the world? I ask you, I implore you, oh agencies of the gods, to tell me what the next step - I wish to be spared, but do not spare me, to heal - if that is what you wish - the world - '

It was not the best prayer I have made, considering my Agent of Godhead was sitting twenty feet from me, but the goetia were doing their best to distract me. First, several hundred gallons of water gushed down the staircase, and swilled about noisily before making for a

---

62   *I wrote to both Trotsky and Lenin urging them to take up the Law of Thelema. I invited them to the Abbey. I received no reply in either case. A.C.*

lower floor of the boat. Then a mincing and effeminate steward followed the water down the steps, shrieking, rolling over and over, all the time holding perfectly upright a small potted palm.

I thought I would make it clear that I was not about to be distracted by these foolish mirages, and then the goetia would cease their strivings against me. But the waves beating against the side of the ship were the waves of chaos, and the goetia, little devils frequently rendered impotent by events on the plane of matter[63] - took the chink in the door of chance, and rushed in.

What happened on the Mundane Plane, or W.W.W.O.W.,[64] was that the chandelier fell down and the room went pitch black.

Yes, *black*. The Soph Lura had been withdrawn, doused by the goetia. The chairs scraped. I knew it was fruitless to search for my Guardian Angel in the dark; she would have felt the presence of opportunistic lower entities, and disembodied herself. I was proved right: when light was brought, the chair which she had been sitting on was empty and she had vanished.

The goetia had not done with me yet: the storm abated as we neared its centre, but I discovered that while my back was turned, our belongings had been dumped in the passage outside, and the cabin I had been offered in exchange for my lecture had been turned into an impromptu operating theatre for injured passengers.

I saw now how the game was going - Whiskers and his friends were operating, albeit unconsciously, as channels of spite for the elementals who were stopping my concourse with my Holy Guardian Angel. Something had to be done, and fast.

I squatted by the luggage, and rapidly produced a Dalai Lama, or

---

63 *Though they always say they are Lords of Outer Darkness, they are nothing of the kind. Trust me when I assure you that self-promotion is rife amongst the diabolic fraternity. A.C.*
64 *What Whispering Whiskers Once Witnessed. A.C.*
65 *Part of the Adept's basic training is to control all bodily functions, and put them under the tutelage of Universal Mind. A.C.*

stool, to Leah's open-jawed astonishment.⁶⁵ Gathering it carefully up, I explained to her that I had discovered that goetia are always sensitive to the intent of evacuations, so they can be used to banish malign influences. Of course the repellent has to be placed correctly. I instructed her to place it in Whiskers' purser's jacket, hanging on the back of the door, in the left hand pocket. The right would have had the reverse effect.

Leah obeyed my instructions and we went back to our pokey little eggshaped hell. It amused me greatly to reflect that on the deck above ours, Whiskers was doubling as ship's surgeon, improvising splints in his shirt-sleeves, effortlessly exuding the melancholy self-importance of doctors everywhere, with no idea his jacket was carrying a powerful message to forces he had no conception of.

As soon as the door closed in our throbbing egg-hell, Leah rounded on me and abused me for allowing her to suffer, making her cart my caca around - 'Next time do it yourself, you pig!' And for not being a proper 'provider'. I told her, mildly at first, that she might just as well accuse the Universe of not being a proper provider, she had about as much chance of being heard: As far as I was considered I had provided royally. It was my operation VIII° that had provided the money for our cosy cabin.

'What do you mean? I got the money from MY mother.' screamed Leah. Leah had clearly put the turd in the wrong pocket, for the goetia were still with us.

I gave her some Anhanolium Lewinii, but then she complained that since the shaft around the propeller shaft thudded, this meant Dracula was trying to get out of his coffin and at her. She would not accept that sex magic would make her headache, or anything better, ever again. She lay with her knees together in the bunk, refusing to allow me to lick her arse or her cunt.

I started to shave my head, in a dirty little basin which held about as much water as my sporran. I was calmly reflecting on my one objective for the evening: to find the mundane name of my Holy Guardian Angel, which would give me the Key to possess her entirely, so that I could command the World by my Will. Since there was no escape from the boat, I felt I was being told that this time she was not going to give me the slip.

'Where are you going?'

'Out.'

'Why?'

'I am going to seek conversation with my Holy Guardian Angel.'

'What's her name?'

'I don't know. Holy Guardian Angel. H.G.A.'

'I'm going away with you, I've paid for the passage, I'm carrying your baby and you are trying to screw the first woman who walks across your path.'

'I'm looking forward to it, particularly since you're not putting out.' Nothing gets you into more trouble than speaking the truth. The next thing I knew was that Leah's little hands were scrabbling at my soapy head, as she tried to gouge out my eyes with her thumbs. Carefully putting aside my cut-throat razor, I attempted to banish the goetia by giving her a smack with the razor-strop. It caught on a peg behind the door, proving without a shadow of doubt there was indeed no room to 'swing a cat' in the room. I had to calm her down by giving her a smack in the chops.

Leah sat down suddenly on the edge of the bed and blubbed. I was disgusted with her. I wanted to kick her. So I did. Do what thou wilt shall be the whole of the Law.

'OK, who is she?' she said, attempting a light, careless tone.

'She's my Holy Guardian Angel, Leah. I've dreamed about her, but she's only ever appeared to me once in the flesh before. This could establish Thelema in our lifetimes,. If I fail to find her, everything we hold dear could fail.'

'I can't believe what a shit-heel I've lucked out with. Everything that Renata said about you is true. I'm pregnant, and look at you.' I was wearing my McGregor tartan kilt with a red silk jacket, rather tight around the waist. Leah was not showing at all, but I was returning from America rather plumper than I had set out. I felt on the whole it suited me, although the added bulk of the Logos' lunch occasionally obscured the view of the Wand of the Aeon.

'What's going to happen when we get to England? Am I going to have to prostitute myself to get money to feed my baby? Am I going to be abandoned? I can't believe I ever agreed to go away with you, Aleister, I can't believe........' The reader does not have to occupy himself with much more, in the same tone. Indeed, neither did I at the time. Although I am hyper-sentient on occasions, clair-audient to the spirit world, I am able to filter out interruptions from the world of matter. Leah carried on whining, occasionally rubbing her jaw while I prepare an extra grain of morphine for injection. The closeness of the cabin was bringing on my asthma again and I did not know how long it was going to take to track down my H.G.A.

'What would you do if she ordered you to kill me?'

'She wouldn't.'

'God told Abraham to kill his son - why not?'

'If she told me to kill you, there'd be a very good reason.'

'I hope your Angel doesn't have something like syphilis. That does *really* nasty things to the foetus.'

I picked up a copy of Liber Legis and pushed it between her thighs.

'What are you doing?'

'It's got more chance of being understood, that end, than the other.'

I saw Leah pretending hurt in her eyes. In fact, she was secretly proud. As Scarlet Woman, her sexual and mediumistic roles would always dominate her intellectual ones. She knew she was still, in my eyes, the Scarlet Woman. She watched, superciliously as I oiled my Wand and its surround with Perfume of Immortality.[66]

'Hey! Are you hoping she takes it up the ass, *right away*?'

I put my rings on, and threw a wrap over my shoulder. Leah was still searching for my Achilles heel, with the ill-forged armoury of her mind. She opened the little book at random.

'This stuff, you know, it *sounds* good, but does anyone know what

---

66   At last the secret is out about what a Scotsman wears under his kilt. Ambergris, musk and civet! A.C.

it means?'

'It is forbidden to study the *Book of the Law*.' I replied. 'In fact, one of the verses of the Book says just that.'

'So whyd'ja keep trying to shove it at me?' said Leah. As I went out, I said coolly,

'Work it out yourself. I don't have the time.'

If I were inclined to write my own tombstone summation, my parting words to Leah could serve as an epitaph as well as any other. But what Poet needs a memento mori, other than his Work? A state funeral at Westminster Abbey? Bah! Camel stale, dowager's hump and codswallop! Bury me in a nameless grave, is my instruction. I am, above all, a poet. If poetic fame does *not* burnish with its golden breath the outline of my (once notorious) skull, lesser reputations are hardly worth striving for.[67]

*'As slithering worms adoringly devour his Wand,
We watch his reputation soar above, Beyond!'*

EDWARD ALEXANDER CROWLEY

---

67 Aiwass is truly the author of the Book of the Law, and not I. Its excremental utterances cannot be laid at my door. A.C.

For the time being, let there be twin granite-graved sphincters upon my notional grave, guarding its eternal Mystery.

Poet
1875- 19**

One day, reader, you may if you please pencil in the true date yourself, to reassure your chambermaids and grooms, your wives and children that Wickedness has a period, that its body has been finally nibbled into Dust by the vermicellic shock-troops of oblivion. But you should bear this in mind. My Dust may never blind any pilgrim's eye: The Secret Chiefs bless them, *may* have told me that I may live for ever.[68]

The boat was rocking gently in the eye of the storm as the Beast stepped out of his cabin.[69] My outfit was extremely striking and drew stares of frank admiration from chambermaids, folding sheets at the end of the corridor.

Now the water was calm again, there was jazz coming from a distant state room, and applause, and laughter. Then a strange notion came over me. I suddenly became sad that I had been forced to leave the bagpipes behind in New York. I felt sure I could have made myself familiar with the pipes, and played a little tune. The truth was I'd played bagpipes only once before, when I involved myself in a magical duel with Willie Yeats, an Irishman of great self-importance who was filching the sacred traditions of the Order of the Golden Dawn and passing them off as his 'poetry'.

I had stormed the temple, puffing at the pipes bravely and squeez-

---

68 *I am forbidden to divulge exactly what the Secret Chiefs have revealed to me about my End. This is not a joke. A.C.*

69 *Bulwer-Lytton himself could not have penned a more catching first line to a yarn. A.C.*

ing the horses' head to keep the goetia at bay. Never having picked them up before, or since that day - the horse's head leaked molasses everywhere - the reader will understand that my skills are probably greater on the *other* Pipes of Pan, the ones I practice daily.

But the deck I was on presented a puzzle. I found that whichever way I walked on it, I was unable to get to my desired destination, and even if I went up stairs, I ended up on the same lowest deck. And tears kept coming to my eyes about my lost bagpipes.

Clearly, I was being tested in some way by an entity. Normally such emotional swamping is carefully measured and documented by me. But now, the uninvited presence was a nuisance. In order to gain admission to the presence of my H.G.A., who would be able to see exactly what sort of things I was trailing round in the ether, I would have to discourage the entity and throw it off the scent, and lose it.

By virtue of *not* following my own inner promptings and sense of direction, and performing the most deliberately stupid searches imaginable for non-existent doors in steel walls, I gradually wore down my opponent. It slowly tired of its ability to mislead me in a steel labyrinth of illusions. Finally as I had planned, it concluded that I was too foolish to have sport with, and left me alone.

As it went I caught a glimpse of a long cloud-like face in a mirror, with melancholy brows like a Velasquez prince. The body was grey, and only partly realised although I could see hands. As it vanished in the mirror, it made a distinctly impolite gesture with its three hands.

With an abruptness that was almost terrifying, I found myself amongst the largest staterooms in the boat, where by rights I should have been given a luxury suite, with a study for writing in the mornings.

The door was slowly opening, to stateroom number 6. Facing me on the other side of the door was a young woman in a maid's uniform, holding a large silver tray which was overflowing with bunches of grapes, on a decorative bed of green vine leaves.

I agree with St Augustine, on one point. Six is a wonderful number, close to god. I leant forward and took a grape.

The woman's name was Ninette and she was going to be intimate companion, while subordinate to Leah, when I set my commune up in Cefalù. She was French, short, with heavy eyebrows and strong, thick calves. She liked most to have her back stroked, before any Operations.

'Can I help you sir?' said Ninette.

'That depends' I said. Ninette had had a child with a French soldier who had been in the trenches, but he had come back to the village shellshocked, and her mother was looking after the child now. When she came to Cefalù, she was able to bring her child.

I took several grapes next. I hadn't meant to, but Anhanolium is a peyote derivative, and the grapes were 'walking' over the plate.

'Go ahead' said Ninette. 'The lady wants them taken away.' *The Lady*! Just beyond the door, I could see a photograph in a silver frame of my H.G.A., in her mundane dimension, standing proudly next to a Russian cavalry officer. I looked at a label on the grapes. The letters arranged themselves, left to right, as A Gift to Madame Poitier, from an Admirer.

'Who sent the grapes to Madame Poitier?' I asked.

'There's a banker, who wants to have her. She tells me to just send everything back.'

'How unfortunate she has confused us. Actually' I lied, 'I sent them. She came to my lecture.' Ninette nodded her understanding. 'She sent me a note thanking me, and asking me to come by. Is she in?' Ninette shook her head.

'Well that's good because I have got something else for her, which she asked for, much better than grapes. Take them away. '

'What do you want me to do with these?' Ninette made the tray do a little pirouette, her right hand steadying the tray. Underneath, unseen, her left hand, her suggestive fingers, with the black hairs on the first joint. Soon to be inside me. Performing one of many *Magna Opera*.

For now, somehow I had to get rid of her without her closing the door. Her other hand with its cheap rolled gold band on the 'wedding' finger was on the doorhandle.

'Take the grapes to F deck, cabin 66. You'll find my wife down there. I'll go in and wait for Madame Poitier -' I pushed in to the room, past her. Ninette's brow clouded, momentarily - 'As we arranged after the lecture.' I added.

Ninette accepted my presence, with the unspoken promise of future intimacy. She sashayed off down the stairs, wiggling her broad peasant behind, holding the tray over her head. I closed the door. I was inside.

I went to the dressing table with its photograph of the handsome Cossack with my H.G.A. How had she acquired a life, as well as human form? It seemed somehow so superfluous to my needs. But everything suggested a credible biography. Her silver backed brush and comb were laid out on a crocheted mat. In the hairbrush, their were streaks of angelic hair. I pulled it out and sniffed it, and I felt my Wand arouse. *Nearer, my God to Thee.*

I went into the bedroom. The air in the room was unimaginably soft, like silk. The bedroom was in half darkness. The visiting moon, at albedo in Virgo, (I should have known better than to push my luck) shone through the snowy dimity curtains round the portholes. Since reaching the eye of the storm, one of the portholes had been recently opened, and the curtains blew softly in the wind.

There was a walk-in wardrobe, full of furs. The door was open. I stepped in. The furs, which had touched her skin, and smelt of her, as well as other animals, excited me intensely. The moon shone down ever brighter. I had taken the precaution of bringing an early volume of my poems, *White Stains,* so that she could become acquainted with her supplicant. Since she was not yet in evidence, I decided to invoke her, by a magickal act.

I opened the book in the middle. I was able shortly to deposit , as one result of a forceful and rapid Operation VIII°, a few million spermatazoons as my Offering to her.

Holding the dripping book in my hand, I was suddenly assaulted with a complete sense-memory of our first meeting. The stateroom in the eye of the storm with its silverbacked hairbrushes, romantic photographs, and ankle length coats of mink dissolved away, and I was transported back to Moscow just before the Great War: still a Moscow of the Tzars.

I was touring with that orgiastically challenged crowd, The Ragged Ragtime Girls, and I first caught sight of 'Madame Poitier' as she now chose to be called - let that be her Name, till her true Name is disclosed later - when I was standing in the wings of an underheated theatre.

The Ragged Ragtime Girls went through their routines sluggishly that night, because of the cold. *I'll go with you you've got the knack Of giving me my laughter back.* They held playing cards in front of their bodies, with some tarot figures on them I was working on the designs of. I had not yet worked out the final form for the Tarot pack for the New Aeon. The cards were two foot by eighteen inches. I had painted them all by hand.

Shuffle me and see
Which one is it to be

One by one, at this stage, the girls threw away their cards, with gestures, which on a warm night, might betoken abandonment to Pan. Then, one embarked on a solo on a dummy violin while the 'orchestra' filled in with whatever musical nonsense they could think of. Her companions moved around her twirling their scarves, in a lethargic imitation of the oriental dancing, from the casbah, which various false messiahs had made popular in Paris.[70] The assistant stage manager

---

70 *I refer to the sordid pimp, carpet salesman and Russian spy, Monsieur Gurdjieff, of which more anon. He came to see the Ragged Ragtime Girls, stole all my staging ideas and made a profitable 'religion' out of them for years. Magus? I ask you! A.C.*

was trying to get me to extinguish my cigar because the smoke was visible from the front row. As if we were in the business of 'illusion'! I was wearing a full-length beaver coat, bowler hat and white silk scarf. I was an impresario.

I did not have the first idea of what I was doing in popular theatre. The gypsy band, out of my eyeline, took up a reprise of the Ragged Ragtime Girls song. In order to avoid the continued irritations of the stage manager I moved out so that I was almost on the stage. Then I saw her.

'Madame Poitier' was seated in the circle of the small theatre, but she seemed to be surrounded by a strong nimbus of yellowish white light, not the Soph Lura this time, more a creative gold. In the instant that I first saw her - remember at this time I had no recollection of her, I had not yet come across her in my dreams other than indistinctly - she glowed and was recognisable. Recognisable from what? I have no idea, but the soul is timeless.

Like a peacock, she suddenly spread her wings, in an explosion of blue and vermilion. She was too far away to speak to me with her eyes, so she had spoken with her blazing aura. Then the light around her died as the Ragged Ragtime Girls, doing what under other circumstances would be called a 'high kick line', obscured the view of my destiny, my mirror, my eternal beloved, the deathless, stern and implacable beauty of my döppelganger-soul. Then she disappeared.

VI The Lovers

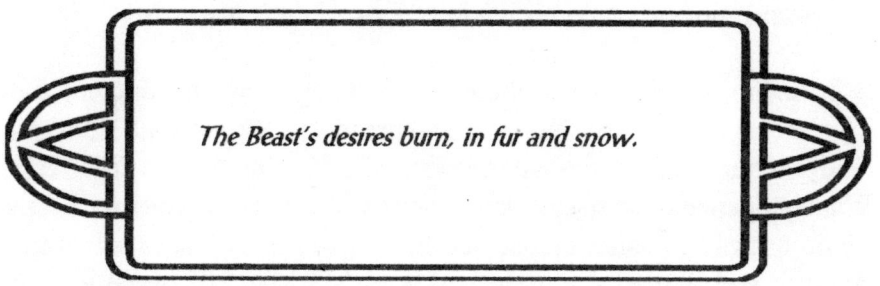

The Beast's desires burn, in fur and snow.

After my H.G.A. had shown herself to me and withdrawn, I found myself midstage in a ridiculous wrangle over fire risks and cigar smoke. On top of that, the wall-eyed runt of a repellent stage management was now withholding our gate money. I had to act fast. I gathered up my 'girls', and announced that anyone who wished to leave 'showbusiness' for full time prostitution could stay, the rest could accompany me on the next train out of Moscow. I was as good as my word.

The train left a bitterly cold Moscow Station at midnight, with the Ragged Ragtime Girls still in costume and makeup.

Day broke find us inching across the frozen wastes of the Russian winter. When I scratched a peep-hole in the frost on the window, the monotony of the view outside was stunning. Inside the carriages, now filled with chill white light, the girls had put on every stitch of clothing that they owned, and huddled together inside a ring of empty suitcases trying to sleep. I sat apart, smoking, and reflecting on whether I was in fact worthy of my destiny. My career as a theatrical producer had landed me in a part of the world that was even beyond 'the sticks'. As far as I understood from the driver of the train our final destination was Siberia: something I had not discussed with the girls.

Beyond the statutory babushka guarding the samovar, the last three carriages were filled with shaven-headed convicts dressed alike, men and women chained together, copulating with their felt boots on, to keep warm under the bored, vicious eyes of their warders.

It seems to me still, remembering those convicts, that all the ingredients of the New Aeon were all present in Russia, smouldering, ready to burst into flame when breathed on by the *Book of the Law*. What happened of course we know now, was a disaster - the Swiss sent Lenin back to Russian in a sealed train, like a bacillus, to infect the country, and like a bacillus he did his job. Instead of plumping for Crowley, the Russians settled foolishly for Marx.

The high kicks of the Ragged Ragtime Girls had cut off my acquaintance with my Holy Guardian Angel like a knife. With the removal to the train, I became depressed, convinced I would never see her again. I had been the vessel for the *Book of the Law*, true, but what had I done that was worthy of her attention in the subsequent eight years? Divorce an alcoholic-paranoid wife? And then? As my father would say from his wayside pulpit, trying to draw out the admission from sceptical yokel passers - by of the final fear of hell-fire.

And then? And then?

In the train, I drew out my copy of the *Book of the Law* from my baggage and tried, once again, to fathom its wisdom.

'*Learn the secret that hath not been revealed. Behold the rituals of the old time are black. Let the evil ones be cast away. Let the good ones be purged by the prophet. Then shall this knowledge go aright.*' I had the uncomfortable feeling, as the doomed train clanked sulkily towards the arctic circle, that the writing of the New Aeon was not as appropriate for running a troop of hoofers in Vladivostok as I wanted it to be.

Then I looked up. I did not know what was prompting me to do so. In the doorway to the compartment, I saw my Holy Guardian Angel again. She was in the body, corporeal, as before in the theatre. She was dressed in furs, the same fur that I was plunged into, in her stateroom six years on. Her face seemed to radiate light from within itself. My boredom and self doubt died in an instant. I half rose, feeling it was now or never. She was about the same height as me. Her brown boots were laced, and though she was too tall to be a ballerina, she had her toes turned out as she stood.

'You have a message for me?' I asked. No reason why one's H.G.A. should not speak English. What was my direction to be?

'*Je suis desolée. J'ai perdue mon place.*' She was about to go. I leapt forward and tried to physically stop her, seize her, fall at her feet. I saw a flash of her flesh. Under the coat she seemed to be wearing nothing but Babylonian cuneiform lettering on her body. As she moved, the lettering moved, as if it had been projected on her skin. And then, although I was convinced I was holding her by her knees, she was gone, and I was left holding nothing but a fox fur stole. I leaped up and followed her.

She flew like the wind, past the copulating convicts. I followed hard behind intoning sonorously from the *Book of the Law* -

'*...I Am The Flame That Burns In Every Heart Of Man, And In The Core Of Every Star. I Am Life, And The Giver Of Life. Yet Therefore Is The Knowledge Of Me The Knowledge Of Death: I Am The Magician And The Exorcist -*'

The words lent wings to my feet, but still she kept ahead of me. I pursued her past the samovar. The babushka screamed a long foul, toothless scream as it fell, inundating her old feet with boiling tea. Why did my H.G.A. not stop? All I wanted to do was worship her properly, and learn from her. She had reached the end of the train and I thought I had her cornered in a windowless carriage. I saw, by the light of a swinging oil lamp over a card game, my H.G.A. was now trying to open the door which led to the frozen wastes outside.

'Stop!' I vaulted over four cossack guards, who were having a game

---

71   '*My God!*' Perceptive fellow. A.C.

of poker.

'*Borshj Moy!*'[71] One of them shouted, astonished. Although I was fast, I was not fast enough. My H.G.A. found the catch and slipped through the door. The frozen wastes outside clanked by at fifteen miles an hour. I realised it was now or never. I jumped.

I found myself alone, as the train trundled away from me over the flat wasteland. Up or down the track, or in the hundred and eighty degrees each side my H.G.A. was nowhere to be seen. The snow was crisp and blinding white on every side but the wind had drifted it over patches of ice so it lay softly in the lee of some sedge. It was there I saw the imprint of a boot the same size as my H.G.A. Further along, there was another footprint.

I set out, on the frozen wastes, on her trail, knowing that any moment she might decide for whatever reason to dematerialise. There was not a moment to waste, if I was to learn my destiny. I discarded my coat and hat, and started an accelerated breathing that precedes access to the Gait of Power.

In New York, when I had given the 'tecs the runaround, I was in a distracting urban environment, which is hardly the best kind of place to practice magic acts which extend the possibilities of the physical realm for the magician. I think I may have been in the Gait in Manhattan, for not more than four minutes.[72]

But now I was in the best possible place for practicing the Gait. There were few obstacles, and exactly the kind of featureless landscape preferred by the adepts who have used it since time immemorial to cross The Waste Land.

The body becomes lighter. The centre of gravity is felt to be around the chest. The step is a long bound. Some adepts use both feet at once,

---

72 *The Gait of Power should not be confused with the compulsive-imitation of gait, which it is possible to use in proximity to victims, and by introducing a sudden stumble in their pattern to bring the hapless subject down- you may have heard of my performing such foolish mountebank stuff on demand - in New York. It is all true or all lies - I forget which, now. A.C.*

recovering during the bounce. Some are able to land on their right and left feet sequentially.

Witnesses who have seen the Gait being used, (It seems to be the same technique, in Mexico or Tibet) say that the runner keeps a steady gaze above the horizon, and if he is not distracted, can achieve twenty five miles an hour or more, for days. I set off, following the footprints, using the Gait. Very shortly I was travelling at close to maximum speed. Occasionally I would glance down to check that the footprints still were in the snow. They were, but I was alarmed to see they became further and further apart. My H.G.A clearly was no stranger to the Gait of Power herself.

By nightfall, I reckon I had covered almost eighty miles, and it had been some time since I had seen a footprint at all. Reluctantly, I returned across the frozen wastes to find a rude hostel close to the railway track. Before I entered, I took care to adjust my weight back to a normal mundane corporeality. It was harder to adjust to the fact that my Holy Guardian Angel had given me the slip. I was heartbroken. I don't think I was able to speak until after I had returned to London.

Oh prophet! Thou hast ill will to learn this writing. Remember all ye that existence is pure joy, and all the sorrows are but as shadows. Up to a point, Lord Aiwass. It's different when you wander the Wasteland, in vain.

Standing in the SS Sirius' best stateroom, I placed the copy of White Stains, with a particularly liquid and copious emanation from the earlier Operation VIII°, as my calling card, on Madame Poitier's bed. But I knew that the brief half-lives of my Wish were beginning to dessicate into nullity, as soon as I closed the pages upon them. She must arrive soon or I would be dismissed. The spell was weakening already.

Very shortly afterwards the door to the stateroom was unlocked and opened. I dived back into the fur coats to hear the muffled accents of her banker admirer, begging for admission in German, Russian, English, French, and when they all failed, Lebanese. Madame Poitier replied, saying Non, in another seven languages, and finally the door closed, and she stepped into the bedroom smiling, holding a bunch of arum lilies against a longsleeved white silk dress.

She stepped out of the dress and dropped it on the bed next to *White Stains*.

From the moment she saw the book, it was clear that she knew she was not alone. She turned and tinkled a little bell, and when nothing happened, she called-

'Ninette!' Ninette was downstairs, sharing grapes with Leah. I decided that it was time to introduce myself. Our eyes met over the fur coats. I stepped out into the room, in my finery. Madame Poitier looked at my kilt and jacket, and stifled a laugh.

'Mighty messenger, ineffable entity, Guardian of the Wasteland, Holy Guardian Angel' I began.

'You were the lecturer, weren't you? I don't recall having had the pleasure........Mr..........' I tried to communicate with her telepathically.

'*Madam. My name is Alastor -*'

'Could you tell me what you are doing in my bedroom, dressed like a highland chief? Has there been a fancy dress ball which I have missed? She tried the little china handbell again. It tinkled, ineffectually. I remember being surprised that an Entity did not use a proper Astral bell.[73]

'Frater Perdurabo awaits his further instructions' I said.

'*Who* does?'

'We met in Moscow, did we not?'

'I don't think so.'

'And subsequently, on a convict train? ' Madame Poitier looked shocked.

---

73   *Composed of metals corresponding to the seven stars. A.C.*

'I've *never* travelled on a convict train.'

'Your are my Holy Guardian Angel. Instruct me. Do you understand?' Madame Poitier shook her head sadly. She had fair hair, on a slender neck, but when she looked down, her expression became pinched, I noticed.

'I am not an angel. I am thirty six years old. I am married to this man. We hope he comes home safe.' She waved at the photograph by the door.

'We?'

'Myself and my two little boys. They go to school in Paris. My husband said the Lycée system is the best.'

I could see she thought she was being sincere.

'This won't make any sense to you now, but let me know when I can elect myself to the grade of Ipsissimus.'

'I shall have to ask you to go.'

'Of course I shall go, if that is your Will.' She went to the door.

'That's my husband. He is fighting the civil war in Russia now. Your Mr Churchill has sent troops, to help us. ' My Holy Guardian Angel was married to a Tsarist Russian. Somehow or other the knowledge of her supreme being was being hid from her. The thing to do was to leave the book and see what it did for her. It might trigger her into understanding her spiritual role.

'By the way' she said, as I was about to step out of the door, 'What is your name?'

'*White Stains*, by A Crowley is on your bed. I am he. I have put my all into the book.'

'Thank you' said my goddess, icily. I bowed to her. The door closed.

Whatever knowledge she had of her spiritual dimension was still being denied her. It was of paramount importance that she read, mark, learn and inwardly digest the book, if her other dimension was to be aroused. If she did not then 'remember' who I was and my importance, the Logos of the Aeon was going to be in for some rocky times.

102 Snoo Wilson

Ninette told me that although she was not blamed, Madame Poitier declares she had never been more terrified in her life, than the night a 'lunatic' came into her room. She was unable to sleep for a week. She immediately locked the door and threw the book out of the porthole, without reading it: nay, she barely opened it.

'There was something slimy in it, she didn't like' Ninette explained, in her bizarrely accented, two-note singsong voice.

One day, Crowleyanity will be everywhere. I foresee twentyfour hour Crowley radio, where the *Book of the Law* is read round the clock. Crowley Cinema, where twin screens project solemn and satiric orgies simultaneously. Everywhere a guilty bondage to sexuality will be reforged as an affirmation. Everywhere the bourgeois boundaries will be overthrown. Peyote, cocaine, and heroin will be as available as the insidious drug of patriotism is today. Everyone will be busy, finding their own True Will, which will constitute the only work. Crowley restaurants will be serving curry too hot to eat, with dog's dirt for dessert. Cut the voucher below out and present it at the till to qualify for your discount.

What began as self-justification, and entertainment has now gone on too far for me to withhold certain secrets of the Adept, which will be buried in these pages, like the wrecked Dutchman on the seashore in this dull, dead town. Those who can see them will profit. And the rest?

Unfortunately there is no card in the Crowleyan Tarot labelled 'The Idiot.'

Watch me as I deal the Magick cards of my life. My Tarot panel will be a guide for you, as you scale the Crowleyan peaks. There are no extra cards up my sleeve, as I sit, trusty Parker pen in hand. The winds of winter howl and rattle the casement, rent is due, nobody (and who can blame them) particularly likes me. The landlord exploits me because of my supposed skills in curing his impotence, but who is kidding who? The stupid old bugger can't get it up because he doesn't know the thelemic meaning of *life*!

The Stephenson's green ink is running low in the bottle. I sit up, writing, night after night. If the wind outside should die for a while, the traditional love song of the travelling salesman may be heard as the other guests break wind in their sleep. Greasy and secular are their midnight farts which bark a dull *basso profundo* through the meanly partitioned boarding-house walls, heard distantly, like the guns of the Somme were on the south coast, two score years ago.

The properly trained mind never wavers. My Mission is to tell the truth - about everything. *Perdurabo.*

The other time I break from my work is to occasionally play myself at chess. I still have a board somewhere, but so many of the pieces are missing it is hard nowadays even to set up a proper end-game puzzle for oneself in reality. Generally I play against myself, in my mind, in three dimensions, until I am refreshed. Like St Augustine, who I named my Confessions after, the apparently limitless quality of my mind still amazes me.

That ringing was not from the astral plane: it was the door bell. A small package of cocaine crystals has arrived unexpectedly from an American well-wisher! Excuse me for a moment while I ingest.

Ah, the wit and wisdom of Peru! The 'snow' is warming my resolve nicely. I even feel a chess problem coming on, and I may turn aside for a while. There are other reasons for taking a breather: I have 'stretched' out my slender resources of Stephenson's Best Green Ink with thimblefuls of my own piss, and blood, until my Stephenson's is Green in name only.[74] Writing in one's own blood (Or other peoples') is a powerful spell, but over the long haul the spell dries up. 'This product may be used for communication, but the makers deny liability. Used undiluted, on warm evenings it tends to clot the nib.' Over the short haul, it works but again, *only if you believe in what you are doing.*

To test this, let us provoke an uncharacteristic act for Frater Perdurabo to perform. Hard to think of one, for I have so many characters I hardly know what to do with them all. But I think I may have one for you:-

To magically abuse my Guardian Angel, in his *masculine* aspect.

As anyone who is familiar with Crowleyanity will tell you, this is a negation of its central creed, and something I, Keeper of the Flame, could not, in all conscience perform.

As a demonstration only, I will write his name in my undiluted blood-

AIWASS=EYEWASH (A.C.)

See? Absolutely nothing happens. Aiwass (Or Aiwaz - there are numerological objections to both spellings that are tiresome, perhaps even to Guardians of the Watchtowers) is silent.

Good ol' Aiw**(+/-*??) knows that *my heart is not in it.*

---

[74] *Not unlike G******'s overrated novelist-brother! What I am writing tonight, on the other hand, is not mere entertainment, but the Magickal Truth. A. C.*

But dear oh dear, what a field day the Bottomleys and the Beaverbrooks *de nos jours* would have, if they knew what Old Crow was up to, d'nights.

Step back, you pale journalistic hypocrites, and let the Master of Lies get his fingers dirty typesetting your titillating and mendacious come-ons. Yes! Let me denounce my own enterprise as the work of the devil!

BLACK MAGICIAN USES OWN BLOOD

As usual, lies, lies, lies. As far as this book goes, I would calculate that not more than 33.3% is written in my own blood. 66.6% [75] is written with conventional materials, and the remaining 0.1% is written with some small sticks of my own poop I have using after mixing with mascara, then moulding and drying carefully.[76] The last is proportionally so low because a tray of my little patent writing sticks, which were turning out quite promisingly, mysteriously found its way into the evening's steak and kidney pie. There was the most ridiculous uproar and although I was clearly innocent, I had to forswear the use my landlord's oven in future for preparing writing materials.

While I am at the business of proving that I never killed Raoul Loveday, I would like to clear my name of another false accusation: that I abandoned the troupe of the 'Ragged Ragtime Girls' in the middle of Siberia, and because I was holding their passports, they were thrown into prison and then sold into white slavery, out of which only one escaped, via Tangier, or Shanghai, I forget which.

Some of them, in any case, had been prostitutes already. I was

---

75   Well spotted. A.C.
76   Semen has been attempted but it seems to dry invisibly, in most circumstances. A.C.

misguided enough to try to give them enough stage skills to put their times in the second oldest profession behind them. They simply relapsed. Crowleyanity says that prostitution is sacred, but in their case most of them were inadequate as Priestesses, quite inept at raising the Sacred Current.

Dearly beloved, young, misinformed one, or ones - (Can there be more than one of you? I suppose that will happen in due course when it is read on the Crowleyan wireless.) - hear my conclusive threefold refutation of these calumnies:-

The first truth is, it was not necessary to possess a passport in the first place, to travel round Europe in 1912. The next truth is, I never abandoned the troupe in the middle of Siberia. They were weeks away from their destination when I returned to London. The clincher is that I left them for a more vital quest, to pursue my second Holy Guardian Angel, over the Wasteland. There can be no more important quest than that, I think you will agree.

But I cannot be angry at these rumour mongers for ever. We must press on with the main story. As Abraham might have said,

'*Revenant à nos moutons*' Translated freely-

'Gumboots on, everyone and off we go up the hillside to catch and court a sheep, and then to cut its throat and offer it to Yahweh!'

Having failed to crack the material carapace of my Holy Guardian Angel's mundane identity, and reveal the spirit-messenger within, I returned rather despondently to the egg hell-hole that was my cabin. On the way down to the throbbing bowels of the ship, two male stewards peered up my kilt as I came down some steps, and one impudently enquired 'If I was nuts, or swish.'

'Swish' was the New York slang for the acts which were allowed to Greek warriors, and have attracted death penalties and worse, subsequently, all during the Vulgar Era we live in now. I remember it being used in homosexual brothels in England, in the 90's. When Oscar Wilde put himself on trial, the word itself disappeared from England and popped up the other side of the Atlantic. In England, after Oscar's impalement by the state, English gentlemen-*somdomites* (Queensberry rules spellings) were described as 'so', as if renaming the act expunged it.

'I am both.' I replied regally. 'I am a little "nuts", all the time. And, since God is sex, and sex is god, I am also a little "swish" all the time. But as a magician, I assure you, I can assume any shape, or being, or desire I need for my purposes.'

'In that case, it's going to be no trouble for you to lose some weight.' said one of the pansies, sneeringly.

I deliberately did not look at him. Unlike Elisha, I believe it is a waste of time to blast the ignorant. I passed on in silence, in maiden meditation, fancy-free.

In my loud little egg-nest, I discovered Leah and Ninette sharing the grapes, as Leah taught Ninette about the imminence of Crowleyanity. Ninette was holding a slim volume of the *Book of the Law*, which Leah had pressed on her, under her nose.

'It is a book of my husband's. He's a magician.' Leah said helpfully.

'That's wonderfool' said Ninette, in her thick French peasant accent, uncertainly. She looked if she was inhaling the book with mixed feelings, as if she suspected any volume of mine could be XI°'d, activated at a distance by its sorcerer-author.

'Naturally I don't understand it' said Leah, more as an aside to me than anything else. Ninette now saw me for the second time in my robes. She allowed her admiration to blossom, briefly.

'Ah, so he is magician! The people I work for are all so bourgeois'

'You could come and work for us. We're certainly not rich and stuck up, so there won't be much money.' Leah was never adverse to pitching Thelema, even the thornier side.

When Ninette flapped her ankles I could smell the cheesy whiff of her feet. It gave me a strong idea of what her cunt would smell like. My worm began to writhe a little.

'I don't like the English weather.' said our princess of France.

'We're going south' countered Leah.

'Where, in the south of France?'

'Aleister's not sure exactly where.' Aleister's worm was sure, though.

'I've got a little boy' said Ninette, sounding a warning note. Leah patted her own stomach reassuringly.

'That's alright. I'll have a little friend for him soon.' Ninette was delighted at her newfound sisterhood.

'Thank you.' said Ninette. She threw a glance at me which I chose to ignore. When they hurl themselves at you, stand back. But before she left our cabin, I gave her surreptitiously, a Serpent's Kiss. She gasped. Leah affected not to notice, saying.

'The only rule we will obey in our new community will be love.'

When Ninette left, I worshiped Leah's body P.V.N. with loud desperation born of hopelessness, drowning out the engine noise till exhaustion overwhelmed me. I had not achieved communion with my Holy Guardian Angel. As Ninette later recounted, Madame Poitier pitched the little book out of the porthole with finger and thumb, mercury finger raised. It must have fluttered down to drown in the wake of the *SS Sirius*, losing its myriad homunculi to digestion by the mute, incurious ocean.

VII The Chariot

*The Abbey founded at last.
W. Somerset Maugham's past contribution to the legend -
Frank Harris is no help at all-*

I was with my true love, my Man, Raoul Loveday, in the British Museum: this time I was no hovering ghost over his head, but myself, in the flesh, alongside Raoul after my return from New York. His first concern, after he met me off the boat, was to bring me to the room which held the Amon-Ra exhibit which he had made his unsettling promise to. He explained to me the details and I listened, wondering what I could do to help his undertaking to the stern god. In between these serious conversations flowed our natural warmth of greeting.

'I'm so glad you're back. Nobody in this country understands anything any more. Is America any better?' Raoul's eyes were bright with hope. He would have followed me to the ends of the earth. I had no intention of testing him, though.

'America is cursed, for me' I said sadly. 'And what's more, I can't wait to leave this country.' Behind us, Leah trailing behind, had become weary and taken off her shoes to ease her swollen ankles. Raoul and I were more concerned with the more serious problem of past action, his curse openly accepted, from Amon Ra. It seemed to me to be a very tricky matter indeed. I heard Raoul out, and his terrible summary;-

'I said I would agree to take any retribution that Amon-Ra might choose to give.' This seemed to put the poor dear boy entirely at the mercy of the god's whim. I determined he should not be unprotected, but I could not express my fears so directly, to him.

'We should immediately perform a ceremony to protect you against any goetia who might be tempted to meddle in the situation.' I said, lightly 'The only problem is we don't have much time. We're going to Italy, Leah and I, tomorrow.' Raoul's luminous, quiescent orbs looked up at me pleadingly.

'You didn't say.' he said. Did I detect a note of accusation? Poor Raoul.

'Don't worry - I'm not going to behave irresponsibly and run off without leaving you with any protection. What we should do, is immediately perform a rite for your purification. We can take a room in a hotel, now. Just you and me.'

'What about Leah?'

I looked back at Leah. She seemed to be completely asleep. Since she had become pregnant, her edge of curiosity had blunted - the great question mark itself pushing out her belly button.

'Don't worry about Leah. She can find her own way home.' I said.

Dear Raoul! How unselfish he was, even when he was in psychic peril! And how bravely we stepped out together, fuelled with ether and peyote, for hikes on the astral plane to find the best protection for him, with our true selves!

The working was extremely effective, in one regard. At the end of the three days, Raoul was begging me to take him with me. But there were no funds for the present, beyond the rail tickets already purchased for myself and the Scarlet Woman. I left my boy in tears, as I stepped out to find Leah.

'Just a short trip' I replied, reassuringly. 'Reconnaissance for the Abbey. You can come later, with Betty.'

'If Betty doesn't want to come with me, I'm coming alone.'

'Don't worry, I'll make a spell for Betty to come, tonight.' I said lightly.

'I want to see you do it.' Raoul had put me on the spot, so I had to do something. The actual event has been documented in Betty's own writings.

I went round to the pokey lodging where Betty and Raoul were staying unannounced, in full Highland *fig*, with a Jeroboam bottle of hock that a wellwisher had bid me carry off from a German wine exhibition in Jermyn Street. I rang the bell, and when Betty saw me, I produced the mighty tribute to Bacchus from beneath my sporran, and greeted her. Raoul behind her of course knew the Thelemic reply to my salute, and Betty did not. I bowed low, and kissed her hand, but deliberately refrained from using the Serpent's Kiss. She didn't seem a bit impressed.

'What do you want?' She said.

'Want? I want you to cook dinner, I suppose.' I replied, as nonchalantly as I could. My right hand was performing an Arabesque behind my back which only Raoul could see. That was the spell I was working, to tie Betty's fate to Raoul's. Raoul's fate I knew was inextricably tied to mine.

'I will not cook dinner for you.' Betty said. My spell-working hand was getting cramp working all the time behind my back, so I concluded the spell over my head, as if I was about to bow to her. I tried to keep her attention the while by smiling, until I could deliver the instruction spell.

I have normally an unremarkable, highish, rather nasal voice, but when I command Magickally, the subtle bodies supervene and everything changes.[77]

'A time will come when you will cook all my meals for me.' I said, in a resonant Voice of Command.

'Not tonight, Mister. You're welcome to do what you like with the food. I'm going out.' Betty clip clopped off down the street outwardly insouciant. But I knew I had got her, right between the eyes.

---

77 *If you want to be like me, the trick is practice, practice, practice, and concentrate on lots of thrilling vibrato, from the diaphragm, if you please. A.C.*

When I left the house, after midnight, the creature who had challenged me was lurking in the shadows, waiting for me to go. Betty was slow to understand that she had been magickally shackled to my Will.

Although I was confident I had performed the spell I was still worried that Betty would hold Raoul's spiritual development back. She had a long history of cocaine addiction, and had recently come out of it and denied her former self. Every time Raoul and I had a working session, which would sometimes go on for three or four days, she would threaten to leave him. The miasma of a horizontal body which had appeared, like a floating corpse, over Raoul's head in their wedding photograph was brought up, again and again, as something to do with me, when I was on another continent at the time, and certainly not thinking of Raoul.

Raoul of course was devoted to Betty. He had fallen in love with her, when he was a schoolboy, and like a schoolboy still, he could not see what a basically coarse and uninteresting woman she was. I made no attempt to get him to leave Betty. That would have been against the Law of Thelema in any case. It was best to enlighten him, if possible, by degrees about his *amour fou*.

I took great pleasure in bidding Raoul farewell later and later in the night. Once, after a long ether session, at four o'clock in the morning, he terrified Betty when he climbed the drainpipe and broke into their bedroom through the window, 'so as not to make a noise in the hall'. I'm surprised he didn't try to fly up there directly. He was immune to Betty's pleadings now. He would tell her he had contracted with Amon Ra to take on any results of her blasphemy and he needed to perform rites to protect himself with me.

And so it was that, with a small but growing number of loyal thelemic supporters promising to join us, I set out with Leah to see if the magickal current might allow us to discover our true wills, in Sicily.

A strange, menacing bald figure, in a striped oriental coarse wool costume could be seen as he strode through the narrow streets of Cefalù, Sicily. His strange garb suggested he was a Turk. The visitor's gaze was deep, penetrating and mysterious. It seemed to speak of other worlds. There were enormous rings on his fingers and he carried a stick, overlaid with snakes, like a demented version of a caduceus. A bizarrely dressed woman was at his back, reproaching him as they walked. Heads turned as the pair, in loud tandem passed by fish vendors with their barrows of Mediterranean fare. The pursuing woman was clearly pregnant, with a flame coloured dress, and henna'ed hair under a large floppy hat. She finally ran and caught up with her theatrically dressed companion and slapped his head. The superstitious peasantry gasped as he shook his pregnant companion roughly off and strode, apparently uncaring, past sacred shrines bedecked with flowers in the walls. Overhead, the hot blue sky was peering down at the pair, curiously, between the faded tiles and the curved lines of washing that hung motionless between the upper stories. But in the end, puzzled, the sky simply shook its head.

This might be how a lesser author than myself, a Somerset Maugham perhaps, would begin an account of our stay in Cefalù. Maugham profiled me in a book, which took several of my biographical threads and woven them into a yarn. *The Magician* was published four years after I composed the *Book of the Law*. Afraid that I would sue him, Maugham changed my name to Oliver Haddo. In fact I was quite amused at his tribute.

Leah and Mr Crowley settled into a café in the main square in Cefalù and after some baked squid and a litre or so of sharp Sicilian wine, tasting of volcanoes, we became agreeable to each other again. Leah had been whining ever since we left England about how she had been abandoned, a defenseless woman in the British Museum, while I went off with Raoul for three days. I had patiently explained that according to the Law of Thelema, it had been my Will to protect Raoul with the necessary celerity. It had taken from London until the Cefalù fish market, before the mixture boiled over into physical resentment. However I was quick to forgive her.

One of the problems had been the fatigue of the heat of the day and the walk from the railway station. All the while, as this was a first visit, in deference to the history of the Knights Templar on the island, I was wearing my Baphomet costume.

Baphomet himself (Again, the spelling is damnably tricky for beginners and I am not even sure if even I have it numerologically correct after all these years) is the mysterious deity revered by the holy Knights Templar, who became a power when they protected travellers to the Holy Land. There is much debate about Baphomet's true identity, which is in fact Mithraic. The Templars - destroyed when they were accused of necromancy - were convicted of paying homage to Baphomet as the devil, with elaborate ceremonies where all present kissed Mr Baphomet's symbolic *vas nefandum* prior to performing like intimacies with each other.

The Knights Templar, having become a rich and prosperous organisation (Clearly, much magically successful Op. IX°) became the object of envy, having so much wealth. They were suppressed, imprisoned, hung drawn, quartered, and burnt at the stake, as sodomitical sorcerers. The Christian Church pounced upon their accumulated wealth. And everyone forgot about Baphomet, till I came along.

I remember thinking, in the Cefalù square, after Leah collapsed and I had to carry her up the winding path to view the house that became the Abbey, that I rather wish I hadn't remembered Baphomet either. I had the costume made made from goat's wool, for symbolic reasons. It was thick and coarse. Wearing it in any heat was something which combined a hair shirt and a turkish bath. Intolerable, and it brought me out in a rash.

We slowly rose above the town. I was beginning to wheeze (I think

I may have been allergic to goat hair, as well, in retrospect), but the view improved with every turn of the path. The slopes had been planted with olives and cypress. Shortly we came upon a particularly fine one storey farmhouse, which looked out north, towards Stromboli. The mighty bulk of Aetna slumbered to the West. The gods had provided me with my Abbey at last. I was to hold it in trust, effectively, for six hundred and sixty six days before the cold lava descended. A black magical current would come, to blight Raoul and my family alike, and finally blast me from Italy. Useless to fight destiny. I was Alastor, Wanderer of The Waste.

I signed the lease jointly with Leah, both using variations of our magickal names, and returned to London to spread the good news, and attract a community of like souls to go to Cefalù and find their True Will. The venture was glorious, innocent, it was the culmination of all my proposals and yet somehow it felt deliciously unplanned. The gods had seemingly agreed to provide us with a banquet, and we duly rejoiced.

Back in London, I was dining with Frank Harris at the Café Royale, in order to see if he had any ideas about raising money. Frank had been a journalist, and while not of the mental calibre of a Thelemite, knew the ropes of commercial publishing.

Frank's estimation of his own work was hilariously overblown. He once said that there are only two writers in English, Shakespeare and himself, and while the Bard goes widely into all aspects of life, Frank in his own estimation 'went deeper'. However, he assured me that in his canon of English literature, I occupy second place equally with W.S.

But in spite of his championing of his own works over mine, he had a broadly tolerant attitude to sexual expression, very unusual at the time. His autobiography is full of comic boasts of conquest. I never found out exactly how old he was but one of his claims to fame was that he worked as a 'groundhog' navvy building the Brooklyn suspension bridge, which meant that he must have been at lest twenty five years older than I.

I entered the Café dining room and went to Frank's table, to give my Thelemic greeting, and was greeted with nothing but gales of laughter from Frank. Leah, catlike, came and sat by my side, ready to defend me. Frank eyed her bump and raised an eyebrow.

'Looks like you have been doing what you wilt, *indeed*, old boy.'

'Frank, I need to ask your advice. I've found somewhere for a community, out of England, in Sicily.'

'Why on earth go there?'

'It's perfect.'

'My name's Leah, by the way.'

'Pleased to meet you, Lear.'

'There are good vertical rock climbs.' added Leah. Frank turned back to me

'Good god , Crowley, are you still at it? I thought you'd stopped when they ran you out of the Alpine Club. This man never gives up!' He eventually smiled on Leah showing his teeth. The effect was like a rather dirty sun coming out.

'Frank, you must tell me about publishers. Since I privately published most of my writing, I'm something of a novice is selling a book.'

'What sort of book, Crowley?'

'I want to write a novel to spread the word about the new community I'm going to be leading.' Frank laughed until he cried at this.

'You can't expect people to believe what you put in in a novel!' he finally gasped. 'Besides, the sort of stuff that you get up to, even if you're quite circumspect, it's going to be absolute dynamite! In the midst of the First World War, there was still time to burn the alleged sanguinary phallocrat and all-round danger man David Herbert Lawrence for a completely innocent book called *The Rainbow*. And poor old Lorenzo's pretty conventional, apart giving it to that Hun-woman up the behind. His crime is that he had married the cousin of a German fighter ace, not simply buggered her.' Frank wiped his mouth free of soup with a napkin the size of a small tablecloth, sadly. He had a way of putting all our literary troubles in perspective. He concluded, 'Alas, all taboos, particularly sexual and patriotic taboos are interchangeable to closed minds, I'm afraid. The gallery that had been prosecuted for showing Lawrence's nude paintings has also run into difficulties with yours, I hear.'

'That's another reason for writing a novel.' I said. Frank started semaphoring with his napkin so hard that Leah, sitting to his right, had to lean back. He was wearing an ancient white linen suit, and had no idea of what a spectacle he was causing to the other diners as he talked at the top of his voice.

'Balls to novels, Crowley! For a start, if it's any good, it'll get banned, and make you nothing. What are you going to do - turn out a potboiler?' Leah was not as familiar with the mainstream of English literature, but she leaped in like a lioness to the rescue.

'Aleister couldn't write a potboiler if he tried. No. He's already told me the plot. It's really good. It's called - *Diary of a Drug Fiend*

'Good title, but I've had a better idea, which may astonish you at first.'

'Aleister should make a movie of his life to get his ideas over.' Leah said.

'Terrible idea' said Frank. Leah continued.

'I don't think so, sir. I mean, have you not seen *Birth of a Nation*? Leah continued. 'We could have a live orchestra playing specially composed music. I'm composing it now, *The Symphony of the Beast*.'

At the time I thought the idea foolish in the extreme. Today, Leah's insight seems to be visionary. She was considering filmic biography ten years before the 'talkies' made anything like that remotely plausible. In Paris, later in the 20's, I had met with, and dismissed all the foolish nonsenses that went under the name of art in that city. A man called R. Mutt, for instance, had introduced a common urinal as an art object, to shock the honest citizens. (If he had been using it, and then thrown the resulting ichor over his audience, I think it would have made a telling Thelemic point about Art. He missed his chance.)

Much later, when I had taken a quantity of Anhanolium, I chanced to see a performance of Abel Gance's film on three screens, *Napoleon*. I confess my first reaction was envy, which then subsided. The musical accompaniment made no appeal to my ear, but the visual experience, with its severe and uplifting message about the price men pay for greatness, made a considerable impression on me. I am compelled to prophesy:

One day, I shall be up there, on the silver screen.

In the Café Royal, Frank was thinking. His ill-fitting dentures, slightly green, lifted and dropped in the groundswell of his thoughts.

'Let's be SERIOUS for a moment. What we should do, Crowley, is to start a NEWSPAPER.' Frank had once been editor of a London Evening paper, which was rather like Oscar Wilde's time editing a woman's magazine. These things happen, and even so, they were still incredible. 'Ownership is the ONLY way to control what people write about you. Look at this! Beaverbrook's been going crazy since you got back.' Leah picked up the paper and dropped it again . I didn't look. She told me later that there was an article about my return to London 'King of Depravity Arrives.' Frank picked it up and waved it round his head like a tic-tac man at the races.

'It's publicity, but it's not good publicity, Crowley. They're going to bury you unless we can all fight back! You have to fight THESE lies with BIGGER lies, if necessary.'

'At the Abbey, we're going to have a rule, no papers. We don't care what the newspapers say.' Leah said flatly. 'It's not important.'

'What gets written may not be true, but is is BLOODY important.' said Frank, losing patience with my beloved one. Poor Frank. He had been reduced to peddling his sexual exploits, in print, which he did. But he did not have a single clue as to why he was driven to do what he did: he was like an atheist taking pictures in a cathedral.

I could see that he and Leah were not getting on, which amused me enormously, but the situation was moved into another dimension by the arrival of Raoul at the table. This was a complete surprise to me as I had only just arrived in London and had made no effort to contact him. He gave the Thelemic greeting, then practically fell on my neck, which made Frank guffaw, pointedly. I introduced them.

'Howjer do, Raoul,' said Frank, and turned to me and leered, oyster-eyed. 'Another *disciple*, I take it. One of each! Congratulations, Crowley!'

'Pleased to meet you sir' said Raoul, politely.

'Raoul's one of the country's top historians and mathematicians' I said.

'Top hole!' said Frank. 'Raoul, did you know that Crowley and I are going to start a newspaper, together?' Raoul looked puzzled.

'A daily or a weekly?'

'That depends on how we're capitalised. Of course you'll have to write for us.' Raoul was flattered. The waiter brought the bill and laid it ostentatiously next to me. Frank suddenly seized it and said to me-

'Let me do this dear boy. At least that way you'll know that you've got ONE friend in the world.' He signed the bill with a flourish and gave it to a waiter who bore it away.

'Now, Raoul, about this newspaper. I think we should begin by printing the names and telephone numbers of all of Beaverbrook's mistresses. For a weekly paper, we'll need about three thousand pounds, say a thousand each, you, me and Raoul.'

'I'm sorry sir, I don't have a job' said Raoul. Frank was unfazed.

'Neither do I.'

'But what I mean is I can't raise a thousand' said Raoul, blushing. Frank beamed.

'Nothing to be ashamed of dear boy, neither can I right now. But later in, ah, six months, who knows?'

'We get money through sex magic' said Leah, irritated at being excluded.

'How absolutely splendid. You really must show me how, one day.'

said Frank.

The head waiter came back this time with the bill and started whispering in Frank's large and whiskery ear. (It's a puzzle. Do old people have larger ears because they need them to hear with?) Frank's smile never faltered for an instant as he said loudly -

'How EMBARRASSING. My CREDIT has been TEMPORARILY WITHDRAWN. Who can lend me fifteen guineas?'

I had no intention of lending Frank anything like fifteen guineas. Raoul said sheepishly, 'I'll do it.'

'Thank you dear boy' said Frank, with the practised ease of the born scrounger. Then he turned to me. 'About the novel, I suppose you could try Collins the publishers, and see if they'd have you. You can have as much stuff about drugs as you like. But you can't do more than hint at normal sex, and - ' his voice rose again to a stage whisper - 'Keep Raoul and his kind out of it!'

'What do you mean, sir?' asked Raoul politely.

'Mathematicians who are also first class historians' replied Frank glibly. 'You have to stick to what the man on the Clapham omnibus understands.' He took the newspaper up and handed it to Raoul, who read the headline with furrowed brow.

'This is slander!' cried my dear boy.

'I know.' said Frank. His tone became confidential. 'Poor old Crow. He doesn't stand a snowball in hell's chance if he sues, either. It's all up for him now.' I doubted somehow Raoul had the money. Leah stood up and I followed her example. As I moved away I could see Raoul emptying his wallet. Frank shouted to me,

'Let's start the paper in Paris, shall we? Then the next time you come to the White Cliffs of Dover, you will be CROWNED with LAUREL leaves dear boy, it will be a TRIUMPH!'

VIII Justice

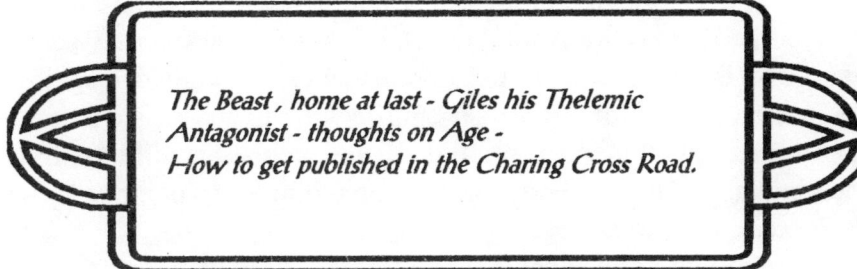

The Beast, home at last - Giles his Thelemic Antagonist - thoughts on Age - How to get published in the Charing Cross Road.

A chapter with this title can hardly avoid the charge of irony, in my history. Truly I have sat in Lord Beaverbrook's scales, until his coffers overflowed. The Justice of Lord Beaverbrook, newspaper proprietor connects to me via a luckless minion, who he sent to spy upon me, in Sicily. The minion's name, I know from laboriously penned telegram receipts at the Cefalù post office, was 'Giles'. Forename, *nom de guerre* or True Surname? Did 'Giles' ever get his expenses paid for those long, incompetent and expensive communiqués to Fleet Street?

I imagine that Giles was tall, with a hunted air, and thin, receding fair hair. He was my undoing, in part, and yet I know nothing about him. How was he corrupted, seduced to come upon his filthy mission of destruction? Has he been knighted yet, for services to society? Did he survive the Second War, to lose the rest of his hair, thicken and breed?

If he has no end, he should at least have a beginning. Let us imagine 'Giles' is the new teaboy in my Lord Beaverbrook's offices in Fleet Street. The War is over. The Roaring Twenties are on their way. Beaverbrook, as everyone knows, is short, hideous, with the face of a rubbery dwarf. I imagine Giles stooping, to conceal his height as he clears away the tea trolley in the Great Man's office.

The Great Canadian, one hand in his pocket, playing with himself is delivering the same energetic 'pep' talk that he does every week to four identical dark suited press executives. The main plank of his argument, over fifteen minutes being that newspapers ignore Moral Duty, at peril from the Almighty. The Beaver's newspaper with St George on the masthead has to provide unsleeping vigilance against the Dragon of Vice, or the British Empire will fall and we shall cease to be a leading nation. And worst of all, the circulation will fall. In an uncertain age, a distant bogeyman is something everyone can focus on. Reader, I was that bogey.

'Mr Crowley has never been tried for his part as a German propagandist and spy during the war with Germany. He is a traitor. He is a self-proclaimed dope addict. He is a con-man, who preys on the innocent. He is a shameless seducer of our youth...' At this stage the Beaver's eyes go glassy and focus in the middle distance, over the heads of his editors. The executives all scribble busily.

Wk on angle to that. Enqs. to the Home Off? Poss. Campaign. MPs if questions asked in H.C. Lambeth Palace dot dot dot.

The Beaver's mind has been invaded, pleasantly by the anticipation of an evening in Fulham, which he will spend flaying the daylights out of some poor drab, a gag in her mouth, for six guineas. The editors' ideas dry up rapidly, and they now look up, uncertain if the great man's instructions have concluded.

The Beaver suddenly realises he is daydreaming. He is expected to take charge, to give instruction. He turns round to see the target of Giles' grey suited behind, bending over the tea cups.

'Here boy!' he barks. 'Want to get ahead?' Giles lives with four maiden aunts: they are an unmarriagible generation: too many men drowned in the Flanders mud. His aunts are all soft-spoken so when people bark at Giles, he jumps.

'Yes, sir!' replies Giles, trembling.

'This is your chance. Drop everything and get out there!'

A moment later, it seems, and Giles is at Thomas Cooks', with his brand-new passport, buying a second class rail ticket for Cefalù, with instructions that he should report regularly on its most famous inhabitant.

A writer, it is said 'gives himself away' every sentence or so, but giving oneself away with only pen and paper for company is a lesser art, just as VIII° is a lower grade than IX°. Leah took down my autobiography, a prodigious feat of memory, in longhand from my dictation, hence her other name, the Ape of Thoth.[78] She was both recorder and audience for the following -

'Ninette saw me as her Saviour and her gratitude soon turned to an ecstasy of romantic love. One superb afternoon, sunny and springlike—it might have been May, after a jesting run, we sat down in a glade, on a bank of soft green moss and without preface of words, fell in each other's arms. We walked home on air and the next few days passed like a pageant of purple pleasure and passion. Ninette could hardly believe my attitude to The Ape had not been altered in any way by my liaison with her.'

What seems like delicious romantic vagueness - it *might* have been May - is in fact a touch of real coyness, in the dictation. Leah could have walked out, and then I'd have to write it myself. Accordingly, as I spoke, uncharacteristically I tempered the wind to the shorn lamb.

In any case my autobiography, which concluded, *de facto* with the departure of the Ape, seems a long way from the wretched business of what I'm doing now.

I haven't had a poke for weeks. I sit here of a night, hunched over a wobbling baize card table, with my half-baked shit-sticks crumbling and falling apart between my arthritic fingers. Promptly at the expiry of every hour, the electricity sub-meter expires, and I have to hunt for

---

78 *Thoth was the Egyptian Mercury, who brought writing, and other communications to them. A.C.*

florins in the dark, to feed it. The money I put in comes from the sale to my landlord of my little pills, which have to be manufactured by other solitary acts of mine. Since I write best at night, the money runs through my hands straight back to whence it came. I am a wizened lonely scribbler, who has to turn aside, periodically for an Op. VIII° just so he can still see what he's writing - if I should share these secrets with you, reader, will you pick up the telephone, and betray my humanity to *The Daily Express*?

MAGUS IN HASTINGS SHOWS HOW HE TURNS LIGHT ON

It seems to me, at the end of my life, that I have lost my following. Eloi, Eloi, Lama Sabaktani? *Ou sont les cuisses, d'antan*? The Ape fell away after, and sank to prostitution in Paris with Norman Mudd, who had himself lost an eye to gonorrhea. Like the poet Ovid, I seem to have appalled my contemporaries who can only see heartlessness when I expose contemporary morality: I have been banished by Augustus, vilified to die in exile,[79] where my life declines.

It was, indeed time to put the wall up. Sometimes the Truth revealed by Adepts can be too overpowering. Let us return to our Sicilian idyll: 'Giles' has dropped everything, and is now 'out there' in Cefalù. He has checked into a local hostel, where he is being cheerfully robbed, by being charged four times the nightly rate even for foreign grandees. He has discovered he will have to go to the local

---

79 *I came back from Cefalù and have spent the last thirty years, mostly in England, but I am obliged as I explained earlier, to throw the occasional inexactitude, to qualify this a harmless work of fiction.. So - be on your toes! A.C.*

post office if he wishes to make phone calls. He has laid out his shaving soap and badger-hair brush, his Wilkinson Safety razor, and his patent hair restorer (A present from Maiden Aunts 3° and 4°) from his brand-new leather suitcase. And now he puts his reporter's notepad in his pocket, and ventures out into the blinding sunlight of the street.

The first thing he notices is that he is a foot taller on average than the local population. Next, he feels the tender skin on his receding widow's peak, stinging under the assault of the Sicilian sun. Deeply shy, the fool does not buy a hat. The Italian for hat, Giles, is 'Capo'. He passes briefly and with some relief into the long shade of the duomo, the huge byzantine cathedral built seven centuries ago by Roger II to create a bulwark of a bishopric against Rome. The cathedral, seven hundred years after Roger's Will planted it in a fishing village, is still many times too vast for the little town.

Giles' Baedeker Guide to Sicily (Aunt 2°, we believe) would have informed him that the arrangement of the church at the base of the tall limestone cliffs is highly unusual: Mediterranean settlements generally welcomed Christianity by erected the new edifice on top of the old temple, which was invariably the highest place near the settlement. Roger's mighty edifice, unsuitably vast, ignores the narrower places on top of the rock which are sacred to the old gods. There, tradition has it, are ruins of Diana's temple. Or perhaps it was another aspect of her, the nymph that presided over the Messina straits that the Templars intuited as the sacred sister of Arthur, Fata Morgana.

Whoever it is, there the Thelemites will make pilgrimage, on occasion, away from their homespun temporary temple, in their robes, genuflecting their way as the sun goes down, seeking the older, truer paganism of our forefathers. And Giles, true to his calling as Judas was to his, will lurk in the growing shadows and spy on them.

The Post Office, where Giles fails to establish a line of credit, is in modern turmoil, as Mussolini's brand new fascist administration locks horns with older and more established practices. The gossip round the square by the duomo is all of whether Il Duce will succeed in modernising Sicily. The Greeks tried, then the Romans, the Normans had a go - in fact it's hard to think of a country that did not, at some time rape and rule this increasingly arid island. So much so that history here flows backwards: A very Crowleyish place.

Posters of Il Duce are going up against the Duomo walls. Bald, with staring eyes. Has Crowley incarnated with his twin in the true Spirit of the Times? Either way, the *caribineri* will find that at night the posters are defaced and torn down. Old habits die hard, in Sicily: orders from Rome are always refused.

Giles finally buys a straw hat, the kind the locals put on asses' heads, and goes towards the sea, where he has heard the Purple Priest would be at that hour of the day, making his ablutions.

The beach next to the wine-dark sea is deserted. Sweat pricks out on Giles' tender brow as he settles down beside a rock in his inappropriate dark suit, with the stiff detachable collar on his shirt already losing its starch and riding up in the heat. He takes his brand new Carl Zeiss of Jena 'DELTRINTREM' 8X30 binoculars (Cordings of Piccadilly, four guineas, Aunt 1°) out of their velvet-lined calfskin case. He turns the right hand lense wheel to compensate for the slight astigmatism caused by a wooden bayonet in a boyhood game of soldiers, when he was obliged to be the unpopular Boche, and looks out -

Giles is colourblind, and he would not see what you and I would see from there. Like Iseult scanning the oceans for Tristan he peers. But the oddly pigmented waters are empty.

Giles turns round to look at the hinterland of the beach. On the road behind his hideaway can be seen two travellers, weaving along in the heat haze. Brushing the sand from his powerful new binoculars, the direct descendant of the telescope that Leonard used to discover Jupiter's moons, Giles is able to see that the road holds a young woman with a suitcase in one hand, and a small child in the other. They are not Sicilians. They are approaching a figure on the beach.

Giles sees the travellers go up to a naked woman breast feeding a small baby. How could he have missed *that*, before? The women kiss, then they all sit down together. Giles does not know their names yet, but I can tell you that Ninette and her little boy have arrived to find that Leah has given birth to our girl child, Poupée. Leah has known they are coming and makes them welcome. Giles is looking at what he has come all this way to see - family life in the Abbey of Thelema. The sun beats down, and little Poupée's cries, tiny painful noises come to Giles, as if the heat haze was sieving them slowly through muslin.

Giles is half-listening to the intermittent eldritch distress, when a greater scream rents the midday heavens. A portly figure erupts from the rocks nearby, and streaks towards the water. It is I, reader, bounding over redhot sand and rocks and howling with pain, in my birthday suit. The scream goes on and on, like a runaway locomotive, until finally the agony is extinguished as the Beast hits the cooling water.

In the water, brushing rivulets of salt water from my eyes, I do not realise yet that Ninette had arrived to take up the Great Work because I had just defecated. I now tread water, watching the slim, curled turd drift slowly away.

That day Ninette arrived, we spent most of the day on the beach, and left when the sun was low. To Ninette's delight, we took Adoration, that is praising Ra in his rising and setting, from the winding path back to the house, as the sun went down. It left a perfect yellow afterglow. In Sicily, as I have observed before, one can always count on two or three hours a day of sheer visual poetry.

At the same moment as we were taking Adoration, in a Fulham lovenest under Brompton Cemetery's greasy skies, the rubbery-faced Beaverbrook no doubt had already donned his mask, to unleash his own amusement. To bloody the wallpaper, 'breaking in' the latest cash-starved, curious or unlucky girls, as the windup gramophone played 'nigger music' to camouflage any gossip-inducing screams.

'It's a respectable address and they are just letting their hair down, having a party, you see, officer. No one is being detained against their Will.'

Giles' three aunts had a ghostly parallel with my own three aunts, who the influenza epidemic carried off at the end of the Great War: nothing showed more clearly the passage of Neptune, that anaesthetic, dreaming transmuter into fiery Leo than the fact that the epidemic carried off more people than had been killed in the whole of the war. The three aunts left me legacies, which I used to secure the lease on the Abbey, but there was nothing left after that, and in spite of Frank's scorn, I kept thinking about Collins, the book publishers, and the idea for a novel.

I confess it is very difficult for me to get myself to the idea of 'selling' anything. My father sold beer, and beer engines, but being a teetotaller himself, he believed that drinkers went to hell. Thus the trade, though lucrative, was quite separate from the rest of his thinking. Not so the hapless writer, who has to spin his wares from the very Founts of his Being. I came down from Cambridge a young man who had the misfortune of never having had to count his wealth: suffice it to say it would have bought me over seven million IX° with the famed 'tuppeny uprights', ladies of the night who famously plied their cutprice trade round the unlit corners under Waterloo Bridge. I had enough in other words, a lifetime of love. Naturally I threw this largesse away, and then, when it was gone, I did what any Beings have done whose message is for mankind. I looked to others to support me.

When I returned to Europe at the end of the Great War, Neptune smiled on me - never trust that watery smile! - my aunts were carried off, one by one, as peremptorily as if they had been in the fifth act of a Jacobean tragedy. Neptune in Leo accomplished what Graf Von Zeppelin had failed to do, and lo, all my aunts were dust.

It left me a little money, and I immediately applied it to The Work, but I have never had any experience of keeping money - in fact, since

I am Ipsissimus and a magus (against my better will and judgement, I have to say) it is fitting that my followers should provide the wherewithal. But - and it is a large but - when one's followers are such a wretched crew,[80] in the end, it falls to the most able to be breadwinners.

It was clear I would have to create an impression in the book trade, in order to secure a realistic advance. In order to make myself known to the world of commercial fiction, it was necessary to impress them with a magickal event. Being magickal it would also contain the core of my being, which had complete contempt for their flaccid outpourings. I woke up one morning with the perfect stratagem that would gain me the full attention of the commercial publishing world. *I would make all their books disappear.*

My plan formed, I went into one of the many bookshops in the Charing Cross Road. The shop was stuffed, floor-to-ceiling with bad novels. There was a hunchbacked, goggle-eyed creature behind a desk, with glasses which made his eyes look like a newborn piglet's. He was slowly selling whatever drivel the public were persuaded to purchase from the packed shelves. But the day had hardly begun and there was no one else in the shop.

'I'm Aleister Crowley' I announced, dispensing with Thelemic greetings, to obvious infidels. 'You will have heard of me.' Piglet-eyes snuffled, and moved some brown wrapping paper and bits of string around his desk.

'Ah yes. You're the magician.'

'I am indeed a magician. A very good one.' I said. Piglet-eyes cocked his head dreamily. If I could hypnotise anyone, I could do it to this specimen of humanity.

---

80 *Doctor Johnson's chief anxieties about the words and acts of Christ the Saviour being properly reported were because his disciples were 'a rude crew.' Quite so. If I had a proper apologist from amongst my rabble, able to tell when I was merely being ironic, as opposed to gnomic, I would not be sitting up at four in the morning on top of my grapes of wrath writing this stuff.* A.C.

Pretending to check the time, I started to swing my fob-watch on the end of its chain. I have the trick of hypnosis - it is no more, I could teach anyone with competence the trade in five minutes. I instinctively made the watch swing at the rate his brain required for complete subjection to my authority.

'I suggest you would like to see a trick' I said. Piglet-eyes grunted. He had fallen so fast, so far into my power that it was extremely amusing.

'You will not remember this watch, but you will remember what Aleister Crowley did when he came into your shop.'

'Aw'right' Piglet-eyes grunted. He really did grunt. Like Circe, I could turn humans into swine.

'Now when I click my fingers once, all the books on your shelves are going to disappear.' I clicked my fingers once, and Piglet-eyes stopped grunting, and looked round in amazement. He could see his shelves bare. The fact that I knew they were still groaning with Arnold Bennett, H.G. Wells, that windbag G.B. Shaw, and other literary mountebanks made no difference. Under my spell, piglet-eyes suddenly could not see them.

'Can you see any books?' I asked.

'No I can't.' He became worried. 'You've made them disappear.'

'Yes I've taken them away.' Piglet-eyes started to riffle in his papers.

'Did I give you a receipt?' He asked, worried.

'Stop.' I used the voice of command.' When I click my fingers again, you are going to wake up, and all your books will be here. ' Piglet-eyes looked at me. His face was a mask of incomprehension and misgiving. I clicked my fingers, and Piglet-eyes' shoulders visibly relaxed as his books swam into view again and settled on the shelves, just as a customer opened the door.

'Don't forget to tell everyone what happened' I said. 'Oh - and tell them as well, I've given you a new name - 'Little Porker'.

In a week, the story of my cleaning out the complete contents of the book trade, and then restoring it was all over London. In a month, I had my commission for a novel entitled *Diary of a Drug Fiend*.[81] Sustained by cocaine, I was able to dictate to Leah at the rate of 5,000 words a day: mindful of the public execration of *The Rainbow* I did not touch on any IX° Operations. This was not from any false modesty. Lawrence's last novels, trash no doubt are banned for the wrong reasons, but banned all the same. In the roaring twenties, I could not afford the penalties of mounting a full frontal assault on sexual hypocrisy. I thought it would be tactical to take the money, and use the book for an advertisement for my own Abbey, where those who wished to learn more about Thelema could visit. How utterly, utterly wrong I was. After a promising start the book was banned, and Collins have never risked reissuing it.

Personally, I blame Pluto. Almost until the year of my bankruptcy, that other watershed, I never even chose to speculate if there was 'anyone there'. I chose to ignore the rumblings of the scientific establishment about the existence of a planet with an orbit even wider of the sun, for the most part, than Neptune. The actions of Uranus had been most effectively described by me, as well as Neptune. The writings were part of a general survey I began on the subject when I was in America, sadly never finished. My assistant had tried to cheat me of all the profits, and then the Abbey called. After the Abbey had been torn from me, I was about to take up my pen again, when in February 1930, the master of the Underworld himself was first seen, floating proudly at the edge of our solar system, captured in a light-reflecting concave mirror: the sort of thing that would have got the perpetrators burnt as sorcerers a few score years ago.

I hardly have the heart to redraw my own natal chart to accommodate him. Let thy servant depart in peace! Pluto and his dark forces lies trine to my Mars, accounting for my volcanic energy, and humanity,

---

81   *A wonderful kind and noble man, wrongfully accused in the press, living on a remote island is able to wean morally bankrupt visitors off their dependence on narcotics. Oh, and he never touches them himself. A.C.*

but 90° square to my Uranus. I would interpret the intercalation of this new God as accounting for the difficulties I have experienced getting my new ideas (Uranus) over in the mass turbulence which attends the birth of the New Aeon. Pluto is also square to my Saturn, which fits with my difficulty with authority figures. My father died of cancer when I was eleven. I have absolved myself of this event, but doubtless the leader of the Viennese school of analysis[82] (now no longer with us, praise Pluto) would have had something else to say about my buried feelings. But as for Pluto's contact with Venus - a quincunx - it relates to compulsive and guilt motivated patterns in love and venery. Oh dear.

Suddenly, now the skies have opened further, my 'fate' doesn't look like the chart of a charmer. It is the chart of someone who would end up rowing with almost everyone he came into contact with. Of course, I say, 'They simply fell away on the Path.' Over the years, I have become inured. What does it matter, in the end? *Perdurabo.* More hock and seltzer, Oscar,[83] and devil take the hindmost, as you know he generally does.

The first evening, Ninette came up the path hand in hand with Leah and her little boy-child, Hermes. The Abbey was a majestic building with five capacious rooms leading off from a large central hall, which I had dedicated, through an exhausting number of Operation IX°'s

---

82 *Sigmund Freud, whose wilful misinterpretation of the Oedipus myth has been taken up with delight by the trickster's paradise, America. It was unnecessary for the Nazis to have burned Freud's books as they did. They could have simply laughed at them. A.C.*

83 *The British never treat their poets properly. They should put Oscar Wilde upright in a glass coffin on Platform 11 of Clapham Junction, with his body preserved like a pharaoh, or Jeremy Bentham. Then with sixpence in a slot, you could listen to a long-playing phonograph record of St. Oscar reciting The Ballad of Reading Gaol. A.C.*

with Leah, as the central temple of the Thelemic Mysteries. On the floor was a Magickal circle, inside that a pentagram and in the middle of the pentagram, there was a six sided altar with six candles upon it and all the necessary Implements, the bell of seven elements; a magickal burin, a carving tool, a sword etc., etc., as well as a Great Book, a record of the Publick & Magickal events of the Abbey. This was quite separate from the Magickal Diaries which all neophytes, or new arrivals were requested to keep, recording all of their inner thoughts which I could peruse to check their spiritual progress.

Before Ninette's arrival, I had been busy painting murals on every wall of every permutation of the sexual act, in order to break down the taboos and ridiculous attitudes which society and civilization had adopted to The Work. Although no door was ever locked, on my instructions, and all the stimulants known to man were available from my study, I had to din it continually in to everyone's head that they were not simply there for pleasure and indulging themselves.

'Every operation is an Opus, and every Opus is serious Work.' The children who arrived would not be constrained against the Wills in the education, but would be permitted to watch whatever we did. If they became curious the rituals would be explained to them, but the main thrust of the Abbey child-rearing philosophy looked like benign neglect. The children were not sacrificed (Unless you read the account in a Beaverbrook paper, consequently banned in the Abbey), they were not coerced against their Wills to do anything. When young Hermes picked up an attraction for cigarettes, little was done to discourage him from smoking. Cigarettes in my view were a low, injurious form of tobacco that the War had popularised, and as soon as Dionysius realised he was not getting the pleasure he could from a pipe, or a fine cigar, no doubt he would wean himself from his fad, just as his swearing and throwing rocks at adults would fade away if it was ignored. The Abbey was Liberty Hall in all but name.

On the first evening, little Hermes did no more than glance at the pictures on the wall of men and women copulating with stars and goats before going back to happily playing in the dust on the verandah. A cool breeze now came in from the sea. In order to welcome Ninette, I went into my study, and put my Baphomet outfit on, some topaz earrings and Perfume of Immortality in the usual places.

A meal of salami, bread and Sicilian wine was prepared. Ninette showed her eagerness for the Work by serving it. We ate it outside, borrowing one of the sacred candles in order to have light. A black dog, a stray which Leah had adopted, lay just outside the circle of candle light. Its ears were bloody with ticks. I had named it Satan.

'I'm so glad you found us on the beach.' Leah gushed. Both of us had been eaten up with anxiety about the health of our own little baby, Poupée.

'It was easy to find you' Ninette said in her curiously accented voice. Sometimes its register was almost subterranean, like the song of a courting woodpigeon. I was in the presence of Pluto, that most subterranean of gods, who would speak through Ninette, and smash the union of myself with Leah, ex-schoolteacher, ex-perpetual student, who signed herself amongst other titles the 'Contessa de Kerval'. Oh, oh, you cruel gods. Those whom you wish to destroy, you first make mad. I was more than a little mad already, and I was about to draw the rest of the Dionysiac crew in my train.

'How was it easy? ' Leah pressed Ninette.

'I just asked for the crazy people.' said Ninette. A long section of salami skin had got caught behind my lower Serpent's Tooth.

Little Hermes pointed at me and tugged at his mother's skirt. The tooth was already a little decayed and I was having to exercise care extracting the skin.

'*Qu'est qu'il fait, maintenant? Pourquoi Le Grand Bête ne mange pas avec un fourchette?*'

After I had signed the lease to the Abbey, and seen its beauties, I had made a decision to teach my own mind a negation of the Western values that had poisoned Europe. I was going to return to a relationship with my food which gave me a better opportunity to fully benefit from its *prana*,[84] which relied on food being as close as possible to its natural condition. In the case of salami, I simply took it with my teeth, as I needed.

Finally, out the salami skin came, longish and white, and I dropped it on one side. Ninette shrugged, the shrug of a million peasants, and Hermes watched as Satan, his hunger aroused, went hunting for the piece of discarded intestine, and snuffled in up, with the dust. Satan's hordes of parasites no doubt rejoiced at the prana which would shortly be coming their way.

'Ninette's going to have to keep a diary. Does she know?' said Leah.

Ninette's position in the Abbey was to be that of helpmeet to the Ape of Thoth. Leah knew that Ninette and I had practised Thelemically together, but it was very clear from Ninette's demeanour and conversation generally, that apart from having a fine, fat firm and juicy yoni, she was not out of the top drawer, intellectually or magickally. She was still suspicious of Leah, and would want to gain exclusive possession of my affection because of her own insecurities. I would have to teach her that the Law of Thelema frees everyone from jealousy. Inside, Poupée was beginning to wail. Overhead, a northward bound shooting star the size of a grain of sand burnt an extravagant green hole in the sky. Then it silently collapsed to a black nothing, too lightweight to fall and blast Rome. Ninette looked at me as if I had caused the phenomenon. I deliberately looked away, as if I wanted nothing to do with it. I took a fig from the bowl on the table and held it up to the candle light.

'What's this Ninette?'

'*C'est un figue, non?*'

'It's a fig, Ninette. That's right, a fig. With the figleaf, Eve covered what? Everything which people were previously ashamed. But the tree you're sitting in at the moment, we're none of us ashamed, we're none

---

84   Prana is life force. Indian adepts can ingest the prana from a meal of twenty oysters before voiding them, leaving the intestine clear. The adepts have fed nonetheless. They are charged with the creatures' prana. A.C.

of us leaves. We're figs.'

'We're all figs' said Leah, unnecessarily. I broke open the fig with my thumbs, and showed her the inside, all succulent pink.

'That's what we're going to do to you. We're going to free you to remake yourself, from the core of your being.' I'd tongued her *vas nefandum* till my tongue-root bled, but clearly no one had ever offered to turn Ninette into a fruit salad before. There was a fresh wail from inside.

'Should I get Poupée?' Ninette asked, warily.

'I'll get her.' Leah said suddenly. 'This is your first night. You stay and...talk.' .

Ninette could not have come at a better time, from one point of view. While I was dictating a letter to Raoul, the previous day, Leah had fallen asleep over the typewriter. She was tired, with puffy eyes, from tiredness, the baby, and the continuous Work. One of her eyes had a tic, from exhaustion. Leah got up slowly. She had henna'ed her hair and was wearing the Robe of Alostrael, the purple robe that I had designed. She went inside, but the crying continued.

IX The Hermit

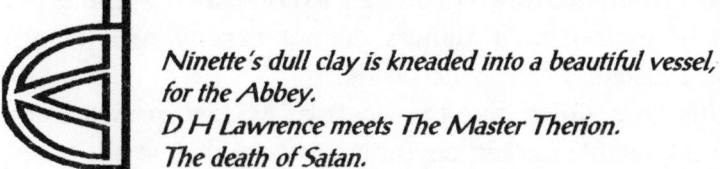

Ninette's dull clay is kneaded into a beautiful vessel, for the Abbey.
D H Lawrence meets The Master Therion.
The death of Satan.

No one who has not tried to start a new religion will appreciate the sheer administrative burden which goes with the job. However, with Leah freed from looking after Poupée after Ninette's arrival, I was able to redouble my efforts to seek out disciples - and hopefully, funds. Leah as always with her American outlook was insistent that the Film Industry should be involved in publicising the new way of life we were practicing, and indeed we managed to attract a number of American visitors, including one actress, over the time we were in Sicily. The Americans on the whole however were however totally corrupted by the sanitised version of the life they had previously lived.

I became tired of explaining to disappointed neophytes that the Abbey had no hot and cold running water, and pointing out that in the absence of built-in sewage systems, natural functions could be easily dealt with in the healthful way which they had been dispersed round the habitations of Man, for thousands of years. In the end, I simply turned my back, inhaled my ether and in order to facilitate the psychic revolution, painted my striking paintings everywhere I could reach on the wall.[85] In England, at the same time, I understand that a section of

---

85 Health warning. Ether enables the user to see deeply into the heart of things, but should not be used to excess, dearly beloved, mainly because it tends to still mental processes! A.C.

the London literary hyena pack, who like to call themselves something like the 'Bloomsbury Elite' stole this idea and daubed the insides of several of their country cottages, including the furniture.

I have not been invited down to Sussex, to compare our results but the writings of their female authors do not exactly reek of all-transcending, pansexual messianic vision.[86]

And all this time, Giles, like the Hosts of Midian, prowled and prowled around, unable to 'get' anything on the Abbey at all.

One morning, I wrote the letter to Raoul, simply letting him know that he should come. I left it open whether he should come alone or accompanied. I had half a mind, if Betty should come of her own free will, that I could get her to accept the Law of Thelema as well.

But for now, it was time to invest Ninette. Whatever the shortcomings in her own understanding and her expertise, she had come to us, and so we should free her, in her own fashion. Then she could become a full member of the Abbey and henna her hair.

Incense was burning at the altar. I was wearing my High Priest's white robe, which I used later to officiate at Raoul's funeral. Leah and Ninette were both wearing the capes of the Abbey. Leah put Poupée down, but she only cried so she held her while Ninette looking terribly solemn was invested. I took Ninette through the formal process, concluding-

'Ninette, your Magickal name for the Abbey shall be Sister Cypris.'

'Does that mean I can't be called Ninette anymore?'

'You can be called Ninette if you wish, but you also have another name, a Magickal name, which expresses your new being.' Ninette shrugged. Leah and I kissed Sister Cypris, ceremonially, repeating her new name.

'And your son is called Hermes' said Leah, flatly.

' *'Urmees'* said Ninette, trying it out for size. She had given him a

---

[86] The apocryphal story - that as soon as Lytton Strachey saw a drawing that Augustus John had done of me, the old queen squawked 'Semen!' - is probably correct. A.C.

maize- paper cigarette to keep him quiet. 'Urmees was busy relighting it behind her, leaning up against the Temple wall. I made a mental note to for Leah to try and obtain some cigarillos the next time she was in the tobacconist's. I was sure the indulgence was doing the boy no good.

'Now Sister Cypris, in celebration it is your task to read the devotional verse, for the day.' Ninette slowly read out the Abbey's credo, its Rights of Man. Ideally she should have learnt it by heart.

'Man has the right to eat what he will, to drink what he will, to dwell where he will, to move as he will on the face of the earth. Man has the right to think what he will, to speak what he will, to write what he will to draw, paint carve, etch, mould, build as he will, to dress as he will.

'Man has the right to love as he will' - She shot me a dirty look, here- 'Man has the right to kill those who thwart these rights.' Ninette closed the book and turned to Leah. 'This is all about a man. Is there another one for woman?'

'*Man* means everyone' said Leah, sharply. I didn't like the attitude that Sister Cypris was developing, either, even as she was concluding her induction. A short sharp shock was needed to let her know that the way to selfhood could be long and arduous.

'As a member of the Abbey, Sister Cypris, you are involved in the business of self-transcendence. That is the work, that is the only work we pledge. As an Abbey neophyte, it is forbidden to you from this day to use the first person singular, at any time. If you do, you can take a razor and cut yourself, on the arm, lightly. This self-punishment is practised regardless of gender. I.'

I took up the burin from the altar, and pushed it into my third finger, to show I meant business. A few drops of blood fell on the altar, from the digit sacred to Apollo. Ninette's eyes started to go blank, as vacant as the eyes of the cow that the followers of Baal worshiped.

'What if I say "I" in French?'

'The penalties are exactly the same for all Indo-European tongues. You may of course speak the First Person in Basque or Portuguese' I concluded, humorously. But Ninette was not to be jollied out of her sullen mood. Leah declared that all in all, our first induction had been a considerable success.

I was musing on my greatness a few days later, while nursing a large brandy in one of the cafés in the square outside the cathedral when I saw a couple crossing the square and going into the street where the post office was. For some reason I cannot to this day fathom, I thought that they might be looking for me. I downed my brandy and followed them.

As I crossed the square, I reflected that one of the reasons that I had been to date unsuccessful in America, was rooted in my complete contempt for the so-called giants of their literature. Take Mark Twain for instance. His genius appears to rest on disguising the frank and decent sexual feeling between a young white man, and a black slave considerably older than him. You would have thought that in the United States, where the pursuit of happiness is a right written into the constitution, it would have been possible to write about the true feelings of the two characters for each other more openly. But then, his wife had to pass every chapter, as fit for publication.

Twain also adopts the position where the character telling us the story openly claims that he has made bits of the story up in order to 'amuse' the reader. We are not amused. I hope I make it clear, that where I am diverging from 'the truth' it is for a higher reason than Twain's tooth-sucking rural excuses for 'stretchers'. If I throw dust in the reader's eyes from time to time, it is not because I like a good yarn. Like Mr Dennis Wheatley - Oh! The very name sends cold shivers down my spine - I have undertaken to my publishers to protect the average reader from acquiring the Means for Magical Wickedness. I can point in that direction, but no more.

With his thin build and red beard the man who I had followed to the post office looked like D H Lawrence. It was indeed The Nottinghamshire Traitor and Smut Peddler, as Beaverbrook referred to him. I had not realised that he had been living in Taormina, the other side of the volcano. He was slim and nervy, standing in the Cefalù post office, holding a bulky manuscript-sized parcel, which he had just received from the *poste restante* counter.

I have not dragged Lawrence into my story in order to praise his writing. On the contrary. His vacuous fictional maunderings, preachy and coyly homoerotic by turns, with no real grasp of the magickal nature of the sexual current were largely the result of his body condition. He was racked with tuberculosis. Lawrence's illness indeed was partly why he moved to Sicily. He looked like a sick fox.

There was a much larger woman standing calmly behind him in a grey dress who I immediately understood was his German wife Freida. He was about to hurl his manuscript back over the counter when Freida caught his thin white wrist in her large paw.

'I am sure we will get someone else to publish it.' said Freida in her guttural voice. Lawrence dropped his hand, and turned to declaim to the post office queue -

'Curse them, the blasted, jelly-boned swines, the slimy bellywriggling invertebrates, the miserable sodding rotters, the flaming sods. The snivelling, dribbling dithering, palsied pulseless lot that make up England!'

The Sicilians, who only recently had fallen under the yoke of a man who made the trains run on time, stared back at him, with the look I would see again on the crowd at Raoul's funeral. They had been oppressed for so long that any extravagant gesture apart from fratricide and parricide were alien to them.

'They've got white of egg in their veins, and their spunk is that watery it's a marvel they can breed!'

'Yours is no better' said Freida. 'You are rotting inside.'

'Why, why, why was I born an Englishman?' howled Mr Lawrence and fell to the floor in a tantrum. Freida raised her eyebrows at me, but did nothing to stop her husband who was now lying on the floor, kicking his heels and screaming. The couple, I was aware had been vilified continuously. Frieda's children had been kept from their mother by detectives after she took off with her young lover. Like me, Frieda had been accused of being a German spy and Lawrence, with his last two books banned, was in rather a similar boat to me. We were both trying to reform society, but our reputations - our only means of drawing attention to our ideas - kept getting in the way. I had half a mind to invite both of them to the Abbey, if the latest paroxysm of 'lorenzo' was not going to prove fatal.

Finally Lawrence's disease-laden spittle-froth and screams subsided.

'Do what thou wilt shall be the whole of the Law' I said, mildly. Frieda cocked a teutonic eyebrow at me.

'Vot?'

Lawrence got up and slowly dusted down his dirty linen suit.

'Do what thou wilt shall be the whole of the Law' I said to him. He put his lean foxy face close to mine.

'Are you Aleister Crowley?' he asked, as if expecting to start a brawl in the Nottinghamshire Working Men's Club.

'The same' I replied. Lawrence clearly didn't think he needed introducing. If people don't offer their names, I never ask.

'Willie Yeats told me about you. You play the bagpipes, don't you?' His face was opening now, in a knowing, shy half-smile.

'I do indeed.' I said, remembering the mucillagenous horse head. Freida moved away, as if she remembered it too.

'You live round here, do you?'

'Yes.'

'I can't stand England either. So - are you on your own?'

'I've started a community here.'

He peered at the bottle I was carrying. I could get Allinson's Gripe Water, which was thirty percent alcohol, from the same pharmacy that supplied me with heroin.

'Have you got a sick baby, then, have you?'

'My little girl's got colic.'

'Your little girl. There's a thought now. I haven't got *any* wains and it's going to stay that way.' Lawrence said. He bent down and picked up a small parcel of unwrapped white calico that he had dropped on the floor during his outrage. Naturally it had become filthy.

'I bought this to make Frieda some knickers. I bet she won't wear them, now. ' he said, and brushed at the dirt on the fabric. 'I can't stand the lacy French ones she buys. The ones she's wearing now make her look like, like ... an '*ore*.' His eyes widened, and his Nottinghamshire accent deepened as he came to the dread word.

Freida loomed in the post office door and shouted at her husband.

'Lorenzo! Kommenzei!' Lawrence turned to me, shrugged and by way of farewell said,

'We're off to America, soon. If they let me in, with my sewing machine.' Then he broke away and joined his wife outside.

I let him go. I make it a point of principle never to pursue converts. But I was sorry I did not convert the Lawrences to Thelema. Illness was his prism, as drugs are mine. I would have liked to have cured him.

Leah said that it was not only insanity but insanitary, to think of inviting tuberculosis cases to where they could infect healthy people, and anyhow, as soon as Lawrence would have seen my Abbey, it would have become the butt of his sick animal rage, and he would accused me of twisting and corrupting the sex act - exactly the things, in fact, that people accused him of doing. And with the spies from the papers hounding Lawrence as well, we would never had had a moment's peace.

She was right, of course. But they both exuded an interesting Magickal Current. I couldn't help feeling that I had missed a trick, there. He could have run up some curtains for us, so that no one could have spied on us.

I can't believe that I've confessed I wanted to cure D H Lawrence. I just can't believe it. I must be even more insane than I suspected. Is

that the truth I swore to tell, or the one I had to withhold? Or is my own confusion truer than either?

Perhaps like Churchill's father I am suffering from syphilis. Aiwass knows I've fucked enough whores. Outbreaks of irrational fear and phobia culminating in general paralysis of the insane. You can get treatment now, but even new-fangled penicillin can't roll back tertiary symptoms. The damage has been done. Oh, not *unconscious* lunacy, please. I have to *know* what I am doing. When I have not been good, my intentions have often been for the public good, the common weal. And often it has looked bad simply because I have been ahead of my time.

And truly I am no madder now than I have been the rest of my life.

People often hate me for nothing other than the constant desire I have to improve the lot of humanity in my lifetime. What cheek! What presumption! I once undertook to cure Lord Tankerville of insanity, by taking all his paranoid delusions seriously and working with him to magically defuse the threats. It ended up with him saying

'I'm fed up with your preaching, preaching, as if you were Jesus Christ Almighty, and I was some poor bloody shit you trod on, in the street.'

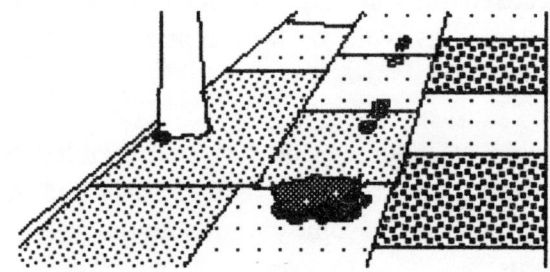

& Did those Feet, in Ancient Times?

It is now six hours, six minutes and six seconds since my last injection. The hour of the wolf! A miserable cold, cloudy dawn will break soon, and at breakfast, the landlord of 'Netherwood' will be wanting his pills. His little goatee beard will have nothing to chomp on if I don't get started.

4.15AM To work, in haste.

4.25AM The meter is making the noise it makes just before the electrical contact is broken. Op. VIII° Copious effusion. Pills almost rolled. Consumed excess myself. *Waste not, want not.*

4.29AM Pills finished. It's gone dark. Those who think I am a mere Gargoyle on the Cathedral of Life, beware! I still Sup upon the Secrets of Eternity.
Half a grain H. To bed, to die, perchance to dream...

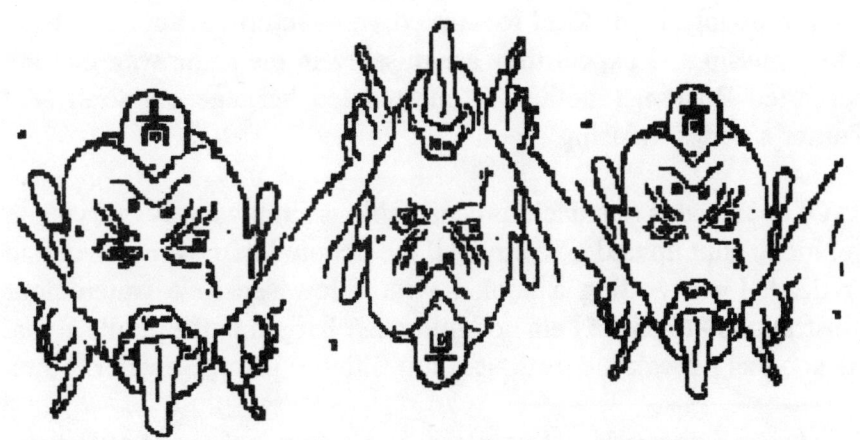

X Fortune

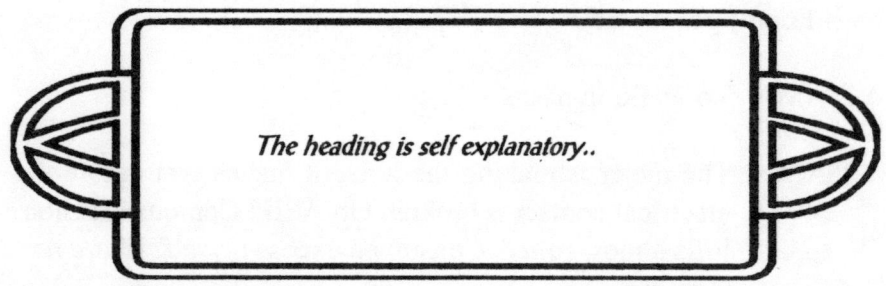

The heading is self explanatory..

Oh, Bollocks. Having set out on this enterprise with firm assurances that my publishers would honour my penmanship, provided its references to magickal incantations were sufficiently veiled, a letter now lies opened at my table, containing the withdrawal of any such undertaking. I now learn that I need to 'tone down' what I have written even further before they can offer an advance. And some of the drawings in the MS I forwarded, (now returned) appear to have gone 'missing'. I expect they are missing in the same way that the perverted Ruskin, (another of our twisted heritage curators) sent Turner's nudes 'missing'.[87]

Of course, this mendacious censorship is simply a way of trying to get me to shut up and go away. All the people I name are either mad or dead. I am writing a book - with a few sensitive watercolour illustrations - to prove I am not guilty, as charged in the public arena. As soon as I speak the truth, it is too filthy to print. Bowdler,[88] thou

---

87 Ruskin's censorship - he destroyed the paintings in the name of Victorian propriety - is a measure of how the Good and Great think they have an obligation to rewrite history. A.C.

88 Dr Bowdler made it his life's work to Bowdler-ise Shakespeare and took out the indelicate passages. This Volume will I hope, be carried far into the New Age of Crowleyanity, when such butchers of poesy will be quite forgotten, except in footnotes such as this. A.C.

shouldst be living at this hour. Only my own candle, lit at my own hallowed altar of innocence drives me on. I shall fight to clear my name as long as I have a hole in my bottom. On we go, with a little help from our friend, crystalline white, dearest Snow. To Sicily.

Up past the rocks above Cefalù to the eagle's eyrie of the Abbey, where superior Beings are in the process of self-development. We wheel above the sunkissed tiles of the blessèd spot as the ranks of the olive grove in front of the house stand guard in the afternoon heat. There is a slight heat haze, over the straits of Messina. A postman, wearing his brand new uniform, (for Fascists, sensitive to the New Aeon, bring stylish change to every corner of Mercury's domain,) approaches the house. A dog begins to bark. The postman hastily tips his letters in the square yellow sheet iron box nailed to the gate at the end of the grove below the house, and goes on up the hill as Satan stands and barks sluggishly, to defend his adopted own. His ears have been rescued from ticks by Ninette's nimble fingers. Behind Satan, stands a plump baldheaded man, dressed in a kilt of the MacGregor Tartan. I say to Satan:

'Sicc'im Satan! Sicc'im! Go on!' Satan does nothing of the sort. He returns, tail drooping and dusty, lopsided tongue panting, to the cool of the northside of the altar.

The Postman has heard the Name of the Dog. He crosses himself, and makes a sign to avert the Evil Eye, in case the strange man in the skirt should have laid it on him. His mother and his brother both were cursed, and it ended badly for both of them.

I, The Beast, go down in stately fashion to the postbox at the gate, and draw the letters out. One of them is from Frank Harris. The other is from Raoul, and I open it immediately, and read, standing in the shade of the olive trees, while the cicadas' song accompanies the eternity that is the Mediterranean afternoon. Raoul's letter sends no money this time but it says that he is coming soon: My beamish boy!

In order to complete the task of creating surroundings which were conducive to the transfer of wounded sensibilities from the old order, accelerating the acceptance of *Liber Legis*, I used to rise in the late afternoon, and paint into the night, often using ether as my stepladder to the artistic empyrean. I would inhale from a pad I kept with me, and simply dive into the project I was currently engaged in.

I had made a number of attempts to portray Madame Poitier as I had first seen her. Aiwass who I had glimpsed imperfectly during his dictation of the *Book of the Law* never presented the same problems: in his more feminine aspect however, my Guardian Angel proved elusive.

The breakthrough came for me when I had a dream in which Madame Poitier appeared, endowed hermaphroditically. This dream was associated with the old temple of Diana in Cefalù, on top of the rock, at what were known as the Baths of Jupiter, where I frequently climbed.

Madame Poitier's choice of association with Jupiter in the dream proved without a doubt that she was a facet of of Jove's wife Juno. Suddenly the peacock feather background the first time I saw her made sense.

Through analectic deduction I proceeded thus: The peacock, παωσ, is a bird sacred to Hera, with its flesh fabled incorruptible: its tailfeathers are the many eyes of Argus, cut by Mercury. So 'Madame Poitier's' true name and identity, so far hidden from me in the story, would be be linked with or close to the bird itself. Pavus is the latin for peacock, the final letters changing to a O and Z for reasons of numerology. This I was able to establish with a rapidity which astonished me, since I was and am still uncertain about the spelling of my other Guardian Angel's name.

In the dream, Ninette and Leah were both present atop the rock at the Temple while I officiated at a sacrifice. The sacrifice cannot have been to PAVOZ for at that stage I had not deduced her Name. I took up an obsidian blade. With Leah holding a tourniquet on Ninette's arm, I slipped the sharp stone knife into Ninette's flesh. She gave a little gasp and bit her lower lip, but then turned and smiled trustingly. Leah selected a small stone bowl and started to catch Ninette's blood. When it was full I placed it on the altar. I can remember no sense of anticipation, but then suddenly, PAVOZ was amongst us, in a dazzlingly bright light, with her mighty wings unfolded, as I had seen her, when I flew with her, across the desert. From the neck down, her downy skin, lit from within, was covered with the same mysterious hieroglyphics that I had seen before. But this time, hung about her neck was a vast, rimless green gemstone on a black leather cord. She finally folded her wings on the word of command,[89] bowed her head, took off the gemstone and handed it to me.

If I had all my life to live again, against that moment, I would choose that moment, when my H.G.A. made submission to me.

PAVOZ stood on her points, like a ballet dancer, and proudly turned round for me, showing me her breasts and her hermaphroditic parts till her whole mystical lexicon was exposed. Every square inch was covered with symbols. I became aware that her own self-generated light was pulsing to her heartbeat. PAVOZ reached out to touch Ninette and the tourniquet fell away. Ninette looked at her arm and there was no mark of a cut.

I took up the gemstone. Both sides had been smoothed and curved so it acted as a magnifying glass. I started to peruse PAVOZ's body at close quarters, dictating the Egyptian and Sumerian symbols which I was able clair-sentiently to pronounce. Leah had taken up a stylus and was writing down the symbols as I dictated them to her. When she had filled one tablet, Ninette would hand her another. I was about to have a record of every scrap of wisdom which PAVOZ had written on her body. At the end, I indicated that I would need to examine the symbols which were between her legs. She lay down and spread her legs for me. The hairs on her yoni were little peacock feathers of gold. I put my finger in her. She moved her leg a little, invitingly. I noted that her male

---

89 *The Word, for obvious reasons, is only disclosed to Ipsissimi. A.C.*

organs were not engorged. I could not see anything written inside her labia. I laid the magnifying glass aside, and tried to penetrate her with my Wand. Unexpectedly, it was difficult and actually painful. I pushed and I pushed manfully.

And suddenly I was falling. Not falling to the ground, but falling like Lucifer, through interstellar space, from where god had chosen to thrust me, to the next place of his choosing. PAVOZ had withdrawn from me.

When I woke up, I was lying on the floor next to the ether bottle with Ninette standing above me, leaning with her uncombed hair round her face, her great tits hanging over me. I touched her arm reassuringly. Would she have remembered her part in my Dream?

'Well done, Ninette!' I said. Ninette's face knotted in a puzzle. Naturally she didn't remember anything of her willing sacrifice. The next time I saw PAVOZ it was after Raoul died.

To London, to watch Betty May purchase the gun which she will use to protect her husband's virtue in general, and in particular, try to kill me. The letter has arrived from Cefalù (Saith The Beast, Come!) and Betty has taken counsel with her friends. The sculptor, Jakob Epstein advised her and Raoul against going, for he prophesied that only one of them would ever come back. Let us tear down Epstein's overpraised lumps of clay, and dig up his body and spit on it, for using the Black Arts to scry the future! How the hell did he know what I was going to commit?

Let Pavoz take you: I would take you, but I am indisposed, all my concentration is required for a dawn rockclimb in Cefalù. Let PAVOZ take you by the hand, and show you to a second-hand shop in Fulham to where Betty has just stepped in through the door.

Betty bought a new dress to travel in. She knew the shop, from her coke-head days, when she popped a number of 'things', never to see them again. She could now see the gun, an army officer's revolver lying with a price tag hanging from the butt under some dirty glass in front of the salesman.

'I need a gun.'

'You'll need a licence, madam.'

'No I won't, you see, I'm going abroad and my life, and the life of my husband may be in danger. He needs a revolver for protection.'

The assistant produced the gun, and a little greasy box containing eighteen dull brass cartridge shells. Betty hadn't enough to pay for both in cash, so she pawned her wedding ring. When she took it off the plain gold band rolled around on the counter for ever, it seemed, before coming to rest, and all that time she was never in any doubt that what she was doing was right. I rather admired Betty in some ways. She was a spirited antagonist.

Meanwhile above Cefalù I was plunging my fingers in a bag of mixed powdered chalk and resin (Professor Crowley's Special Climbing Formula) to give my hands grip as I ascended the rock towards the Baths of Jupiter. After my meeting with PAVOZ in my dream, I proposed to perform an operation VIII° on the spot with the object of breaking the code of the symbols on her body. I had been fluent and confident in my reading of them in my dream, but the knowledge became hidden from me, when I awoke.

As I went higher on the limestone, I decided to try an unusually risky chimney. Pulling myself up round the overhang, I came on a section of limestone face that was invisible from above and below. An amazing sight greeted me.

A large birds' nest, three or four foot across, with dried twigs pasted together with grey birdlime lay before me in the early dawn light. Draped round the inside of the nest was a thin brittle, papery material that I could have sworn was a complete human skin, cut away neatly, with everything present except the hands, feet and head. It was grey. I examined the debris at the back of the ledge, and found a number of fragments of egg considerably larger than an ostriches'. The creature that had lived on the nest must have been enormous. The eggs were not fossils, certainly, so there had been something there in the historic past. There were also bones of a sheep or ram that the creature had plucked up to consume at leisure. Having no great interest in ornithology, stupidly, I thought little more about it but continued my climb up to the summit, handicapped only by a slight attack of asthma.

I performed the Opus VIII° as King Sol himself rose. At first I was confident that Giles and his binoculars would not be up that early, but then I became distracted, and I concluded with an invocation to PAVOZ, then sat down on the rock and I cleaned out my meerschaum pipe and had a smoke.

I was intending to sit for a moment, but when I got up again, five hours had passed! I was summoned home by a prearranged signal of Leah flashing a mirror from the Abbey verandah in the direction of the rockface; this was to tell me that the mail had arrived. I came down the easy way. It was only when I reached the ground that the thought struck me that the nest, which I had dismissed so casually could have been the true temple of PAVOZ. This would account for my lack of success further up the rock.

I cursed myself.

Later on I tried till the blood flowed down to my armpits, from all my fingers, but I was never able to find that particular ledge again. It was the most extraordinary business.

Leah and Ninette had nominally reached an accommodation about sharing my favours in The Work, but it was an arrangement that was more honoured in the breach than the observance. I would observe scenes where the same antagonism played itself out again and again. The two of them would pretend to want to collaborate on household affairs, but in fact they would immediately fall out. They were baffled as to how it happened. Neither of them could explain it rationally. It was really quite amusing.

When I got back from the Rock, Ninette had bought some pig's trotters and was showing them off proudly.

'What do you call these?' She stood them up danced them across the table. Leah stared at her coldly.

'Where on earth did you get those? Are we meant to eat them?'

'They will make a nice broth for Poupée.' said Ninette, quietly. In the background the baby screamed.

'You do whatever you like.' said Leah, dismissively. She walked Poupée around, patting her back till she stopped crying then she put her back in her cot and started to finish a large announcement over the Temple doorway. LOVE IS THE LAW. LOVE UNDER WILL. The paint dribbled down from the L's onto the brick floor, and Ninette's bare feet carried the splashes over the painted temple floor, which immediately started another row.

I calmly sat and opened my letters, and tried to give them the sense of existing in a world which was not wholly spiteful.

'Listen to this. Raoul is coming very shortly, and he can bring at least fifteen pounds.'

'Only fifteen?' said Ninette. 'It should be more.'

'Food's not expensive' said Leah. Ninette hissed at her,

'Yes it is, and also he may be bring his wife so there will be two of them.' A number of the operations with both Leah and Ninette had been for the attraction of money, which we were in great need of. Both of them were behaving as if my performing sex magic with the other, hated, partner had the reverse effect and actually driven money away.

'I think you should write to him and tell him, Beast' said Ninette.

'Tell him what? He'll have already left' I said. I was spending a very large proportion of my time trying to find sources of money. When I was not performing Operations for its arrival, I was dictating letters in the hope that some of the ripples caused would result in money coming in the direction of the Abbey.

The next letter I opened was from Frank Harris, so it did not include Thelemic greetings. Nevertheless he and I had been thinking along the same lines.

'Dear Crowley, sorry not to be able to join you in foreign parts, ha ha. Here is something that you might turn to your advantage. There has been understandably a great furore in the press over the publication of *Diary of a Drug Fiend*. No one can quite put their finger on why it should be since you have boxed clever in the story. You don't even mention your little weakness, the Dick's Hat Band stuff that you are so fond of, not to mention the drugs. But people still seem to be in awe of your wickedness and think there is something evil about you when your friends like me know you are the most genial fellow in the world. Collins however will not reprint. Now you are well acquainted with nine day wonders and the short memory of the public, so you should cash in on the public appetite for prurience and press home any advantage, now. You would be able to get at least a hundred pounds advance for an autobiography. Yours, a fellow penniless Priapus, Frank Harris. P. S. Then we can start the newspaper together.'

I looked up at Leah.

'I will make a start on my autobiography this afternoon.' Leah was thumbing through the remaining envelopes, head down. Then she said, 'Someone's opening all of these envelopes before they get here.' It was true, mine had been opened already.

'It's the caribineri. They've got their orders.' said Ninette.

'They're stealing the money that should be coming to us. I'm going straight to the American Consulate.' said Leah.

'You're foreigners. Crazy people. They spy on you, of course. I told you.' said Ninette.

She had used the 'I' word again. The 'I' that was not free to criticise; the 'I' that was trapped in a world of want.

'Ninette' I said mildly. 'You should take up the razor ' Ninette looked daggers at me. 'I have warned you' I went on. 'Only I shall use I with impunity. All others will discipline themselves away from the detested pronoun until they have found their true Wills.' Ninette stared at Leah, who turned her back on her.

'If you want to stay at the Abbey' I said, 'you must go and do as we agreed, in your room.'

Ninette went to her room, slammed the door and noisily put a chair against it, in a completely futile gesture of exclusion. I judged that her rage would have soon subsided and would have been replaced by self pity of the worst kind. It was time to give her a chance to help lift herself out of the swamp of the Self. I picked up the jug of wine, went to Ninette's door and pushed it open with my toe.

The chair fell over and the door opened to show Ninette sitting at a small table, with a mirror propped against the wall. She sat hunched, glowering at me over her shoulder. Her outside forearms had a few scratches, nothing more. The razor lay on the floor where she had thrown it down, after her first few tries, the edge of its blade thinly red. I calmly sat down to go through her Magickal Diary which was open at the table, putting a circle in red ink round every 'I' in the torrent of malicious spleen that the girl had expressed. When she picked up the razor, I paused, looked up at her raised one eyebrow quizzically, then when she did nothing, I bent my head, exposing my neck, and completed the task.

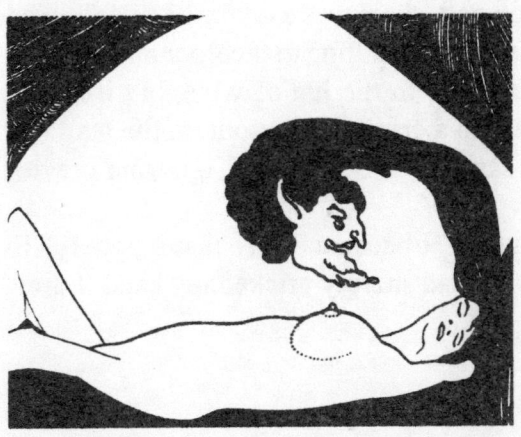

XI Lust

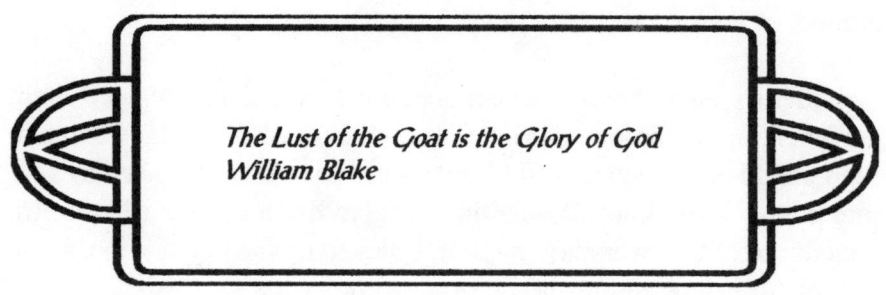

The Lust of the Goat is the Glory of God
William Blake

'You and your wife are ganging up on me' Ninette finally said. This was the sort of unmemorable tosh, trawled from penny dreadfuls, if not shilling shockers, that was shackling Ninette's soul. I continued to mark her diary, as if she had not spoken. The red circles targeted the 'I's with monotonous regularity through the corrupt text. There was a melancholy satisfaction available in my didacticism, as a Magus. Was I was above such feelings, or could I allow myself to enjoy what I was doing? I concluded I could not. I would remain aloof and serene.

I had finished the marking and was about to put the cap back on the pen. It was an Osmiroid which I had consecrated to The Work by performing a Magickal Act with Leah. Just as my demurring with myself, had concluded, there was a loud whack, followed instantly by the noise of pottery shards falling to the floor and on the table. Ninette had taken aim at me with the jug of wine, but it had sailed past its target, and burst into a crimson blossom on the wall.

'Why can't I say 'I'?' she screamed, ignoring previous strictures, yet again.

'Because I say so.' I became aware that a pottery sliver from the domestic explosion had sharply pricked my hand. I drew out the slip of pottery, and sucked my own blood thoughtfully.[90] The blood reminded me of Ninette's other, dream self, acquiescent to The Work. But now her hot little face was blotched with anger.

'Why can you say I and not me?'

'Because when I say 'I', I don't mean it in the restricted way which you do. I am the Logos of the Aeon.' Ninette's gown was hanging open. I could feel my Wand arouse. For the last seven words, only, I used my Voice of Power.

Making a rapid invocation for Raoul's safe arrival, I approached Ninette, in a clear state of readiness for worshipful Work. Wordlessly she showed she understood. I then demonstrated my trust for her new willingness to Work, by allowing her to put her lips and teeth around my Wand.

It is at this stage in the story, that I think it is suitable to introduce a lighter note.[91] It has often been remarked that my writing has been devoid of the better, indeed, any kind of humour. Witty, yes, profound, certainly to those whose minds can touch profundity, but lacking the soufflé touch.[92]

The lightness of touch in this piece of love poetry will come as a welcome surprise: my poem, Nepali Love Song, deserves a wider readership. In fact on re-reading it, I think it deserves every reader it can get.

I dedicate the following stanzas to those whose minds will be sated, in the future New Aeon, through reading endlessly about hot purple

---

90 Readers of 'The Rime of the Ancient Mariner' will recall what a tonic effect this has on the system. 'I bit my arm, I sucked the blood, I cried, 'A sail! A sail!' A.C.

91 Humorous question: 'Which Oxford college has been flooded with undergraduate applications by Sapphic students?' Answer, 'Radclyffe Hall.' I made that one up myself. A.C.

92 Why am I going on about writing 'lightly', when it was a promise made to

158 Snoo Wilson

knobs pulsing, yearning clits, and imaginations temporarily dulled and made vacant by twenty-four hour Crowleyvision. I have no doubt that all that will happen, for mark my words, Crowleyanity Will Come. But I assure you, O Disciples Yet Unborn, there will be humorous interludes, for as this poem shows, humour will be born along with the rest of the New Aeon.

> O kissable Tarshitering![93] The wild bird calls its mate ، and I?
> Come to my tent this night of May, and cuddle close and crown me king
> Drink, drink our fill of love at last—a little while and we shall die,
>   O kissable Tarshitering!
>
> Droop the long lashes; close the eyes with eyelids like a beetle's wing!
> Light the slow smile, ephemeral as ever a painted butterfly,
> Certain to close into a kiss, certain to fasten on me and sting!
>
> May? Are you coy? Then I will catch your hips and hold you wild and shy
> Until your very struggles set your velvet buttocks all a-swing
> Until their music lulls you to unfathomable ecstasy,
>   O kissable Tarshitering!

---

    publishers who betrayed me shamelessly, and I am engaged in possibly the most important introductory document in the New Aeon? I am a trusting fool. The next time I send them the MS I shall secure the pictures to the text with a properly consecrated magickal talisman. One of the ingredients I am sure you will have no trouble identifying - though the likelihood of it holding together the volume presently in your hands is small. As for the other, rest assured Frater Perdurabo will see the New Aeon right. It may be harder to obtain menstrual sanguis *at short notice, but one of the whores on the promenade will be sure to oblige on one of her days 'off work'. A.C.

93   'Tarshitering' sounds like a process for painfully covering Macadamised streets. I wrote it, prophetically, before tarred roads touched every horizon. Aiwass at the wheel! Progress, pain and continuous smashes. Advance, New Age! A.C.

Back to the story: I have been engaged in Op, IX° P.V.N., doggy fashion, with Mmlle. Shumway, spinster, for the duration of the reading of the poem. For those unversed or uninterested in Magickal practice, I will also record it in the canting tones of a popular modern fiction. But whatever my publishers say, I shall put it the footnotes, where its leering jauntiness need not affect the thrust of the main text.[94]

Through the open door, Hermes watched his mother in a matter-of-fact manner. After coming into the room to help himself to cigarettes, he wandered off. I was glad to note that Hermes seemed unimpressed that I was Raising the Ecstatic Current with his grunting mother. This was in line with my theory and practice. I believe when the sexual act has been stripped of its shame, its sacred qualities will emerge all the more easily.

I was concentrating on invoking Pan at the orgasm, and so heard nothing mundane, but Ninette claimed that at the same time she heard a gunshot, outside.

There had been a number of psychic events around the Abbey: footsteps in empty rooms: astral bells which struck spontaneously without anyone being near them. In retrospect I can put this down to the black Magickal Current which was tightening its grip about our little ship, so that every board creaked. Certainly, the mixed effluvium of the Working was copious, and dense.[95]

What is certain is that the Magickal Working went wrong. Ninette did not improve, and from that moment she was ceaselessly intriguing against me. I do not hold it against her. It was simply the direction of

---

94   'His sleek, suave John Thomas now locked juicily into Ninette's wide, powerful rump.' (After D.H.L.) A.C.
95   This is one of the central sacraments of Crowleyanity. I have insisted on this communion contribution from all my partners, whatever their sex, colour or creed. A.C.

her puny and malicious Will.[96]

What happened on the mundane plane after the fateful gunshot was that we never saw Satan alive again. The day after, Hermes found a brass cartridge case on the hill behind the house. I filled it full of snuff, for him. Sadly his cigarette addiction continued, unabated.

While Satan had fallen victim to the casual malice of the islanders, I had no doubt that the timing confirmed that the execution was another malefic Magickal Act.

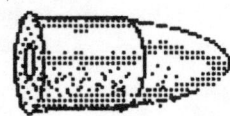

Ninette lay exhausted after our Working, in a pool of sweat, while I stood up. In order to understand her mind more clearly and help her, I deliberately put her dressing gown on, and two of her earrings, against her protests. She of course, the stupid girl thought I was taking them away from her as punishment. I sat down to read her diary, my feet cooling in the wine on the floor. I was able to reach a conclusion with great rapidity.

'You have very little real understanding of who you are' I began. 'This diary simply reveals that you are a whorish little slut. There's nothing wrong with that, provided it is done without this pretence at covering up.'

I continued in this vein, for some time, but I might just as well have 'saved my breath to cool my porridge', as the Glaswegian prostitutes used to remark, when I shipped them out to Boleskine[97] for Magickal

---

96 *Time after time, Fr. Perdurabo always came up against this barrier with the men and women who were chosen for the Great Work. How could they, who were mere clay, sustain the inner fire of someone who had been, willy-nilly, the mouthpiece of Aiwass? A.C.*

97 *Boleskine was a noble building, like the Abbey it existed on one storey without this detracting from its striking nature. In consequence of my occupancy of the house, on the shores of Loch Ness, I was able to call myself 'The Laird of*

Acts. I used to try to enlighten my partners endlessly, even in those days. Perhaps, like my father, preaching is my worst fault.

In the end, I retired to my own room, and took some Anhanolium Lewinii, and meditated on the best structure for my autobiography. If it was to also provide an introduction to the *Book of the Law*, I was in something of a cleft stick, because the Book forbids its own study. Could I blaspheme against Myself?

Upon enquiry from the *I King*,[98] I learned that self-blasphemy was permissible, if it was a continuation of the Great Work. Leah then announced herself ready for dictation. She made no comment on my wearing of Ninette's clothes. A true Thelemite will allow another to practice their Will. I went out to the hammock on the verandah, and began dictation.

It was the most devilish thing, but at the outset of dictation I was suddenly taken with what I can only describe as 'stage fright'. I suddenly realised that I could take any of fifty meanings of my life, illustrate them with carefully chosen facts, and there would be nothing to choose between them. What was The Truth about Aleister Crowley? With my magical achievements I had broken the scales on which normal truth can be weighed. Could I expect the common reader to accept that? I pleaded an attack of asthma, while I tried to collect my thoughts.

When Leah returned I had worked out to my own satisfaction at

---

    Boleskine.' *I have, it is true, a fondness for titles, but I am trying to give back the one presented to me by the Press Lords, and so let us press on with the story. A.C.*

98 *I am happy to take the credit for introducing this oriental Oracle into the lives of Clapham Junction Man. I have to confess to a crudity in my system which robbed it of weak, or moving lines, so my trigrams never could evolve. Later users, the heirs and inheritors of the Thelemic stellar mantle - [for every Man and every Woman is a Star] will appreciate the subtlety of Destiny revealed better than I. Another Weakness confessed! Clearly tonight I am feeling unusually humble. A.C.*

least, a position of compelling veracity, combined with authorial modesty. As soon as she settled on her three legged stool, near the hammock, I began-

'It would be absurd to apologise for the form of this autobiography, Excuses are always nauseating. I mention merely as a matter of general interest the difficulties attending the composition. From the start, my position has been precarious. I am practically penniless, and I have been betrayed in the most shameless and senseless way by everyone with whom I was in business relations.'

At this stage, Ninette's guardianship of Poupée collapsed in wails of tearful abandonment from the back of the house, and Leah went off to rescue the poor mite. Although the start had been interrupted, I felt confident that I had introduced myself in a way which won the reader's sympathies. Anything further from Aiwass' style in the *Book of the Law* would be hard to imagine: the detractors who claim I wrote both to flatter my prophetic side by making light of *Liber Legis*.

It would be amusing to allow another authorship for one's autobiography. Indeed it would be useful to the Publishers of this book to claim that that during my invocations with Victor Neuburg I became permanently possessed by a diabolic entity who goes by the name Choronzon: if it was proven, they could be free from any obligations to pay the author.[99] Nothing is further from the truth, of course. And as to how my various inconsistencies were treated in the book, I don't think it did *Liber Legis* any harm. The shortcomings of a multi-faceted Magus may be interesting. In the end they are unimportant.

---

99 *If Choronzon is the author of my Confessions, then he's written half a million words for me for nothing!* A.C.

(Footnote[100])

When Leah went in, I allowed the Anhanolium to draw me to heights of contemplation, but I at the same time, was hyper-audient. I could hear entities moving amongst the olive trees, and my nerves were so alert that without being aware it had was even feasting on me, I swatted a huge mosquito on my head.

Like the reports of the man condemned to be hanged in the newspaper, who always had a hearty breakfast, my mosquito had dined not wisely, but too well, and the result capped my left hand Saturn finger, its body mixed with my blood.

A few seconds later, little Hermes came by, trailing a stick and announced to me that he had found the body of Satan. For a moment, I saw the eye of Anubis, golden in the sky. A hundred and fifty drops of Anhanolium was enough to inhibit all but the most orotund. However my Training in mental discipline meant that I was perfectly capable, even in my heightened state, of soberly dictating. I calmly asked little Hermes where he was going. There had been three of him, but they all came back together again when he spoke.

'I'm going to bury him, and then I'll have his magic power, and I will be the Beast myself' he said. He pointed his little stick at me, and stared fiercely. His words seemed to make ripples, and as he went away, the stick made a tinkling noise against the hard dry ground, and the olive branches moved in time.

---

100 *This drawing contains two deliberate errors. Can you spot them? A.C.*

164 Snoo Wilson

Drifting between sleep and hallucination, I wandered the waste for seemed like an eternity before I fell into another troubled sleep. As it turned out, I did not take up dictating the story of my life again, until after Raoul had died and the acolytes of the Abbey had been scattered to the four corners of the earth.

The days before Raoul's arrival were characterised by the same theme: I would begin something - a commentary on the *Book of the Law*, say, or a design for a new Abbey, to be built on the site of the Temple of Diana, atop the Rock - only to be interrupted by something seemingly equally important, and everything would fly to the four winds and have to be started again from scratch. As the man who took the one copy of *Liber Legis* and forgot about it, only discovering it when he went up to the attic in Boleskine to look for some skis, I cannot claim consistency at the best of times. But there was something disquieting about the way nothing ever seemed to be more than begun.

In the days before Raoul arrived, I was also going through a period where I was deliberately allowing my body to be poisoned by ever-greater doses of morphine. I was interested to see what happened when my whole system had made an 'enemy' out of the drug - would I spontaneously lose all craving for it? Naturally this harsh treatment ruined all my repose at night. Soon the only sleep I was able to get was during the day, after Operation IX°s that would have tired out ten donkeys, followed by heroic draughts of brandy.

At the same time, In England, Betty will have been angrily doing the packing for both herself, and her husband Raoul, with words of warning ringing in her ears:-

'One of you will never come back.'

Raoul Loveday, my beloved, and Betty May, the much-married ex-cocaine fiend and authoress of *Tiger Woman* finally arrived at Cefalù by train, a train which Il Duce had tried and failed in this case to make run on time.

The journey had been full of little adventures. Raoul told me, with laughter in his eyes, about how they had been in Paris and had run into a noble Lord, who was still prepared to offer him employment at a thousand pounds a year in England. Raoul, in front of Betty had turned him down, saying that he preferred to voyage penniless to me. The Lord had got up and in a frosty manner, indicated that he was not going to have anything more to do with a man who was so hell-bent as to subject himself to the King of Depravity. Betty then tried to get Raoul drunk in Paris in order to forget me, which failed. They had travelled through Italy in a third class train, and by the time they arrived in Sicily they had no money at all.

In Palermo, Betty pawned her second wedding ring.[101] With the money, they managed to buy their tickets for the train from Palermo to Cefalù. Immediately Betty realised that her fate was sealed, she had an attack of blue funk and bolted from Raoul at the station, in order to seek sanctuary in the British Consulate.

'You know, when she went off like that, I was perfectly prepared to let her go, if it was her Will.' Raoul, always the perfect Thelemite, said to me later. Not being able to find the Consulate, Betty came back. Since the train had failed to leave on time, Betty discovered Raoul sitting bolt upright in a crowded carriage. She did not mention where she had been and Raoul's training and forbearance enabled him to not refer to her absence.

'I want to say something to you, Raoul.'
'Love is the Law, Love under Will.'
'Shut up and don't be stupid.'
'If I'm stupid, why did you marry me?'

---

101   Betty, you have to remember, had been married more than once and so had more than a few tricks up her sleeve, in a number of directions. A.C.

166 Snoo Wilson

'I'm beginning to wonder that myself. Listen, Raoul, I just want to say, before we arrive, that I don't want him *corrupting* you any more.'

'I've no idea what you mean.' Betty of course had no idea the extent or significance of the rites we practised. I told Raoul it was better his wife did not know.

'Ether...... and all that. I want you to tell me you're not going to do it.' said Betty.

' I will do whatever is required of me to become his Magickal Son.' replied Raoul, which, to Betty's mind, left a hole the size of a coffin in any undertakings on his part. *One of you will never come back.*

Finally, the Train for Palermo crawled out of the station, its weight in the scales of destiny akin to the poet Shelley's Car of the Hour. But in contrast to Shelley's gilded and triumphant Vehicle 'gainst Tyrants, Raoul and Betty were travelling in a carriage which, according to Betty, was full of pigs, baskets of chickens and mean-looking Sicilians, spitting everywhere, including the ceiling.

Almost  *There!*

XII The Hanged Man

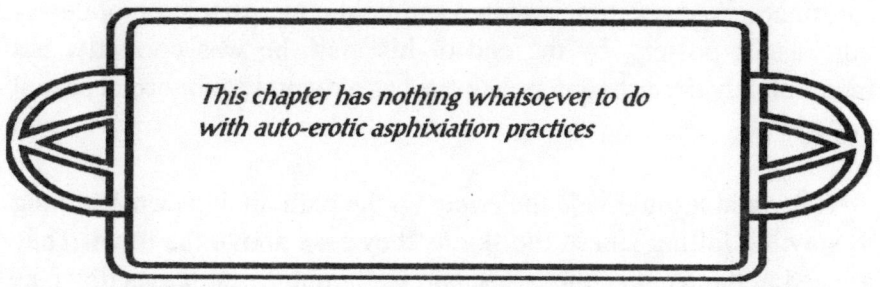

This chapter has nothing whatsoever to do with auto-erotic asphixiation practices

Betty's own account in her sensationalist book *Tiger Woman* (sic) of the arrival at the Abbey is a tissue of lies, which is hardly worth pulling apart to reassemble as a correct impression of the event. When the Big Cat asserts it was night, naturally enough it was day. She claims I greeted them in full ceremonial robes, admitted Raoul, and slammed the door furiously, 'quivering with rage' in her face after she did not respond to my Thelemic Greeting. If it was her Will not to answer, it was hardly my position to be angry with her. And the Abbey was famous, if anything, for *not* being a closed door to anyone who wanted to find their True Will.

She claimed that I was called 'The Mystic', and was known in the countryside around as the 'Purple Priest'. Her erratic account is full of attempts to be fair, but her mind has been damaged by her own drug excesses, and she fails to make much of an impression as an Authoress, beyond an admiring description of how well I taught her, and little Hermes rock climbing. Of the rites which Raoul came to participate in, and the magical grades through which he so rapidly ascended, her account is naturally silent: she had neither the wit nor the insight to speak of such things.

The truth is Betty and Raoul arrived in daylight, having been observed leaving the square by Giles, whose suspicious antics were in turn being reported on in ill-kept, irregular reports by the lounging caribineri.[102] At one time arrested and held under suspicion of defacing Fascist posters, by the end of his visit, he was correctly, but incompletely described in police files as a mentaly subnormal sexual voyeur.

Betty and Raoul made their way up the path, their ascent seeming to stay the falling sun in the sky as they rose above the town. They arrived at the front of the house and Betty put the suitcases down as Raoul looked around admiringly. The verandah was deserted. Betty wandered over to critically examine Leah's prophetic ordure-coloured slogan of redemption, its runaway dribbles now baked hard in the sun. In the shade, on a rope tied round an age-thickened olive tree, a goat chewed at its cud, malevolently, and eyed the new visitors through its rhomboid pupils.

If all of the details of the above are not completely correct, since I was not present, fear not. The Beast is now within and can authorise every last detail.

Leah was first to greet them, as I hastily changed inside, in order to greet my new Magical Son.[103] Leah, like all the female Abbey members wore her hair heavily henna'ed, and a long formal robe, for occasions. On other occasions she wore nothing at all.

Betty hadn't met Leah, but she had heard about her. For Leah had earlier passed like a shooting star through the thick fog of London society, astonishing everyone whose path crossed hers with her Thelemic poise and and unaffected bearing. Betty held out her hand to the famous Scarlet Woman.

---

102 'The Word of a Magus is always a falsehood, for it is a creative word; there would be no point in uttering it if merely stated an existing fact in nature.' (A.C.) Is this statement true, or false? Answer, using lined paper and taking not less than six hours. A.C.

103 A proper Magickal rank, awarded in due course to Raoul, sometimes confused by the infantile with Babe of the Abyss. A.C.

'Mrs Crowley?' Betty said. Leah was embarrassed. She could hear me getting ready behind the shutters, closed against the noonday sun.

'You can call me Leah, if you like' Leah said softly. 'My magical name's Alostrael.'

'I'll stick with Betty' said Tiger Woman, bravely.

Raoul kissed Leah formally on both cheeks.

'What a wonderful place you have here!' said Betty sincerely, relieved not to find me ensconced. Raoul turned away and opened his arms, towards the sea.

'We're in heaven' he said.

Having heard all this as I prepared myself, I opened the door of the Temple, and emerged. I did not slam the door in Betty's face. I intoned the formal greeting, 'Do what thou wilt shall be the whole of the Law.' then had it finished by Raoul: 'Love is the law, love under will'

That was the conclusion of any exclusively Crowleyan ceremony.

'Miss May. Delighted that you could come after all.' I lied. I've heard so much about you, some of it must be true.' I joked. I then turned and embraced Raoul warmly, who in turn made a joke about the return of the Magickal Son. We both laughed.

Raoul and Betty went to the room which had been cleaned and prepared for them. When Raoul emerged he began to find out, to his delight, the details of daily life in the Abbey, where worship and life went hand in hand.

Betty affected to be amused when she discovered that the candles, the source of illumination in the temple on the altar when night fell, were ones purchased from the Cathedral.

'Oh, so they were sold to you when they were too *short* for Christian worship,' she laughed. It was time to remind her of my prophecy. I had wound up a spell, and she had obeyed. No wonder she hadn't been able to break away from Raoul in London or Palermo: her fate and his were magickally intertwined.

'So you have come to me, to cook, as I told you would happen ' I innocently observed.

She turned sourly and looked at the altar. It had seven sides which were painted in accordance with the magic values of each. I made a mental note how long it had taken her to laugh on the other side of her face. Betty's disappointed attention moved now to the altar.

'Do tell me Mr Crowley, why are two panels yellow, two green and three purple? Is purple your all-time favourite?' There was no point in replying to such mockery which only served to expose her own ignorance. I opened the Magickal Record on the top of the altar.

'There is a book here containing the laws of the Abbey, which everyone who stays here has to sign.' Betty at first dug her toes in. But I gave her twenty four hours to comply, and retired to my room, where Raoul followed me and we talked. Oh, how we talked!

All through the night I could hear Betty banging about. I'm sure she didn't get a minute's sleep. I permitted Raoul to go back to his restless, disillusioned bride, who had signed the Record after all. Raoul went to his room at five o'clock in the morning. And even then, he didn't seem to want to go.

Betty as I had expected declined to keep a diary, so the task of opening up her inmost thoughts to the healing currents of the Abbey was restricted. She took up her tasks of cooking and buying the food willingly, and took pleasure in apparently fulfilling the prophecy I had made to her. But all the time her heart was mistrustful.

In order to allay her fears I took her rock climbing, and she gained a measure of trust for me that way. But then when we returned to the house she would attempt to capitalise on her privileged position and I would have to make it clear to her that away from the perils of the rock, she was nothing special in the life of the Abbey. She was outside its rituals through a choice of her own and if she cared to learn more, she would have to keep a diary like everyone else.

When I gave her a razor for her personal use, she threw it away. She claimed that Raoul's own self-inflicted tiny scratches on his arms led to a bleeding which weakened his constitution, and she may in hindsight have been right about that.

However it was Raoul's Will to follow the path of Adeptship, and the accidents which occurred along it cannot be laid at my door.

I made the rule that silence should be observed in the mornings. I generally did not emerge from 'Koshmah', as my private room was called, till late in the day. I have to admit that this was mainly because of the difficulties with narcotics that I referred to earlier. I would take luncheon with Leah in my room, and come out around five, and then eat simple fare together with he rest of the acolytes in the early evening: cheese, bread, and wine, perhaps a goat stew that Betty had prepared.

Having made my vow of renunciation, I was breaking bread and eating with my hands, in other words eating meals very much as Christ[104] would have done, on the shores of Galilee, at the beginning of the Aeon of the Fish.

I had Betty bring a towel and basin while I made a ceremonial ablution, at the beginning of the meal, and even more importantly, at the end. I never ceased to openly criticise her ridiculous position. Since she was vain, and had been an 'artist's model', I taunted her about every aspect of her body in order that she would not be completely stuck in her self-satisfaction. She did not realise that I did not mean what I said and one evening instead of holding out the bowl for me to wash the grease off my fingers, she poured it over my head. I thought it best to ignore the outburst. I simply pretended that nothing had happened and did not refer to it.

Much later, when Betty appeared to have forgotten about her outburst of weeks ago, in order to test her again, I announced calmly that Betty had been chosen for a human sacrifice that evening at eight o'clock.

Her hands holding the bowl started to shake.

---

104 *I do not think he would have been familiar with the stock of a very good 1888 Corvoisier brandy that I had some bottles of. A.C.*

'What have I done?' she finally gasped. Everyone sat silent, watching us.

'You know very well what you have done, Sister Sybilline' I replied, icily. Betty would not answer to her magical name but she knew who she was, well enough.

'Raoul! You wouldn't let him?' Betty now appealed to her husband. Raoul obediently put his eyes down upon his plate. Betty realised that no one would help her.

'You are an evil spirit. You cannot be allowed to remain in the abbey to break every one of its rules in violation of the oath you took when you signed the book.'

Betty thought now she was in trouble, and in response to my threat, she bolted again. It was twelve hours before she returned, in a thunderstorm.

I told Raoul to treat her return, like when she bolted from the train, as the most natural thing in the world. Sure enough she came back later that night and he followed my instructions.

The following morning I woke very early. I was having a pipe of opium when I heard someone moving about in the courtyard at the back of the house. I was thinking that it must be another psychic visitation, then they swore, softly. It was Betty.

I left my room without making a sound and went round the house, so that I could look at her. She was standing in the dawn light where the clothes were washed at the back of the house, washing herself without a stitch on. I admired without liking her strong active body. There was something pure about it, without a trace of sensuality, so I was able to look at her without the torrent of lust that would accompany a normal man who is witness to a woman vigorously soaping and rinsing her breasts, torso and thighs.

Betty finally finished her ablutions, but would never have known I was there if she hadn't smelt my opium pipe, which was still alight in my mouth. She turned round and our eyes met. I gave her the Look of Power, but it failed. It was as if I had only been allowed one magick spell with Betty, the one tying her fate to Raoul's. The rest of the time she was immune to being suborned, although she could still on occasions show a healthy fear. But there was no fear in her face or body that morning, though.

'How long have you been there?' She asked. I did not reply. 'When I was an artist's model, it was half a guinea an hour to look. So what do you think you owe me?'

'For half a guinea, I'd need to do more that look' I said, lightly.

'Go on and look' said Betty. 'You've been trying to break me down at every mealtime, making cutting remarks about my body. But it's not what *real* artists say. They can see beauty.'

She thought she had found a weak spot at last. Of course, my indifference to her body was quite irrelevant, but the opium was giving me a headache instead of calming me. I felt like hitting her. Instead, I offered her the pipe. She refused it extravagantly.

'I don't, thank you. All that is behind me.' The precious bitch. I nodded an approval she knew I did not feel. What is the point of retreating from drugs if the alternative is even more mindless, and further from one's True Will?

'I see you have discovered that the dragon is not for the weak' I said.

'Oh I know. In the end, it just destroys your peace of mind completely' Betty said. The last thing I wanted was a lecture on opium from a woman who two years before, would have gone with anyone for a fix of cocaine. One of her tits hung slightly lower than the other, I noticed, and the nipples pointed away from each other, creating a faintly disorientating squint. I shouldn't have been feeling that nauseous under opium. I had successfully poisoned myself with the last month's increasing doses, as had been my intention.

'It is true that there is a price to pay for the insights it offers' I said.

'It destroys you in the end' Betty said. I nodded, as sagely as I could, in the circumstances.

'You're absolutely right. It's done for me' I said. Betty gave me a strange look. It was as if she could never accept that the task of a magus is transpersonal. If he has surpassed himself and discovered his true Will, it does not matter what happens to his body.

'I know about opium' Betty said sharply. 'Two of my best friends died from it. And they weren't even dirty old men.'

Ah yes. This was because Raoul had told her that the full cast-list of my magickal personae included Alys, the feminine form of Aleister, and she had finally tumbled to the fact that it was as Alys that I intended to draw Raoul into the ultimate bliss as we soared through the aether, as one.

'I'm not a dirty old man' I said. 'I asked Raoul here because he wanted to study magick.'

'So that's what you call it' said Betty. She gathered her clothes together where they had been hanging on the hand pump, and went back towards the house. It was the same accusation as had been levelled at the Knights Templar. Even though they had meant so well, things had ended badly for them as well. Outside the sun rose, banishing the creatures of the night.

I examined all my personalities in vain for the dirty old man that Betty pretended to have found. If I was who she said I was, why did she wait on me at table, who was not even invited to my bed, as were Scarlet Women #1 and #2? It was pure jealousy on her part, retribution for the fact that I had not made a pass at her as she soaped her cunt.

I listed my attributes. I was forty seven, in my prime. My serpent teeth were still in place. I was able to astral travel, to make love on occasion, all day and night, to write poetry of all kinds and taut prose with equal facility. I was intrepid in my transgressions against society's foolishnesses. I was in a word, fearless. For that I had been chosen as vessel of Aiwass, to bring in the New Aeon, with its attendant (and otherwise inexplicable) showers of blood.

In the end, I ran out of superlatives for myself. In Koshmah, red snakes writhed dully in my peripheral vision as I lay sleepless in my bed. The penalties of the drug habit, the glittering stairway to other worlds was getting to even Frater Perdurabo.

There are times when I look back on experiences like the one I have just narrated, with the fond regret of an explorer who is examining his toes, blackened with frostbite, which he has cut off as a sacrifice to the stern demon of the Five Peaks. Sacrifice is a scenario distressing only to the fainthearted. For the explorer, scaling and defeating the previously undefeated and unvisited far outweigh the drawbacks. Furthermore, and closer to home perhaps, for you, O follower of the Pale Galilean, the Only Begotten Son of God recommends that if your right eye offend you, you should pluck it out.[105]

The eye, according to the latest medical wisdom is a part of the brain. In all cases the message is the same. It does not matter that any of our faculties perish, as long as we discover our True Wills.

---

105 *The well-known Moslem tradition of cutting off of the hand- dexterotomy -for theft shows, the two rival religions are far closer than their respective practitioners discern. Both advocate mutilation, on the road to improvement. In the long run, it is not important, because Crowleyanity reduces the fruit of both the Tree as well as Islam to a pulpy fermentation, which when imbibed will intoxicate the world refreshingly in the New Age. A.C.*

XIII Death

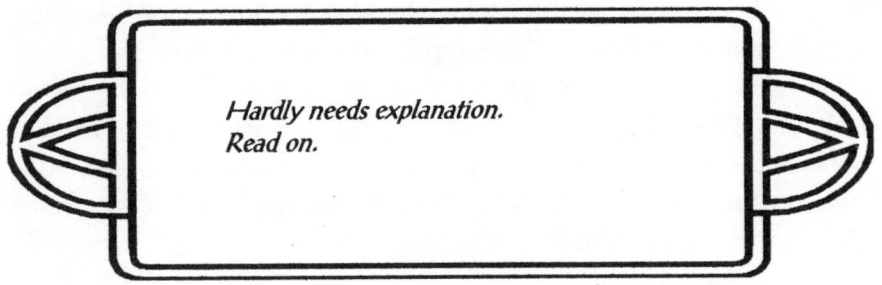

*Hardly needs explanation.
Read on.*

Hastings, England. The war is over. The anti-aircraft batteries have melted away, leaving only concrete patches which the fireweed and the sea kale now invade. A seedy garrison town of an Empire-that-never-was, for Churchill has been sent packing, and the British Empire is dis-assembling itself, like a fakir mutilating himself at an oriental bazaar, with arms and legs flying this way and that. Soon there will be nothing left. Food rationing continues. From time to time, the cliffs to the east of the town crumble another few feet into the sea and the earth opens under some unlucky cow, which stumbles, and tumbles down to the brine where it bellows, its legs broken and uselessly flailing for hours, till the butcher comes with his poleaxe.

The young men in their suits issued for demobilisation, lean, clean-shaven and thick-thewed, get out of the railway carriages. They step up the little path to home, to discover the blushing bride they left behind has in his absence filled her mouth of Isis to overflowing, and it has sported twins. One black, and one caucasian, in one case. One night of passion, two American GI's of different hue, *et voila*.

Do what thou Wilt shall be the whole of the Law.
According to the local papers, this kind of thing has happened in Hastings more than anywhere else in the country. I expect to be tarred

and feathered and run out of town on a rail any moment,

How did I do it? It is not I, it is the New Age. The divorce courts are thronged, as people exercise their Wills. And how you could possibly expect to maintain the facade of Victorian morality after illusion-prone Neptune's entry into Libra, the House of marriage?

I am all for astrology, if practised by someone who knows what they are doing. That is not to say that the news from the stars is all good. In this modern age, about to tip over into the second half of the century, I do not like the way that Neptune, planet of deception, is sidling up to my sun in Libra. Nearer and nearer the Lord of the Ocean sidles, to cement a 'completeness with nature'. I am old, father William! It is almost certain that I will die before the Great Anesthetist leaves the sign. Although he does not slither the middle prong of his trident through my pulsating, throbbing *Sol Genethliacus*[106] for another four years, he has staked his claim on my vitality already. My lungs are weak, and any sixpenny end-of-the-pier astrologer will tell you, there is something in the outer planet's *influenza* that prefigures actual arrival. Hastings is a town of ends rather than beginnings: I could fade away tonight.

But I won't, for I am still carrying the story of my innocence, like a babe above a violent rushing torrent. I see it as the poet sees it, foaming, like Roman Tiber, with much blood. So much to tell, so little time.

Help me, doctor. Bronchitis and asthma are alleviated by the same tinctures that comfort the elderly up and down the country: I simply need a biblical forty times the usual dose. You must have met others who have become habituated. Of course you have, doctor!

As often as not, I have noticed frequently it is the physician himself, who has discovered (clandestinely, reader) the merits of opiates to dull the ache of administering to the sick faceless drone-workers of the Old Aeon, who stumble in darkness, breaking their shins and kicking

---

106 *Neptune's exact conjunction to my natal Sun will be in 1951 e.v.. A.C.*

against the pricks.

The cure, as always, is the reading and study of the *Book of the Law*. It's a pity I have not interpreted it all yet to my satisfaction. But you need a little core of mystery for a religion, and it's probably just as well that the enlightenment for the New Age doesn't happen all at once.

The next two thousand years! I can't decide if it is best to have a twenty year training in Magick before *Liber Legis* is studied, or whether it is best to come on it fresh, as soon as one can read. I can only offer the same sort of direction that were given to Marco Polo when he set off across the Gobi Desert.

'Where the road forks, there will be a way that leads to annihilation, and a way that leads to settlement and safety, and it will be hard to choose between them, for both Ways are lined with the bones of travellers who have fallen by the wayside, and perished with their animals.'[107]

Away from the abodes of excrement, and night, to Sicily. Oh, my lemon-yellow Sicilian dawn, with bare feet treading the smell of thyme and rosemary from the crevices in the rock, as the Abbey ascends in their purple robes with heavy monk hoods, to make salutations to Ra!

Come, Betty, come, my Scarlet Women. Come, Raoul: come any number of dazed and impressionable visitors, astounded that a man can climb rocks and take several grains of heroin a day. But then, I am above suffering. In this respect, I feel very much like Herr Nietszche's superior being, Superman.[108]

What a scene do I behold, if I look back, in my Masonic regalia! We are all unroped. If we fall, it will be our Will. But Frater Perdurabo,

---

107 *The above paragraph used up the last of my experimental plumes de ma merde.* A.C.

108 *In fact I was often too ill when Raoul arrived to do this. But the reader has the benefit here of a composite picture which gives a good idea of the ideals of the Abbey.* A.C.

mindful of little Hermes' inexperience, has chosen an easy climb and he is on hand, moving up and down the climb chimney, passing out his patent handhold mixture to any neophytes who threaten to slip off the rock, into the abyss.

When we reach the top, we recite our hymn, with varying degrees of confidence, from myself (360°) to Hermes (0°) who is sitting at the back ruining his health as usual with coffin nails, or 'gaspers'. But it is wrong to force an apprehension of godhead on the infant sensibility. Like his sexual awakening, it will come in good time, by adult example. First I say-

'Hail unto thee who art Ra in thy Rising, even unto thee who art Ra in thy strength, who travelest over the Heavens in the bark, at the Uprising of the Sun. Hail unto thee, from the Abodes of Night!

Then there is the collective response and affirmation.

'Hail to thee from the Abodes of Night!'

Finally, Ra rises, and the little steam train which is pulling out of Cefalù railway station gives a fascist toot on its whistle, and the grey steam puffs up to disappear like ectoplasm, in the warm morning air. Everything's on time, this morning.

Ninette's recently renewed rivalry with Leah means that both Sisters have elected to climb the rock to catch the sun, but now Leah, like Solomon's true mother, is hastening down the rock again, to the Abbey, to tend to her increasingly colicky and distempered baby. I have suggested goats milk, which nourished Jupiter, but Poupée will have none of it. She can't, it seems, keep anything down. My tortoiseshell predictors, and my studies of her natal chart do not yield much hope.

At the end of the ceremony, I feel deflated, and I start to follow Leah down. Ninette comes up to me and says I shouldn't worry about Poupée, because she has good news. I say I am not in a mood for hearing good news, and I move away.

In fact I was completely preoccupied with solving the dilemmas of the day. The overall health of the Abbey was deteriorating. I was realising by degrees that the key to the situation, was to initiate Raoul into being my Magickal Son as soon as possible, in an act which also was structured to invoke a powerful healing current for Poupée. It seemed to me that Raoul was ready to accept his initiation at the time I dictated. I set myself the task of observing closely any hints or signs which could be interpreted as possible encouragement for the complex and difficult double magickal Act.

At night Raoul and I would recite together:

'Thrill with the lissom lust of light
Oh man, my man!
Come careering out of the night
Io Pan! Io Pan!
Come over the sea
From Sicily &.....

I cannot go on slapping down the *Hymn to Pan* here. For a start, it is my best work, not to be confused with limericks and brown Nepali bum-boy songs. And then, when I got to write 'Sicily', I found myself weeping, weeping, like the stupid old man I am.

I wanted to save the world, and I am dreadfully afraid that I have failed, and the judgement on maguses is not like the judgement on others. But at least I am a poet. That much is a Fact.

'From Sicily and Arcadie
Roaring with Bacchus, with fawns and pards
And nymphs and satyrs for thy guards.........'

There were cypresses around the Abbey, which are believed to be dwellings of the souls of the dead. Strange if it is true, to think that one moment, Raoul would have been in the room, the next he would be making his way into a tree.

When we recited together, Betty would bang on the door, with excuses so offensive it was impossible not to smile-

'Would you mind keeping your voices down, you two? Your dirty ditties are giving me a headache.' Love is the law, love under Will.

There is not better example of *amour fou* than Raoul's position with his wife. All of his ambition for Magick left Betty cold. He was the quickest study of any pupil I have ever had, but Betty could only ever consider me as a predator upon her husband's mind and body.

I was tiring of the accusations from one who was under my roof. So one day I showed her a collection of old ties and I told her they had belonged to Jack the Ripper. Her eyes almost went out on stalks. As she stared, I told her softly, in my most hypnotic voice, that her husband's mind was his own, and as for what I wanted him to accomplish by being my Magickal Son, it was firstly for the public good, and second, entirely on his own recognition.

'We are both Thelemites. "Alys" cannot force the issue, she can only beg and use her womanly weakness as weapons. But whatever you do, it will be highly dangerous to interrupt.' I am not sure she had understood that I was telling her I would be adopting a female persona for Raoul's investiture. But at least she now knew at some level, not to interrupt the ceremony.

A few days later, I had escaped from the oppressive heat in Koshmah and was dictating letters to Leah, whilst lying in the hammock. Leah had taken Poupée on a number of trips to the hospital in Palermo, without any relief to her symptoms, and was questioning the worth of sending yet another proposal to Frank Harris that we should start a newspaper. I recently had had the first rate notion that it could be funded by a lottery, and was outlining this to Leah when she stopped writing down my words.

'A lottery with weekly prizes of five thousand pounds would be bound to attract enormous attention - '

'I think that's a really dumb idea' said Leah, my seer. 'It's bound to fail.' I was so shocked at her desertion of Thelemic duty I practically fell out of the hammock there and then.

'Do you not want Thelema to succeed?' I asked.

'I just want the baby to be well again' said Leah, flatly, and put down her little stub of pencil and her yellow pad of paper, and went into the house where Poupée was crying. I had not told Leah, but when I consulted the *I King*, it gave a judgement on Poupée's predicament as 'Exhaustion', meaning it might not be her Will to live.

I had recently reduced my intake of heroin somewhat, which had reached such impossible proportions, by Will. I was consequently very much more alert to psychic phenomenon that afternoon. It occurred to me as I sat in the hammock in the dappled shade, that the growing illnesses of Poupée, the grating superiority of Ninette, and our own financial difficulties had a common cause: goetia. We were being somehow cursed.

The realisation struck me like a thunderbolt. But I also realised I had no clues to support my dazzling insight. Just at that moment, it came to me that we were supporting one too many cats. I looked out over the canvas lip of the hammock and a mangy tawny cat was staring me in the eye, unblinkingly, from fifteen feet away. It was clear it was under the control of the same malicious force that was affecting Poupée.

A Magus' life is one of continually cutting through the Gordian knot of paradoxes that compose existence. I decided I would rid the Abbey of its misfortune and invest Raoul in the same Ceremony, which would include sacrificing the cat.

The animal's back stiffened, and its eyes blazed with terror, as soon as I had the thought. Its demeanour proved everything that I had feared, and confirmed the course of action that I would have to take.

I thought I would pause here, and send it off to the aforesaid publishers, in order to shame them into honouring their previous commitment. By dint of unprecedented production of Doctor Crowley's

Pills, gaining a modest popularity in the whole of the boarding house now, I was able to stump up enough to send the unfinished manuscript off first class mail, with the new pictures adhering in place. The script came back, like a boomerang, with a rejection slip, and two densely spaced, smudgy carbon copy pages of personal abuse.

READER'S REPORT

20th June 1947

The author has set out, nominally, to prove his innocence of certain charges laid against him in the Popular Press. There is not doubt he has been victimised. His frankness, where it does not repel, is admirable, and very much in advance of its time. On the way he confesses, or boasts a number of homosexual acts. He should know that this document could be used by the police as a basis for criminal proceeding against him. Some of these have been illustrated by him, which would make a conviction a certainty.

I understand that an early fragment of this still incomplete MS. was shown to another reader, and some advice tendered to the author about the laws of the land. But in my thirty years as Editor for this company I have not come across a manuscript which was still so openly actionable.

Of the living, Lord Beaverbrook is the most prominent person repeatedly slandered. While the charges may well have substance, their tone is reckless, their context is depraved, so the chances of winning any action brought against us by a powerful newspaper group, nil.

The author is not a Christian, but a self-confessed magician . In order to clear himself of the charge of being a practitioner of the Black Arts against the life of a certain student of his, he has boasted about practicing the same Arts, using a cat.

In addition to charges of Blasphemy which might be served on the company, (which would reflect poorly on our sale of Bibles), there is also the strong possibility that the prominent member of the Royal Society for the Protection of Animals on the board would be obliged to resign as a consequence of our issuing this material.

The author has further claimed in an (abusive) letter to the Chairman that there had been an undertaking by us to commission but my enquiries show the allegation has no substance.

A.N. Upex.

P.S.I am taking the unusual step of including a copy of my report to the author, to explain why we are unable to offer publication. One of the English-language Paris presses might be induced to bring out a private edition, if the author has the means to pay for printing.

Copy to Le Compte de Kerval, Esq
            c/o 'Netherwood'
            High Ridge
            Hastings
            Sussex

I have been done for by the three British B's: Buggery, Bestiality and Black Magic. As before, many of the pictures were removed, entirely without explanation. As soon as yonis or lingams are depicted it seems that the British lose all sense of property, and feel free to deface or confiscate anything that takes their fancy.

Instead of flying into a frenzy at my rejection, and behaving like Lawrence had done in my sight in the post office at Cefalù, I decided on making an example of A.N.Upex. He had foolishly made the mistake of including his judgement. I saw it had been penned on the exact day of a lunar eclipse in Taurus. It was not necessary for me to travel to London to execute my Will. It would be, I calculated, perfectly possible to blast him magickally simply by speaking to him on the phone.

Claiming that I needed to offer condolences to a widow after a close relative had died, I was grudgingly allowed to move the telephone in the main hall to the dining room and almost close the door. The landlord's curiosity aroused, he now hung around in the hall, constantly poking his little goatee beard into the room, asking if I 'wanted anything'. Finally he got bored with the seeming lack of action and went away. I immediately placed the trunk call through to the publishers.

'I'd like to speak to Mr Upex, please.'

'There's no such person here.'

'Yes there is. Mr A.N. Upex.'

'Could you say what it is in connection with?'

There was no point in beating about the bush at this stage.

'I'm going to blast him.'

'You've got some plasters for him? Alright. Hang on.'

A long pause, and some whispering at the other end. Had Upex got wind of my intentions and gone into hiding already? Another ill-bred voice came to my ear.

'Can I help you, sir?'

'Only if you can find Mr Upex and bring him to the phone, I have some important news to impart to him.' Goatee was already snuffling about in the hall again. Perhaps, through my physic, he had had a successful XI° at last. I concentrated my Will and shortly he went away again. The ill-bred voice returned.

'Are you acquainted with Mr Upex?'

'I'm acquainted with his views, very thoroughly.'

'The only Upex I can find is a Miss Upex, who's one of our readers. Her initials are A.N.'

The magickal current was about to curl around some dried up spinster now, some grey mingey yoni that due to foolish customs and a shortage of tongues, had never been licked. Very well.

'Of course. Miss Upex, please.' Long pause.

'I'm sorry, sir, but Miss Upex wasn't feeling well before the weekend, and went home. We've just heard she passed away unexpectedly, last night.'

'I'm sorry to hear that' I lied.

'Yes, she was a very nice old lady, and very popular in the office, looking forward to her retirement too. It seems so unfair.'

'It was entirely deserved' I snapped, and replaced the bakelite receiver so hard that it broke, and Goatee came running in from the hall, and started bleating.

The 20th, when she had written her report, had been a Friday. She had clearly felt the Magickal Current emanating from the book, resisted it, and over the weekend, it had destroyed her at home, because of her blasphemy against Crowleyanity, all of this in advance of my knowledge and conscious intentions, at the time. As soon as I had put the phone down, I started glowing with pride at the achievement. There were occasions where the workings of my unconscious Will was a pleasure to watch. It is sometimes very handy being an Ipsissimus.

Frown not, reader. I have *taken* life from Miss Upex in the same spirit that Elisha cursed the little children who mocked him. I have however done more than Elisha. I have *given* life back to her, which she would not otherwise have. Miss Upex will live forever, albeit only as a metaphoric figtree blasted by the Master's contempt. She will become an important Example as unforgettable as Lot's wife, who was you remember turned to a pillar of salt when she had second thoughts about Sodom. Let me explain three important **Facts** of Life in the Future.

FACT† There will come a time when the six hundred and sixty sixth millionth copy of this Testament is chaired through the cheering crowds to be entombed, as a substitute for my body, in Westminster Abbey. (I wish to be buried, as I indicated, in a Nameless Grave, and my Wishes shall naturally, in my Aeon, be observed.)

FACT† The book procession will wind past the giant 'flick' houses showing fifty filmed versions of my life and entwinements, on multiple screens. In Crowleytime, nothing will be hidden from anyone during the whole Aeon. Everyone in the rejoicing throng will have been conceived in public, ten Lunar months before their birth, on twenty-four hour Crowleyvision.

FACT† Every seaside resort will have Aleister Crowley lookalike competitions, to mark the day, and the Testament will be third, second and first prizes in ascending order of gold-leaf lavishness. In schools, this Book will be required reading[109] and pudgy, inkstained fingers will be pushing pens over paper, attempting essays on 'Crowley - His Struggle', 'The Importance of Being Crowley', or for the advanced classes, 'Numerological and Symbolic Importance of 666'.

So you see, Miss Upex will be in there, too, in the gallery of immortals, somewhere in Chapter XIII, Death in the Crowleyan Tarot.

---

109 *Something that will, thankfully, never happen to Lawrence. A.C.*

(Chapter XIII in case you have forgotten already, is what you have just read.)

That's enough for tonight. Outside of my window I know the flickering fingers of light from Beachy Head lighthouse to the west will be growing dim: Ra with his immortal cohorts of the orient steals o'er Dungeness; shortly they will be amongst us,

Ra softly inviting with his Light,
'Step forth unashamed, Oh creatures of the night....'

What am I saying, oh people, people of the future, *my* people?

I am saying it is time for a stab in the groin with the old bent needle. When the resurrection then runs through the flesh hanging off my tired old bones, I shall then be in a fit state to stand naked at the window, (no doubt shocking to death more old ladies rash enough be watching,) and make my 'solitary salutation' to the dawn.

You wanted to know what 'a whim-wham to wind up the sun' was? Reader, now you know.

Euphuistically yours,

A.C.

XIV Art, or Temperance

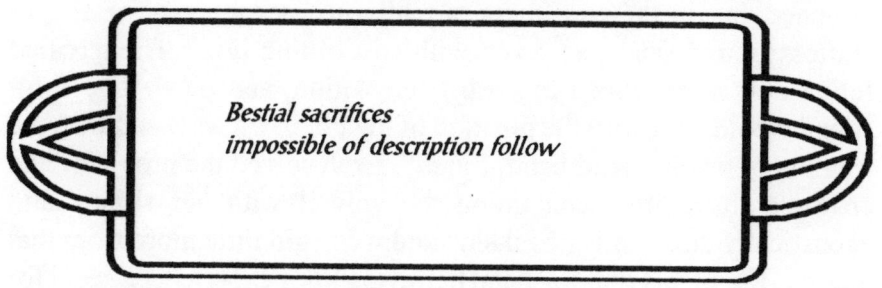

Bestial sacrifices impossible of description follow

I do not imagine that Abraham was ever asked why he chose a ram, rather than his son for a burnt-offering, but I am sure there were ignorant voices raised against the zoömorphic trend of sacrifice, even at the dawn of that Aeon. Abraham, like me, would have had to deal with them, had he been prone to memoirs.

It is true that once I sacrificed a cat. As it turned out it was in vain. But counted against the millions of animals tortured to death in the name of science, the millions of humanity sacrificed in the name of patriotism, one cat in the name of magick seems to sit lightly in the scales. I failed, in this case, but Magick will in the long run, triumph. Today, the mathematician Heisenberg has shown that the lattice of matter cannot be entirely predictable, for the observer himself alters the phenomenon. Time I predict will be the next bogey to disappear.

In the future, my blasting of Miss Upex will be well understood, as just as the fact that 'white strikes spot, and then the red' means a cannon to the cue-holder, in billiards. In summary -

At the dawn of the New Aeon, Science finally and grudgingly is beginning to recognise the Thelemic Will. Watch this space.

Having identified the cat as a malefic channel, I set about capturing it in a large aluminium saucepan. Proof that I was correct in my deductions was provided by the animal's inventive attempts to escape. When I finally caught it, it scratched my arm with pugnacious violence, but in the end, there is really no escape even for shape-shifters from a saucepan, even with an illfitting lid.[110] The terrified feline now commenced to push from within, and mew. The fitful sound would alter with the position of the lid, like a wow-mute on the trumpet of a Dixie-land band. Finally, Leah solved the problem. She crowned the edifice containing the animal with her skinny and acoustically uninventive backside and we heard little more from that quarter. Raoul, his shaking hand betraying his inexperience, asked for help expanding his invocation, but I pointed out that he had covered the main points a number of times and if he added any more, it threatened to become otiose, even to higher intelligences, such as Aiwass.

I mention this only because donkeys like Yeats have claimed that I have not the gift of creating rhetoric to match a ceremony. I am not only a creator, but a keen critic of such matters.

Incense was lit in the temple, and I poured a portion of ether into the saucepan to make the animal easier for Raoul to handle.

I spoke the sacred words of Enochian in a chant of my own devising, re-dedicating Raoul to his magickal name, Adonis.[111] I then stood by my Scarlet Woman for a full two minutes and inhaled her inner being, and dedicated myself as Alys. I was, and I repeat this to make myself clear to the general reader, now getting myself ready for the culminating event, which offering myself as high priest(ess). In

---

110 *If the saucepan ever made it back to England it would have been itself sacrificed on the pyre of Beaverbrook's own vanity as he demanded that Britain's housewives give up their casseroles to further the war effort: a piece of entirely superfluous jingoism that made the war years even harder to bear than they were already. A.C.*

111 *Adonis, a beautiful youth, was killed by a boar while hunting. Raoul took his Magickal name clearly foreseeing that his end was going to be brought about by an animal of some sort. A.C.*

which ecstatic personae, if all went well, I would penetrated by my beloved.

It is when the reader sees a sentence such as the above that visions arise. Cherry lips, forests of lingams with a dense undergrowth of asterisks, trim haunches, bold yonis weeping for jissum and other disconnective tissues, all clump together in a Satanic knot of lust. It was not, I may say, what was going on in my mind. 'Alys' herself might have been looking forward to it, but that was another matter. Aleister was too busy to get remotely aroused.

In the case of 'dedicated' ceremonies, such as the one I was creating, every detail has to be correct, or the invocation simply will not work. Far from looking forward, lubriciously, to my role, my mind was cluttered with detail, as bare of sensuality as a staff officer's making sure that a softening up bombardment went smoothly, before sending the troops over the top.

The fact that the whole business was taking place in the sight of an Unbeliever, Betty, was not so important. Aleister knew that Betty simply closed her eyes to what she did not wish to see, or believe.

I motioned Raoul to begin.

Unfortunately, Raoul had written a very long invocation, and holding the cat at arms' length the while became tiring. Meanwhile the cursed creature started to revive from its ether bath and squirm. I held a pad to its nose, but it appeared to have developed a tolerance for the etheric planes of consciousness that was remarkable. The Entity was clearly acting through the animal.

Finally Raoul, who had conscientiously not missed a syllable of his text, raised the oriental Kukri knife I had sharpened specially, and made a hack at the cat's neck. He failed to sever the body and simply made a gash in its neck.

Ninette was waiting with a bowl to catch the drops. Instead of its essence - the blood - being caught, the cat sprang spitting from Raoul's hands and spreading blood all over the place, made a dash for freedom.

What was serious in Magickal terms was that much of the blood fell outside the consecrated area of the pentagram, and therefore was still in the control of the malefic forces.

After the cat had been caught and sedated in the Beaverbrook Casserole as before, we went through the whole business again, at a much more subdued and cautious tempo. This time Raoul was able to execute the miscreant, whose body was laid on the altar.

In the end, when I gave him the silver cup, there was little blood in it for Raoul to consume. He drained it, manfully, but was so shaken by the power of the ceremony that he fainted afterwards. I saw that he was not going to be in any position to raise the Magickal current, accordingly I made an immediate ceremony to disperse the energies of 'Alys', and after a rite of purification, closed the temple.

That description, reader, deliberately does not give you enough of the technical details to build your own atomic bomb of Magick. However I think that in general terms I think you can see where things went wrong. This last part of this account will be an attempt to truthfully describe the disastrous outcome of the Working, in terms of magickal cause and effect.

I have no hesitation in averring that our worst troubles in the Abbey began from the moment Raoul's grip on the cat failed. There was a crisis in the midst of our formal application of Magickal force, and like a wrestler, caught off balance, we were subsequently dispersed, thrown with terrible force away from our little Eden, the forcing-house of the New Aeon. Perhaps it should be so. Fortunately the establishment of the New Aeon does not depend on the fate of individuals.[112]

The next day, Leah decided that Poupée should go into Palermo, for a prolonged stay at the hospital.

That night I dreamed I saw again the memorable green gem that PAVOZ had earlier brought me. The gemstone had now sprouted a metal handle. But this new steely excrescence was plunged deep into the heart of Raoul. He lay as if slain, with the gemstone protruding stiffly from his bloodied breast. I took his pulse but there was not a flutter in his wrist.

All about Raoul's limp body, scattered on the floor were the clay tablets that Leah had once been so assiduous with, recording every mark on the immortal body of PAVOZ. Even in the dream, now they were all defaced and rendered unreadable, with sharp claw marks as if the very Erinyes[113] had visited us. My Holy Guardian was nowhere to be seen.

I looked around, and to my horror the Pentagram on the floor was being obscured by a rising tide of blood. Leah was gibbering faintly in a corner. I had the feeling that there was a powerful force in the room. There was a noise of tearing, breaking wind which would have put any of 'Netherwood's' nocturnal competitors to shame.

I turned around. I recognised the clarion call of Nimerup, an entity who was manifesting to me as a misshapen green, slimy thing with claws. It was Nimerup who had been scrabbling desecration over the tablets, puking a twin dribble of bile the while. Nimerup finished obliterating the last tablet and then sneeringly looked up at me, ready for battle, breaking wind again in a snarling, arrogant tenor, rising to falsetto.

There was not time to lose. I took up my wand and immediately went into the Golden Dawn blasting position, drawing down power from above with my free hand, and pointing with my brass ferrule at the demon.

---

112 *The deterministic argument has been used, scurrilously, by the inferior maguses of Marxism to suggest that individual failures do not mean that their theories are cracked. I can accept no responsibility for the failures of Bolshevism. No one can accuse me of not trying to convert Russia, by letter, throughout the twenties, at the highest levels. A.C.*

113 *The Magickal name of the euphemistically called 'Kindly Ones', or Furies. A.C.*

There was a most satisfying crackle from the end of the wand and Nimerup disappeared, to the sound of wind, but growing fainter and lower, as if his demonic taking-off was accompanied by a Döppler effect.

I had succeeded in banishing Nimerup. On awaking, although it had been technically a magickal victory I felt extremely uneasy.

It was decided that Leah should stay in Palermo to be near Poupée for the next few days. Ninette was weeping, hypocritically, as she kissed Leah and Poupée farewell the following afternoon. Needless to say, I knew what her little secret was, because I had read her Magickal Diary. What was it? Later, reader, later. With Leah gone, Ninette recovered her equilibrium with rapidity, and came with the reminder of the Abbey who elected to go and bathe in the sea. Betty was the only one to sport a bathing costume, but the rest (Doubtless to Giles' readers' prurient delight) went naked.

SEX SLAVES OF BEAST IN NUDE ROMP

No doubt the blue Mediterranean sky may have appalled at the novel sight of humanity without the intervening veil of clothing: I know not. What is more, I do not care.

I was at the Hastings Public Library this morning, on my way back from my delightful Doctor, who has bent to my every whim for the last six months on my dosage, when I saw an item in the Picture Post.

W.B.Yeats' grave is to be exhumed and the old Fenian and delinquent thief of the rituals of the Golden Dawn is to be reburied in Sligo! A naval destroyer has been detailed to bring the bones of the old fraudster, cheat and con-artist home. Being dead these seven years, he has already arranged his future epitaph: now mark this for originality.

Cast a cold eye
On Life, on Death
Horseman, pass by.

This is all very illuminating. Whence came this arresting imagery? I, alone of this tribe, the human race, can tell you. (The rest are full of passionate uncertainty.)

In my illustrations for the Crowleyan Tarot, carried out for me under close instruction, the Knight of Cups ascends over the water on a white steed. He reaches beyond, to the Crab. Beneath the horses' hooves PAVOS is represented by the peacock, whose tail is the breaking wave. If you look at the Knight, you will see he is the inspiration for Yeats' horseman. You will not read this elsewhere, why?

W B Yeats continues his lucrative literary fraud, posthumously.

Let me be charitable. In life he was probably already too far gone to know who he was stealing from. His geriatric state when, in pursuit of revitalisation, Yeats went to continental quacks to be solemnly injected with a purée of monkey glands, is merely hilarious. The triumph of science!

It is a pity there were no reporters from Beaverbrook empire in the bushes around the clinic to document the spurious suffering of the donors of the glands to the Nobel Prize winner. We could have all been enormously entertained with tear-jerking pictures of the bewildered caged monkeys, about to be 'scientifically' sacrificed for an old man's vanity.

Give me a wild Sicilian *catto* and an aluminium casserole dish, any day.

Ninette was shaving her legs, on the Cefalù beach, using a bar of soap and a cutthroat razor. This was less revolutionary than it sounds, for there was not running water of any temperature at the Abbey. It seemed that every time that she missed a stroke and cut herself, she would turn to me and smile. I steadfastly ignored her blandishments. As an Adept, I could admit her secret.[114] As a man, it would have to wait to be entered into the Book of the Abbey.

The blood was rolling down Ninette's calves into the sand, as the razor plied its trade. I had given up on the crusade on the first person, when I felt the magical current threaten the Abbey. After the invocation, this was probably my other vital mistake. The third was to come.

Troops in the trenches in the Great War believed they should never light three cigarettes off the same match. At the first light, the snipers cock their rifles. At the second they aim. At the third, they fire.

Betty plumped herself down beside me on the sand, wearing something in black and silver, with a lot of diagonal stripes. Several long black strands of pubic hair were in evidence outside the garment. Their convolutions must have been the cause of much wasted charcoal when she posed for the Slade students, and they now hung out of her suit to meet the midday sun. I offered her Ninette's razor, an offer she deliberately misunderstood.[115]

'You know I don't cut myself. Mr Crowley, what is a Magickal Son, exactly?' I always found Betty's antagonism more attractive than I was prepared to admit. Not many people have the guts to stand up to maguses.

'It's someone who takes on all the attributes of the senior magician, without necessarily being related.'

'How exactly do you initiate your sons?' Betty knew exactly what we were talking about. I knew she knew. I was not going to reply. She pulled at her snake-like pubes, distractedly.

---

114 The reader will have no doubt deduced by now that my perusal of of Ninette's Magickal diary revealed that she had deliberately conceived, as an attempt to oust Leah as Scarlet Woman #1. A.C.

115 By now, Betty would have removed the price tag from her Smith & Wesson .45, and greased the trigger mechanisms and bearings of its revolving chamber with a thimbleful of olive oil from the kitchen, as she prepared the weapon for her own Magickal Battle over Raoul's body. How frustrating for her that her implacable foe did nothing but smile kindly on her! A.C.

'Couldn't you just have a son normally, like ordinary people do?'

'Apart from Raoul's own magickal investiture, which he has come fifteen hundred miles for, there's not time to act like ordinary people. Poupée needs all the help she can get, now.'

'Are you confident that you've been able to support her, magically?' The woman was an unmitigated pest. I continued to smile.

'If it is truly her Will, we will have been able to support it. '

'But if her will is paramount, why should you need to intervene?'

'Because I want to help.' I got up and started to walk towards the sea. I had a heat rash which lay irritatingly between my scrotum and my upper leg. The salt sea first stung it violently, and then the pain subsided to a dull tingle as I stood with the water waist-high about me. Betty followed me in.

'Did you ever get any reply from those world leaders you wrote to? King Farouk? Leon Trotsky?' I sat down in the water. The dazzle off the ripples made my eyes hurt. Betty sat down too.

'Trotsky's in charge of the largest social experiment in the history of the planet. When I wrote to him, I merely told him that it was a great pity that so soon after the revolution, they should have stopped free love. No reply was called for.'

'But what are your politics? Are you on the side of the Red Army then?' My patriotism was under scrutiny now, by the Chelsea Arts Club selection committee.

'While it's true that the *Communist Manifesto* foreshadows certain aspects of Thelemic teaching, for the rest of it I never read such piffle in my life. Personally, I hope Churchill knocks the Bolshies for six.' After gambling hundreds of thousands of soldiers' lives, and losing them, in the Dardanelles fiasco, Churchill had recently bounced back into the public eye with a series of self aggrandising campaigns using British regiments to support the dwindling White armies, in vain.

'Mr Crowley, are you a patriot as well as a pet lover?'[116]

'I still have hopes for England' I replied. 'But the war killed patriotism for me. The war brought hysteria, jingoism and profiteering to the fore. They were the things that the British seemed to do best. I couldn't be part of that world.'

As I said that, I remembered Lawrence, rolling in the dirt of the Cefalù post office floor, spitting out his feeble curses in a diseased orgasm of hatred at being cast off and rejected.

Betty for all her lack of intellectual prowess had a straightforwardness which was part of the new world rather than the old. Perhaps things were changing after all.

'Mr Crowley, you have chosen a fascist country to live in. What's your position on fascism?' I had not, as it happened chosen a Fascist country to live in. The Fascists had chosen to take over Italy, while I was in it.[117]

'Mussolini's a windbag. Vain, extravagant, theatrical, a traitor to everything except his own desire to hog the limelight. One would have to be a theatre critic to deal with him on the right level.' I was tiring of Betty's keen interrogation. The sun was shining, but the previous night's business still hung heavy and dark with me. However, a Logos' mission is to enlighten, whatever the personal cost.

'Have you given any thought to keeping a Magickal Diary yet?' I asked. Betty broke into a vigorous backstroke and started to swim away from me. After the sixth splash she shouted a 'NO!' and laughed.[118] I was not to be thrown off so easily. I started to swim, using a tantric version of the Australian crawl I had stumbled upon while

---

116 *Churchill defended the bloodbath as a legitimate gamble of war. However, his career was blighted till the rise of Hitler by disgrace and the hatred he had incurred as First Sea Lord. The Dardanelles venture, incidentally, was five years before little Mischette was detected as the carrier of a malefic current..* A.C.

117 *I had been in Rome at the time of the coup, and the excitement was so great that the Roman whores reduced, and in some cases entirely abolished their prices, for three days.* A.C.

practising endurance swimming in the Yangste Kiang, and very shortly I had caught up with her.

'You will free yourself when you realise that your so-called privacy is a worthless product, and not worth defending,' I said. She broke away from me again, and when she had created a distance of sixty six feet between us she shouted -

'I like my privacy!' I allowed her to swim away, knowing she would return with a load of questions she thought were deep and penetrating. I returned to sit on the sand, and sure enough, when I opened my eyes again, there was Betty dripping on the sand beside me, thinking that she had surprised me.

'Mr Crowley, what if I doubt the fact that the gods, whoever they are chose you?' I deliberately smiled my most beatific smile. I have seen the smile in photographs, and it would melt the heart of a stone. Not however, Tiger Woman.

'Strictly speaking, you're a bit of a fraud, aren't you?' I could have uttered a Word of Power that would have blasted her. I did nothing. I merely rolled over on my side, and looked at the cathedral through the heat haze. After an eternity of waiting for an answer, Betty said,

'Well, *aren't* you a fraud?'

'You should keep a diary of these thoughts' I replied, in my quietest voice.

'Why?' said Betty.

It was and is my policy never to force discipleship on anyone. If they should come to you, well and good. But you cannot force the process: you have to allow the scales to fall from the eyes of humanity in their own time.

'Mr Crowley, have you ever been wrong?' Betty asked.

'Of course.' I said. 'For years I ignored the *Book of the Law*. But Aiwass must have known about my own vanities and incompletenesses when he chose me, so presumably my failure is not so important.'

---

118 *She was consciously resisting at the same time as inviting me, through her own unconscious numerics, to continue expounding 666's teachings.* A.C.

In the middle distance, Hermes had drawn a picture of Anubis in the sand, which had been partly obliterated by the incoming tide. It was time to go up the hill, and take Adoration, before the evening meal. Beyond Anubis, I knew in the back of my mind, Giles would be in attendance, somewhere. I had ceased to think of him except as a remote reminder of the life I had left behind in England. Over the last ten years, first in London with police, then in New York with foolish Federal agents, there had always been the forces of law and order trailing far behind. A journalist seemed like harmless light relief.

They'd bagged Oscar, but the Logos of the Aeon seemingly could do whatever he liked.

XV The Devil

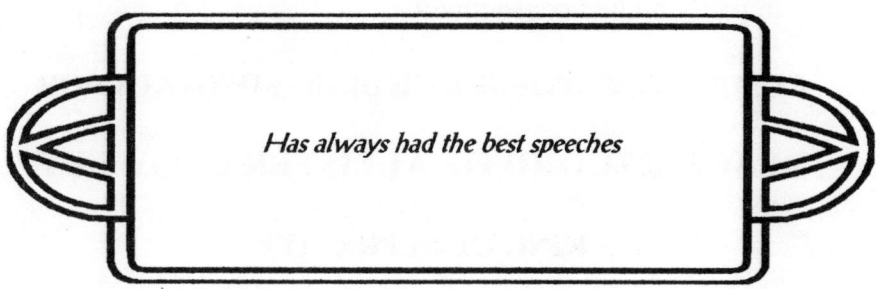

Has always had the best speeches

I didn't know it yet, but the cat which scratched me, and whose blood Raoul drank, had poisoned us both. Enteritis ulcerates the colon, and can cause death through internal bleeding with any sudden movement. It is carried by such feral creatures with great frequency.

First I became feverish, and exhausted, while Raoul, whose constitution was so much less robust, sickened till he could hardly leave his room.

In Palermo, Poupée lay in her little cot with the mosquito curtains round it, in the high-ceilinged ward, while her mother sat at her side, with her face looking as if she was about to cry, the same feeling that Leah said she had had all her life, ever since she could remember -

I had a failure dream about this time which involved Frank Harris, and even more ominously, I found him on an English beach, not unlike the beaches here, where I shall most likely die: (my heart giving out as I am performing a Magickal Act on the wreck?)

In the dream, Frank looked dapper in a most refulgent white suit, with shiny black walking stick. But the sea below him was transparent, and repellent, thick as jellied gravy, falling in waves of slow motion. Inside the waves rolled and floated rags of headlines from newspapers. It was as if the ink from the newsprint had floated off the page and into the water, but the letters kept their distances from each other with great exactness, as the headlines were on cellophane which was twisting slowly in partly melted consommé:-

COMPLETE EXPOSURE OF DRUG FIEND AUTHOR

BLACK RECORD OF ALEISTER CROWLEY

KING OF DEPRAVITY

I began by loudly laughing at the ridiculous caricature presented of myself, and shouting to Frank to watch me, I plunged into the water after what I could see clearly was an Italian lottery ticket, floating on the swell. The lottery ticket was within my grasp. Its number was 66 66 66. I shouted excitedly for Frank.

'Frank! Frank! I've got the winning number! Help me!'

But as I stood up and lifted the ticket up out of the water, it disintegrated in my hands, draining away through my fingers in a mess of incomprehensible fragments.

I remember I was wearing nothing but a large natural sponge over my wand, like a sporran. I had indeed worn a sponge such as this, on another occasion, to demonstrate the body movements in yogic breathing for a photographer. The coyly placed sponge meant that the pictures could be widely disseminated for educational purposes without upsetting the sensibilities and imbalancing the juices of the nation.

I stepped out of the water, and walked up to Frank, who looked at me with some amused disdain. Threads of gold ran through the material of Frank's lapels. I knew the suit was woven from white samite, the same material that even inferior poets are aware covered the arm that took Arthur's sword back into the water.[119]

---

119 'But ere he dipt the surface, rose an arm
 Clothed in white samite, mystic, wonderful,
 And caught him by the hilt.......'.[Tennyson, Morte d'Arthur]

I realised that the headlines were now all over my body. I had become the walking billboard of my adversaries, which flowed over the sponge and then back and around my loins. I tried to tear off the unwanted nominations, but could not remove the lettering from my skin. A middle section of the lettering of 'Depravity' even seemed to have become dyed into the sponge.

When, in an effort to begin cleansing myself and my reputation, I tried to pull the whole sponge off, it was as if it had rooting in me, and was becoming now part of my body. I felt as if I was somehow being colonised by a parasite, an external agency who I could not identify. This made me very anxious.

The letters on the sponge read **EPRAVI**. Even in my dreams, my method of mental control over forces has been to name and therefore control by identifying them. So immediately I named the sponge. But I still could not now remove the procrustinated deity, perhaps Choronzon's plebeian cousin, from his inseparable succubation on me. We were one flesh. I gave up the struggle with EPRAVI, and turned my attention back to Frank.

'The lottery, Frank. That way, we can raise the money for a newspaper.'

'Sadly my friend, we need a newspaper first, otherwise, how *on earth* can we publicise a lottery? It's a chicken-and egg situation and we have neither omelette, nor *poule*.' Frank's dazzling black stick described a circle, taking in the vault of the heavens, where contradictory to all expectations, the stars shone brightly down from a hard purple sky, with the Zodiacal house divisions clearly visible.[120]

'We are lost, Crowley, men out of time. A newspaper for our kind of people is a great idea. The only problem is it is the wrong time.'

---

120 *There were a number of other features of the sky, too many and too technical for the general reader. I shall be accused of bamboozling, if I include them all. I will mention two: a circle close to the Pole Star which I instantly recognised as a perfect geometric representation of the equinoctial precession, and chillingly, an unidentified planet [which I now* ad scribendum, *recognise as Pluto] ominously square my natal midheaven. A.C.*

Hideous Malpractice Knows No Bounds

His stick calmly flicked the strapline back into the water off the toe of his waxed, two-tone brogues. Then he leant forward and tugged mischievously at my sponge. But the brand new deity **EPRAVI**, unlike the strapline refused to budge. I felt increasingly it was part of me. But how could I continue with the Work if my Wand had turned into a sponge?

'I wish you all the luck in the world, with the missionary position, old boy. However you are on your own. I am too old for this game.' Frank straightened up, put a smart straw boater over the remains of his slicked back, silver hair, and winked at me slowly. His half closed eye with its red, loose, old man's lid, now looked more like an oyster than ever.

'It's every man for himself,' said Frank over his shoulder, then he walked off. Brighton's West pier was visible, some way away.

In three steps towards the pier, Frank disappeared into thin air, and the pier somehow became close. I was left peering into the preternaturally clear-etched struts and gantries of the pier's supports for my last ally. At the same time, the purple sky darkened, the wind arose, and the sea, loosed suddenly from its gelatinous chains, began to pound and roar amongst the grunions and palings. The waves broke hotly on the shore, with showers of sharp, fluorescent light. I waded into the breakers, filled with a perverse, Ibsenite anxiety that I would find Frank had been dragged out to sea in an undertow. My arms and body now glowed with clotted phosphorescence as I moved among the giant breakers, crying out for Frank.

I could see as each green wave lit up as it curled, that I was the only one on the shore, but I never ceased my halloo's, in my solitary hue and cry. It came to me again, that I was the last one on earth. I had in mind an Opus VIII° with Venus' own birthplace, displacing the Uranian seafoam with some of my own, and thus become an immortal progenitor in yet another guise, but EPRAVI would not budge, and the fancy left me abruptly, as it does sometimes in dreams.

After an eternity, when I had quite forgot what I was looking for, I came upon Frank's white suit, gleaming on a quietly retreating wave. It was empty. The jacket was neatly next to the trousers, as if his body had been ironed out of it as it lay flat onto the top of the water. But Frank was gone. I was racked with grief. I picked the suit up, in my arms, and only water fell out of it. My heart was filled with inconsolable loss as I contemplated all that remained of my old companion, still holding together but draped over my forearms like a cloth mannequin, devoid of any life.

When I woke up, **EPRAVI** was gone, to my relief but I found I was so weak I could not get out of bed. For the next ten days neither I nor my wand could hardly move.

Betty had awoken to find Raoul had gone out. Assuming that he would come back, she lay and listened to the Mediterranean dawn chorus. When the noise quieted and still he had not come back to the room, suspecting an abduction by The Mystic, Betty put her revolver in the pocket of her dressing gown, and went out to seek him. She found Raoul lying on his own, passed out on the verandah.

Enteritis had now laid us both low. So a solemn, fat Sicilian doctor arrived, a perfect example of a Mediterranean mesomorph. He was not able to speak without waving his hands. He had black stubble on his chin that seemed to go all over his head, even around his ears. He was grotesquely over-hung whatever time of day or night he arrived, and wore a morning suit, stained with the blood of patients, to proclaim the higher nature of his calling. More comfortable in Sicilian than Italian, he was still keen to practise his English, and on his third visit proclaimed the following over Raoul, with much sawing of the air:

'He must lie down, flat. Two months.' Betty was scribbling as he spoke. ' Very soft. food. You unnerstan'? Like bambino. You chew it for him. Or the ulcers in his colon break and he die.'

I was standing, or rather I was propped up by the altar as the good Doctor left Betty indicated me to the doctor.

'What about Signor Crowley? Shouldn't he be lying down too?'

'Yes of course'

'What else should he do?'

'He should not take drugs' I was proposing to vanquish the disease with a diet of brandy, in order to clean the system from within, but I had no intention of provoking a crisis in my already weakened system by dispensing with my other medical aids.

'Will he die if he doesn't stop taking drugs? Will he die?' Betty asked, brightly. The doctor shrugged.

'He's strong. Perhaps.'

Later, Ninette came into my room, filched a ball of hashish the size of a pigeon's egg, and solely in order to make trouble, gobbled it all up. She then started seeing things going up the wall, could not control which etheric plane she entered, and fell into Raoul's room, where she started to wail. I was at the altar in the middle of the evening Pentagram service when Betty came out and interrupted me in mid-sentence of my incantation with the news that Ninette was hallucinating her imminent end and trying to climb under the bed.

When things had calmed down, I gave Ninette a public lecture about the vices of drug abuse.

'You may have your opium, your hashish' I said. But they are to be used to further your spiritual journey. You have merely abused them.' Ninette, pleased with the attention, smiled like the cat that had got away, after stealing all the cream.

I was too weak to go out, so I lay in my bed, dictating letters to Leah. I had just finished a lengthy missive to Kemal Ataturk, who was in my opinion, the one man who could forge a Thelemic country out Turkey.[121] Betty burst in as I was signing it. Somehow the presence of

Leah in the room, sorrowful Leah, loosened Betty's tongue.

'I asked the doctor if it was possible to catch enteritis from drinking infected blood. He said it was.'

'I don't see how he could have conducted a test on Mischette.' I said. The cat had been dead a week.

'You know what I mean' said Betty, darkly.

'I always know what you mean, Betty' I said. 'But so do you know what I mean. When I told you you would be coming to cook all my meals for me, I meant that. And it happened.' Betty was not to be beaten down.

'The doctor said Raoul could have caught enteritis from the cat's blood. Well I have this prediction to make you you. If Raoul dies, I'm holding you directly responsible, Mr Crowley. So don't make any mistakes with that, or I'm going to have to put you down, like a cat, yourself.'

Leah gasped at the effrontery of the woman. Betty withdrew and shortly we could hear her shouting at poor little Hermes, who had last used the shovel, then left it by the grave after he had found and buried his four legged friend Satan. By the time I had come outside to take Adoration that evening, Betty had found a variety of digging implements, mostly unsuitable, and was now waist high in a hole in the ground outside the house, furiously trying to crowbar a stone the size of a howitzer shell out of the bottom of her pit.

I watched her, suddenly calm, pleased that she felt so angry.

'What are you doing?'

'I'm digging a latrine. What I don't understand, Mr Crowley, is why you didn't take some elementary precautions for health around this insanitary cottage before your daughter had to go into hospital.' The dirt flew up from the hole, and alighted on a conical heap, where it slowly slid back till it fell over the lip of the digging and onto Betty's feet.

---

121   *Having successfully opposed Churchill's Dardanelles adventure, but being opposed to siding with Germany, Ataturk's ruthless modernising of the 'sick man of Europe' seemed in 1920, a clear way forward. A.C.*

'I'm going to erect a hygienic barrier in our room, as well, Mr Crowley. I don't want to see you inside it.'

Later, Betty took a sheet and soaked it in disinfectant, so that its smell wafted out and competed with incense around the altar. She then hung it over the door to Raoul's room, against his protests.

Standing in the pentagram I could hear them chatting behind the sheet, and see Betty's busy shadow undressing against it by the candlelight within as she prepared to be all things to Raoul; wife, mother, whore, and now weaver of his shroud.

'From now on, we're going to be very, *very* clean in here. I'm going to be standing over you with a gun.'

'That's rather extreme, isn't it Betty? I thought you wanted me to get well' said Raoul's voice, querulously.

'That exactly it. I want you to get well, and I am perfectly prepared to use the gun if anyone tries any mumbo-jumbo on you.'

'It won't get that far, I'm sure.' Raoul was always the peace-maker the dear boy.

'It can get as far as it likes. But the Purple Priest is not coming in here.'

'Do what thou wilt shall be the whole of the Law' said Raoul. 'How is the Master, anyway?'

'Full of his rollicking good humour' Betty replied, bitterly.

'It's funny' said Raoul, 'You're the only one he doesn't mind making fun of him.'

'I'm not making fun of him. I've just said he's not coming in here' said Betty. By the sound of things, she was combing out her hair, standing naked at the foot of the bed. Then she blew the candle out and the sheet lost its inner luminescence. The altar candles were burning low. I snuffed them one by one. I could hear Raoul settling down with Betty for the night.

'He's the only one to save me.' Raoul said.

'What do you mean?'

'I mean no one else has the knowledge to save me.'

'I do.' said Betty, contradicting him. Either Raoul was too tired to reply or he spoke so low that I could not hear.

I went within Koshmah, and comforted Leah in her sorrow in conventional way well known down the ages. At the moment of orgasm, I wished, silently for a son. To my relief, in a few days Leah announced that she 'knew' she was pregnant.

This was welcome, for it could take some of the sting out of Poupée's exit, which I was preparing myself to think of as inevitable. In addition, Leah being pregnant might smother her jealousy of the time bomb with its own agenda now growing in Ninette's womb. Leah was bound to hear about it sooner or later; already Hermes had prattled in front of her in vague and uncertain terms about a 'little beast' bursting with its five limbs out of his panting mother.

A week later I had crawled to the verandah, and was seated at the table just before noon, my *I King* tortoise shell sticks in my hand. I felt about a hundred and three. The sun fell on my hands with unparalleled ferocity. I cannot remember why it did not sear my head. Perhaps I was wearing a hat. I forget. I had just drawn a highly unfavourable answer to an enquiry about Raoul's ability to recover and carry on The Work, and I must have dozed off for a moment, for the next thing I knew Raoul had lightly touched my shoulder with his hand. He saw I had the *I King* open. I hurriedly closed it, so that he should not see his own hexagrams. He was so weak he could hardly stand up.

'What are you doing, Raoul? I insist you go and lie down this minute.'

I got up and turned him round with hot, dry hands, with an aching fever in every joint. I started to guide my Magickal Son back towards his room across the verandah, praying that he and I would not collapse together.

'I heard the tortoise shell predictors clicking. What says the Oracle to our little problems?' Raoul asked. Finally we went into the cool of the temple.

'It says you should be lying down' I said. As I passed the altar I felt some strength come into my limbs, which was just as well. Raoul stumbled and I more or less carried him through the sheet on the door, and helped him get into the bed.

'Aren't you going to tell me, what the *I King* said, then?' Raoul pleaded.

'I wasn't asking it about you' I lied, and turned to go. At that moment, Betty swaggered in bearing a boiled egg and beside it, three bread and butter soldiers on a tray.

'That's enough, Aleister. The new rules say, you're out. This is our club in here, and you've been blackballed.' Nurse Betty lifted up a kitchen knife from the tray and pointed it at me. I raised my hand in benediction.

'Put up your bright swords, for the dew will rust them.' Raoul smiled in recognition of the Other Poet.

'It's alright, he's leaving Betty. It's a quote from Othello.'

'He didn't say he was leaving though.'

'But I am leaving. No blackball required, as the Moor of Venice remarked.' Raoul started to snicker, but was quelled by a look from Betty. So with that witty remark, I drew the sheet aside, and left the sickchamber, standing upright with some difficulty.

Next week, I was able to hobble down the path towards Cefalù. A third of the way down it widens into a mule track which is wide enough to take a horse-drawn taxi. In this fashion I was borne into the town, in order to visit Poupée in Palermo, and then on the return, discuss planning permission with the local police for my projected Academy on the top of the rock.

As I passed the post office on my return from Palermo, I noticed a tall English looking head poking up above one of the two open phone cubicles. There was a small queue of Sicilians waiting to get on the phone as the post office now resounded to the tones of Giles trying to justify his expenses to the Beaverbrook organisation. His overall ineffectualness I put down to two factors. Firstly his youth and general inexperience, secondly his total lack of any role models such as 'hardened reporters' which came in with the 'Talkies' ten years later, in the heyday of the Hearst Papers.

At any rate, there was Giles, in red braces, and shirt sleeves, doing what the English abroad do so much of, shouting very slowly.

Giles was in this case, trying to make himself heard to another Englishman, along the gutta-percha covered Marconi cable laid under the Straits of Messina, thence to Rome, thence to Paris, thence through Calais and Dover to Fleet Street, London. Oh, New Aeon! Instantaneous will be thy Pleasures!

'Front desk? Front desk? This is Giles Guilfoyle[122] in Sicily. SICILY!! Are your ready? Crowley swims naked with women. NAKED. WITH AT LEAST TWO WOMEN.' There was a pause when he must have been straining to hear some low instruction from his masters for he next yelped,

' I can't do that!! Suppose I get caught?' I did not think it was worth staying to hear the rest of the conversation. It was really all far too predictable.

After I had finished my polite but inconclusive interview with the police over planning procedures, I was sitting in the main square when I spotted Betty, who had been shopping for delicacies for Raoul. She went and sat down at a nearby table round the corner from my table.[123] Betty was shortly joined by Giles, fresh from his headline-grabbing triumph in the post office.

'Excuse me madam. Could I ask you a few questions?' Betty

---

122 *That was the name he said. It may of course have been an alias.* A.C.
123 *I was sitting inconspicuously in a corner and so it was not necessary to cloak myself in invisibility.* A.C.

shrugged. We all knew about Giles by now. Clearly he had been told to come up with the goods by the front office, or else.

'It depends.'

'Does Mr Crowley do all those things that people say he does?'

'I don't know what people say. What *do* people say?' said Betty.

'Dirty things' said Giles, uncertainly. He knocked over Betty's coffee cup, to his intense embarrassment. 'Sorry, I'm always doing that' said Giles.

'Are you asking if he does dirty things to me?' Very slowly, a grimy waiter with a stained apron detached himself from the primal horde of waiters at the end of the cafe, and came forward to examine the coffee stains.

'Does he?' said Giles. ' Do dirty things?'

Betty held up her marriage finger, bare of its ring, in a profoundly ambiguous gesture.

'It doesn't look like it, but I'm still married' she said. 'I don't know what you are talking about.'

'Do you know where Mr Crowley is right now?' Instead of saying

'I think he has gone to Palermo to visit his daughter in hospital, and then on to consultations with local planning departments' Betty said, 'He's right behind you.' Giles turned, and found himself staring into my eyes.

I had had enough of him. I used the Look of Power. Giles rose to his feet, trembling, knocked over another coffee cup and dashed through the rest of the tables, running across the square as if he had a pack of hellhounds at his heels.

XVI The Blasted Tower

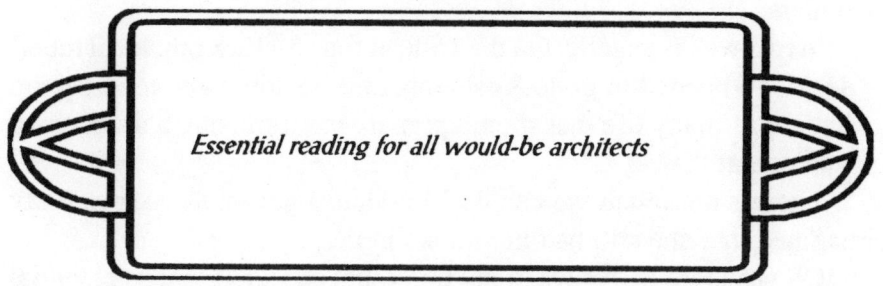

Essential reading for all would-be architects

'Whatever has got into him?' Betty asked as I sat down at the table with her. I said nothing and kept my eyes low. 'Mr Crowley, can you explain?'

'I doubt it' I said, humbly. 'Perhaps you mentioned masturbation.'

'I did no such thing. The young man was plying me with questions, then he saw you and fled.'

'It's inexplicable' I said, solemnly, adjusting my cloak.

It was always comical when, after a Magickal act had happened in broad daylight, people would relate the most bizarre trains of events in order to 'explain' what had actually gone on.

'How is Poupée?'

'Sinking. Leah thinks it's the heat.'

The waiters, who while Giles had been in evidence had all fled to the other end of the cafe, now flocked to the table, and a bottle of brandy appeared from nowhere.[124]

'Mr Crowley, what does Raoul's horoscope really say?' Betty knew perfectly well that horoscopes did not 'say' things.

'The horoscope simply shows a malefic transit' replied the Logos, and held his glass out for more brandy.

---

124 *A figure of speech, in this case.* A.C.

'And when is that transit going to take place, exactly?' Betty pressed forward, her eyes boring into me as if she too could work wonders.

'In two weeks exactly. On the 16th, at four o'clock pm, local time.' I decided I needed to go to Koshmah, and lie down and meditate on what it was in my life that should prepare me for losing a daughter, a loved one at that.

'There's not much we can do.' I added. I got up to go, but Betty imagined that she still had her hooks in me.

'Oh yes there is. It says in my book that strict hygiene is essential if you want to recover from enteritis. There hasn't been much hygiene at the cottage, to date, has there?' On one of her trips into Palermo, Betty had got a copy of 'Handy Hints for a Healthy Empire' from an English tourist bookstall, and had left it prominently on the altar at the Abbey, with some passages on Intimate Hygiene underlined in shaky pencil.

'The Abbey is for the development of the Will -' Betty interrupted and did not let me finish.

'And did your little baby fail the test of being one of your pupils? You're meant to be looking after your people. And you're not, you're not!'

Her accusations pricked me to the heart. I was not looking after my people. They were all of them, including me, sick.

I found myself clutching the back of the chair, unable to move. Betty swept by me imperiously and flounced into the sunlight of the square.

After that, Betty continued to defy me in other ways. She continued to exclude me from Raoul's room, and started keeping copies of newspapers, which were forbidden at the Abbey. My position on the gutter papers and yellow press was that it was all lies anyhow, a distraction from the real Work and the Abbey. Betty's Handy Hints recommended a Cooling Draught so the sheet of disinfectant was hung over the door to a room that was never closed. One morning while I was at the altar I caught the following conversation between them.

'Is that today's paper?' Raoul began.

'Don't be ridiculous' Betty replied, tactful as ever.

'Then what is the date on it?'

'It's at least three weeks old.' There was a rustle and Raoul's weak voice said insistently,

'Betty, he knows when I'm going to die, doesn't he?'

'Of course not!' Betty snapped.

'Has he told you when, Betty?'

'The hell he knows.' said Betty. ' A pity I can't carry you out of here right now.'

'This is all my fault' said Raoul, my Adonis. 'I failed the test to be his Magickal Son. If I had not failed, then there would not be the misfortune we are all suffering.'

'You're an intelligent man' said Betty, patronisingly. 'How you can think any of that stuff works is beyond me.'

'It works if you believe it' said Raoul. The woman was truly astonishing. Betty had seen me reduce a stranger to a state of panic and gibbering fright with a single look, and still did not believe in the power of occultism. She was now outlining her plans for the future, which included her own comforts. Raoul was not going to be given a say in where they were.

'Do you think I like being cooped up here living on with the stink of disinfectant? As soon as you are better, we're going *straight* back to London. And I don't care if I don't smell another piece of goat's cheese, or goat stew for the rest of my life. But If I turn my back on you here for one minute, the Beast will be in here, trying out some more special magical medicine on you and poisoning you again, and that will be it! Curtains!'

'He doesn't want me to die, does he?' said Raoul, plaintively.

'Oh yes he does! He likes to meddle anywhere he's not allowed! But he's not going to get at you while I'm here. Over my dead body!' Raoul judged that the little tiff was almost blown out.

'I'm sorry, Betty. Why don't you go for a swim today?'

'I can't leave you here.' said Betty.

'I won't let anyone in, I promise.'

'Swear' said Betty.

'Cross my heart and hope to die' said Raoul. The chance of speaking with Raoul uninterrupted was too good to miss. I tiptoed away, elated, leaving the door to Koshmah ostentatiously ajar, announcing to the world that the Beast had left his lair, and gone forth.

I withdrew to a rocky vantage point above the path. I could now look down and see the house as well as where Hermes had buried Satan, Betty was already on the path to the beach when she was joined by Ninette. Their voices floated up to me past the grey limestone rocks.

'I think I'd rather be here than anywhere else in the world.' said Ninette.

'Raoul and I are leaving soon - I don't think this paradise is for us,' Betty replied.

'He is doing his best to protect Raoul. You will be safe while you stay' said Ninette, a touch of threat in the voice. 'People blame the Beast for everything. The dog that died, I know he did not do it. He was inside me when I heard the shot.'

The path wound away out of sight, and I waited till their voices died, before standing up.

I thought I would give Raoul a surprise. I made a wide circle round the house and started to approach the patio from the other side. It was then I heard sticks breaking, on the other side of the house, as if some clumsy Frankensteinian monster was coming down the hill to the house from above.

Leah was in Palermo with Poupée. Hermes would be following his mother, his principal source of nicotine, to the beach. There should have been no one there except Raoul, who was too weak to get out of bed.

It sounded as if someone was trying to get into the house, through the woodshed at the back of the house. It was where Randy slept, but the only thing in it apart from his cot was a little box with a blanket in it, sacred to Satan's memory. There was nothing there of value so I settled down to wait and see who the gods had sent.

After ten minutes, a tall bald figure wearing fawn trousers and fawn braces over a white collarless office shirt came round the corner of the house onto the patio. It was Giles.

Giles went and stood straw hat in hand at the door, which was the only one open to the house. He tapped on a shutter, so softly that I could not hear. Then, taking this inaudibility as an excuse for an announcement of his entry, he boldly stepped into the main hall where the temple and the Altar was. I was rejoicing in what was happening. An agent of the Beaverbrook press was engaged in trespass on my leasehold, and I was about to have him caught in the act. I noiselessly moved onto the verandah and waited for Giles to emerge with whatever larcenous booty his masters would have him steal from us, so I could confront him with his misdeeds.

The inside of the house was so quiet I could hear Raoul's snores. After a while he stopped, and called out.

'Betty, if that's you, could I have a drink?' Moved now by a desire to protect my beloved from the shocking depredations of the yellow press, I stepped inside the door myself. The six doors to the rooms off off the main temple, three on one side, and three on the other suggested six possible hiding places for Giles. The sheet hung immobile over Raoul's door, so he was not in that one. It was then that I heard the crash of a dropped glass coming from Koshmah. I concluded either Giles was a very clumsy burglar, or he had passed out at the sight of my depictions of supernatural sexual acts.

A moment later he emerged from Koshmah with a loose leafed manuscript in his hands.

I made the mistake of leaving the doorway unguarded. He vaulted over the altar, and dashed past me, out through the front door over the verandah. It had all taken less than five seconds. It was over so fast that I had not thought to use the Voice of Power.

I discovered from checking my papers that his hasty theft was the carbon copy Leah had made of the manuscript of *Diary of a Drug Fiend*. Raoul stayed curiously listless, uninterested in our visitor when I put my head round the door to tell him all about it. So I withdrew. I was in the middle of composing a rebuking letter to Lord Beaverbrook pointing out the asinine and illegal performance of his so-called representative, when I was greeted by the postman, arriving at the front door.

He had become considerably more friendly now that his target practice on the dog had been so successful. He gave me a telegram, which Leah had sent from Palermo. Poupée had died, and the registrar required that both parents as resident aliens signed the death certificate. I left the letter to Beaverbrook unfinished, and set out for the railway station, feeling my heart contract to a cold stone, as the only defense against the waves of hopeless emotion that beat in a frenzy on my defenseless head. So this was destiny.

On my way to the station, I passed the post office, where Giles would no doubt be trying to read extracts of my work down the crackling Marconi cable to Fleet Street. Giles would be slow to accept that what he had stolen was a worthless prize.

'What do you mean, how can 'Diary of a Drug Fiend' be a book? I have his diary in my hand. He's the drug fiend, is that not correct sir? I don't understand. You mean it's not his real *diary*....?....'

I went by the police station. The caribineri eyed me curiously, in silence. They filled the cafe next door to the police station where they sat in large numbers, with their leather boots out as if to trip pedestrians. I did not stop to report the theft: I had other things on my mind.

I was placing myself by a magickal act, into Betty's imagination. I felt clair-sentiently that she would be swimming underwater at that moment, with her shadow underneath her on the silver sand. I know that underwater she would be believing she had removed herself from my purlieu. It was time to teach her a lesson.

I commanded her to open her eyes, and there she would see me, underwater, crosslegged and mirthful, a Buddha who was at home in any of the five[125] elements. I made welcoming gestures with my hands to her. Welcome to Crowley's Aquatic Kingdom! She turned her face away? The Buddha would fade, only to reappear in her eyeline a few moments later. And if she looked out to the sands either side of her shadow, there on the bottom would be a chequerboard pattern of the faces of the Master Therion, stretching away under the blue haze either side, staring straight up from the bottom of the sea. No escape from the fact that life is about the discovery of your True Will.

Leah met me in tears at the coroner's office. The coroner was in the midst of slowly and imperiously filling in several forms to do with the death of one small baby. After watching twenty minutes of this farce, I went and stood in the corridor outside for some air and had to be called back by Leah to pay for the pompous seals by which the documents were authenticated.

Afterwards, arm in arm, Leah and I went down a corridor. Like every public building in Italy, it had a brand new picture of Mussolini on the wall.

'That chap gets absolutely everywhere, doesn't he?' I said, lightly.

---

125 *The Chinese believe that wood is an element, and who am I to contradict them?*
    A.C.

I was trying to lift our shared mood which was so black I did not believe I would ever survive it.

Leah then attacked me.

'Get away from me, you monster!' She screamed.

I can think of no other explanation than the fact that she must have looked up, seen the picture of Mussolini, and momentarily confused the two of us, in her grief. She ran away, screaming, down the corridor and it was some time before I caught her and cured her hysterics by giving her a good hard slap on the face. When she had recovered, she said quite calmly,

'You've got that little hooker pregnant, haven't you?'

'Which hooker?' I asked, innocently.

'Ninette.' Ninette had never been paid for sex in her life. 'Anyhow, I'm telling you. If you've got her pregnant, out she goes.' This was against the Law of Thelema, but Leah was herself pregnant at the time, and I made a mental reservation that I might have to do as she demanded if she was not to lose the foetus she was carrying now, out of sheer grief.

On the evening of the tenth, four days before Raoul's projected danger period, I decided to act. I took Ninette's Magickal Diary, ostensibly in order to see what events in it should be incorporated into the Abbey Magickal Diary, but in fact I was performing a good, old-fashioned witch hunt on a girl I had got pregnant. I was looking for evidence to ostracise her, and I found it in reams in her confessions. Swift and severe expulsion was to be mooted at ten that night.

As all show-trials are meant to be, it was impressive. I donned my Masonic regalia, and with vast, smoking brands (Again, second-hand from the church festivities) each side of the table, sat down to give judgement. The rest of the Abbey, in their robes, were sat in the half darkness behind me. Ninette Shumway was summoned, wearing only a shift, trembling, from her room to face her menacing, hooded accusers.

'At Poupée's death, we felt the brunt of an encircling Magickal force, heavy, black and silent, which was engulfing the Abbey.' I began. 'Although it has withdrawn, we have to take precautions for the survival of the other members before it strikes again.' I laid my hand, solemnly, on Ninette's incriminating diary. At the same time, I felt my features settle into the same expression I used to observe on my father's face when he was about to pronounce on some particularly juicy piece of predestination. I continued-

'This catalogue of spite is not the evidence of laudable frankness I thought it once was. In fact, it is a willed and directed malicious current against myself, against the Scarlet Woman and against our health -'

'- And against Poupée -' Leah interjected, needlessly.

'- And against the aims of the Abbey' I continued. 'It was made clear to you at the start that you would never be my Scarlet Woman, however we have bid you a warm welcome.'

Ninette shrugged. The strap fell down from her negligée off one shoulder.

'I wrote down everything just like you said, and now you are using it against me.' This was so clearly true and obvious that I could not allow it to be examined. Beyond the olive grove, lines of other flaming torches could be seen approaching the house along the path, in a swift jogging motion. Something wicked was coming this way. It was time to thunder, and like Jove, I did.

'Either you reform, or your soul will be constrained to purge itself by feeding on its accumulated poisons in solitude. You have three days to make amends, before I sentence you to banishment from the Abbey.'

As I finished my judgement, the first of the caribineri's torch bearers arrived on the verandah. Then the complete contents of the police station cafe had tipped out of the square and poured up the hill, every man jack of them holding a police issue flaming brand, of considerably better quality than the ones we had purchased from the church. Mussolini's shock-troops of the new social order demonstrated their readiness to act by running at the double, but then had to wait until the stouter and older members of the patrol, who had the paperwork, made their way up the path. Meanwhile Ninette had a captive audience.

' 'Ave they come to arrest me, Beast?' she asked facetiously, as the caribineri stood on the edge of the verandah, like a herd of young heifers uncertain whether to charge. 'Alright so you stuck your tongue up my arse, but that was your idea, not mine.' Ninette said. There was no flicker of understanding on the impassive faces of the caribineri standing there, in the torch light, in their dark, hot uniforms. I had no idea what had brought them there, so I ignored them until the commanding officer, a man of impressive girth, finally arrived at the top of the path and pushed through the little crowd of his subordinates to perform a Fascist salute to me.

'Viva Il Duce.'

'Viva Il Duce!' bellowed the Caribineri, suddenly, as if we had not got the idea the first time. The officer then spoke to me in Italian.

'We have something important we believe is yours at the police station. Come immediately to identify it, and bring your passport.'

'Can you tell me what it is?'

'A manuscript. In English.' Somehow the manuscript of *Diary of a Drug Fiend* had found its way out of Giles' thieving hands. I expect that when he found it was of no value, he left it in the post office.

'Could you not have brought it with you?'

'You have to identify it before it leaves the station.'

Since we were outside, the officer had no chance of looking around at the 'dirty' pictures which was why, presumably, the whole police station had turned out in force. Pleading a sprained ankle, I promised to come and collect the script at the earliest possible opportunity. And as quickly as they had arrived, the Caribineri melted away down the path again, and their lights were swallowed up in the night.

XVII The Star

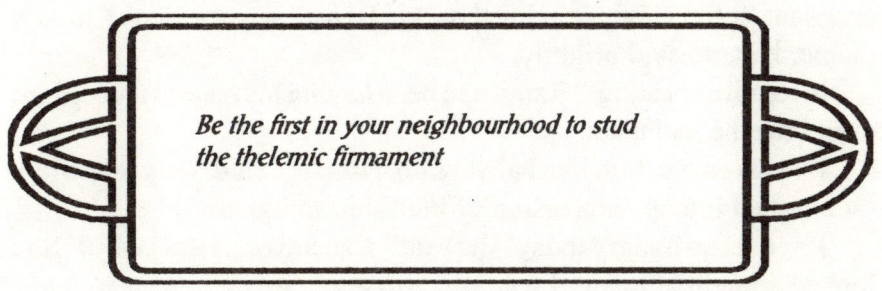

Be the first in your neighbourhood to stud the thelemic firmament

I wrote up the Official Magickal Diary of the Abbey. Ninette was under official threat of excommunication. She had also been ordered by Leah to take over Betty's tasks, that of preparing the food. The following day, as if she was going to live at the Abbey forever, she ignored her kitchen duties to henna her hair. In the end, Leah started to make the evening meal herself, only to have Ninette take a piece of goat's cheese out from under her nose. We observed her stuff it greedily into her maw, with dirty, henna covered hands. It was not a pleasant sight.

'Tastes good?' Leah said, politely. Ninette grunted her approval, then went to the pump at the back of the house, where she stood in the middle of an enormous grey puddle of henna, impudently sluicing herself, while the dirty water spread all round and even into the kitchen.

Later, when we had sat down to eat, Betty was ministering to me as usual. I asked her if she had had any unusual experiences when swimming underwater.

'We didn't go in the water that day' said Betty.

'You will' I said. Betty gave me a strange look. That evening there was flat Sicilian bread, good red wine, and some boiled squid. I made a short peroration about the transmigration of souls, and the likelihood of Poupée being born again. The soul does not enter into the body for reincarnation until the foetus is three months old. So Leah could very easily be carrying the 'new' Poupée, even though she had been pregnant before Poupée passed away. Before anyone spoke to this theme, Ninette said brightly,

'Is Raoul not eating?' Raoul had been having his meals taken to him ever since he had taken sick.

'I've taken it to him like I always do, Ninette.' said Betty. Ninette's face settled into an expression of ineffable smugness.

'I'm ever so hungry today' she said. 'Can anyone guess why?' She looked straight at Leah. 'Leah, can you guess why?'

'Are you pregnant?' said Leah. Ninette nodded, and stuffed some prosciutto ham into her greedy little mouth. Leah knocked over a tumbler full of wine, and it poured onto the concrete floor of the verandah.

'Just two more days of this, then out you go.' said Leah. Ninette's eyes sparkled with hate and I felt her dirty little foot working its way up inside my robe, under the table.

I went to Ninette's room later that evening, and we performed some of the most exhaustive Works that I can remember, with the objective of strengthening the Will of the individuals in the Abbey. Even without ether, the power of it left both of us dazed. Whatever Leah's feelings on the matter, if Ninette's soul development led through the performance of such important Opera, I was not inclined to throw her out at once.

Later I could hear Leah typing, in Koshmah, which was strange, since there had been no advance on the autobiography for weeks. At three in the morning, I went to investigate the phenomenon.

Leah had put two pieces of paper and a carbon in the old Underwood, and put the day and date at the top of the page in the English sequence, as I had taught her. Then she had put Ninette's name in the middle of the page.

She was now crossing every letter out with a heavy, repeated capital, in a frenzy of rage, carrying on until the carbon and both papers were torn in a tiny horizontal slit. I stood and wondered at it, for five minutes before she even was aware that I was in the room.

I should say in its defence that it was a crude but extremely powerful and effective piece of Magick, which was being directed with great force by her Will.

The next day, the storm between Ninette and Leah broke.

I was striving for ecstasy in a lengthy daytime romp with Ninette during which I encouraged her to draw blood. She bit my lip most avidly. I came. *Sanguis et semen*!

At the same time Leah invaded Raoul's room and tried to get hold of Betty's revolver, presumably in order to put Ninette down, as one might get rid of an unwanted bitch.

Betty was reading the forbidden newspaper, when Leah burst in through the Hygienic Sheet and demanded 'it' as if everyone knew what she was talking about. 'Where is it?' she kept demanding of the peaceful scene in the bedroom.

Leah then threw all the clothes from the suitcases on the floor, found the gun at the bottom of one of them, and waved it at Betty.

'Careful, it's loaded' said Betty.

'This time, I'm going to kill him' she said. The two harridans then joined in a high arm wrestle for the prospective murder weapon. Raoul watched them sway and struggle across the room. Leah was half a head taller than Betty, but Betty was fitter, and true to her Tiger Woman name. Betty finally took control of her gun again, and the two women stood panting for a moment. Outside I had had the most tremendous and unexpected second orgasm, during which I loudly invoked Aiwass for enough energy to ride all the steeds to a standstill that the Abbey could furnish me with.

'For lust's sake, let us Lust!'

On hearing my paeon to joy, and then more joy, Leah's murderous impulse changed direction, and she left the room having decided to kick Ninette to death.

Outside, she found Ninette squatting on my face in the pentagram. I was trying unsuccessfully to suck some shit out of her, when Leah laid into Ninette with her shod feet, denouncing her repeatedly, the while, as 'You fucking cow', like a cracked gramophone record.

In the midst of this delightful sylvan scene, Betty arrived like the peacemaking Sheriff of Moose Jaw, North Dakota, but having laid aside the gun and prudently hidden it.

'Pull yourselves together, you two! For heaven's sake!' She tried manfully to separate the scrapping sisterhood by thrusting herself between them. Finally she managed to calm Leah down enough to push her into her room. This left Ninette standing in the pentagram, seething silently but denied detonation, as Nimerup, and no doubt newer misbegotten deities such as Epravi poured their mischievous bile into her bowels of darkness.[126]

Nurse Betty was still acting the part of Miss Hygienic Curtain: but the black current continued to wind about us, and shortly her own even-handedness would be thrown into Nimerup's Plutonian meatgrinder. For the present moment, however she was still sweetness and light.[127]

---

126 Copraphagia by the Adept is not the foolish perversion that deserves a prurient footnote in Krafft-Ebing, but a conscious attempt to magickally tap this potent energy source. As before; this product comes with a health warning: don't try this one at home unless you've got written permission from the Secret Chiefs! A.C.

127 Arnold's book of the same title bizarrely fails to mention that buggery is the one activity that preserves, by generational iteration, the British public school system. A.C.

'Er, Ninette darling would you go out and feed the goat? It looks just starving.....' Ninette, unhearing, stared at the doorway of Koshmah, her eyes twin disks of fathomless hate. Her piss, which she had promised me, snaked down her legs now, and dribbled out of the pentagram, unchecked.

I realised that I had suppressed an accusation which Leah had made against me, in the dream where Nimerup visited me. Leah's strangulated voice came to me from afar -

........*'You left the circle'*........

So this was why all our troubles were on us! I had failed to take Magickal Precautions in a dream. Truly, the standards for Magi are not as for common mortals.

'Ninette, I warn you. I can feel myself losing my temper' coo'ed turtledove Betty, as if she had never lost her temper and never would. Curious as to how much longer Betty would manage to remain sweet, I deliberately pushed aside the sheet and stepped behind her back into the forbidden zone of Raoul's room.

Raoul was lying in bed, reading newspapers.
'Caught you redhanded!' I said, jocosely.
'I know' he replied, in a tone of weary surrender.
'I, I, I.' I said, reproving him with a stern smile. ' Repeat after me. It's a fair cop, guv, and I'm reaching for the razor as we speak.' We both knew that Raoul's condition, and my own affection for him,

made any attempt at conventional Abbey discipline impossible now.

'You know who the *real* enemy is?' Raoul volunteered. 'Cheap newspapers, and Fascists, well, they're all the evidence for something sick inside everyone. They're the boils on the neck, the evidence for the deathwish of a whole society.' I wish he had not mentioned boils. Mine had been particularly troublesome over the last few weeks.

Further communication was made impossible as Saint Betty, having introduced Ninette to the ever-hungry goat, brushed aside the Hygienic Curtain and sailed into the room, to dock between us on a high tide of righteousness. Betty deliberately straddled the bed between us, so I could no longer even see my beloved.

'Oh, Mr Crowley, since you've pushed your way in here, against your word given earlier, I wondered - did you see your review in the Daily Express? It's the story that starts 'Profligacy and Vice in Sicily.' She threw down the paper. I got no further than the headline, before I was rendered helpless with laughter, even as I read them out.

' "Unspeakable orgies impossible of description." - and; listen - "Madman who Feeds his Debased Appetite with Slavish Disciples."'

'So tell me what do you think of all this?' said Betty.

'I think that Giles must have been busier than we thought' I replied. 'Tapping out his reports every night at the hotel. Considering he's had to make it all up, he's done rather well, don't you think?'

'I wonder what they'd say if they knew you couldn't keep order amongst your concubines and wives' Betty said.

'You're not my concubine - yet' I said to Betty. I was not able to make the required hand movement to make my wish come true, because I was now engaged in a tug of war with Betty, with the newspapers.

'Let go. It is going to be infinitely more hygienic in here if I burn these stinking lies.' I quipped. And then Betty snapped.

'No you won't burn them. These are my papers. And it's not all lies. It says you are a hopeless drug addict. Well, you *are!*'

My hands are small, but in those days I was still a highly proficient rock-climber. I used the Grip of Power. Betty realised that nothing she could do would make me dislodge my grasp on the forbidden newspapers. So with her left hand, she held onto Beaverbrook's valued publication, while her right hand sought out the gun which she had secreted from Leah under Raoul's pillow. She pulled it out and clicked the safety catch off with her teeth - something which she had probably learnt in her days as an Apache's trollop in Paris - and pressed the barrel of the gun into my forehead. Right at the spot where the Third Eye sprouts.

'I am not part of your mènage. I have not finished reading this yet. Let go of my newspaper or *I'm going to kill you*.' Betty said, keeping her tone remarkably even, considering the content.

'Betty - *don't!*' cried Raoul, naturally alarmed.

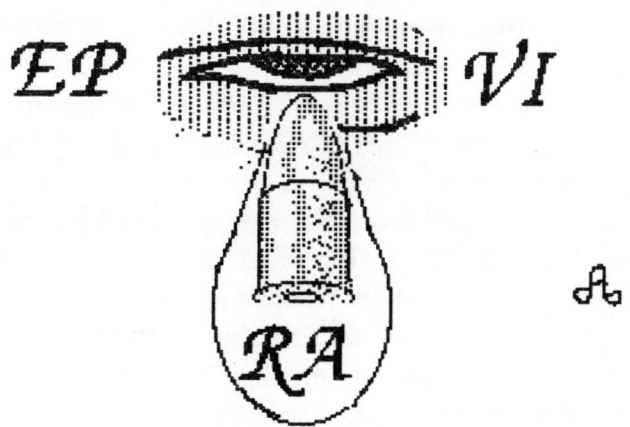

XVIII The Moon

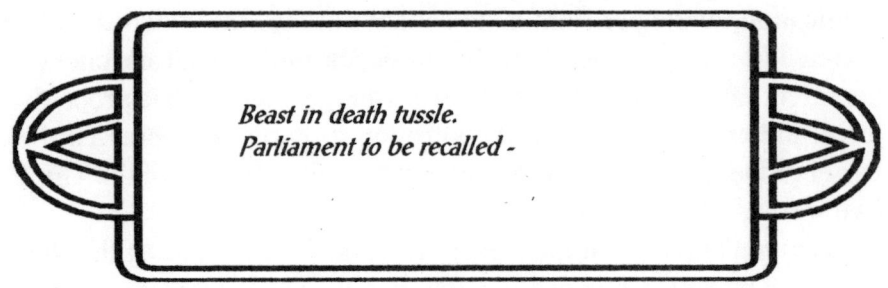

Beast in death tussle.
Parliament to be recalled -

'I shall count to three' said Betty. She half-cocked the hammer using her teeth, again. I suspected that the girl knew her stuff with a pistol. There were empty cartridge cases on the window. She'd been practising.

'You two are being incredibly stupid' said Raoul, feebly.

'One. Two -' said Betty. 'Three.' I'd carried a Webley of that design when I had traversed lower China: in fact I'd used it on a raft of mutinous Chinese. At half cock, the hammer can be drawn back relatively easily with the trigger finger and it has no choice but to fall on the percussion cap when it has reached its full extent.

Betty's trigger finger whitened, as she started to squeeze the hammer back. I thought it beneath my dignity to acknowledge what was going on, rather like the Roman senators who sat, motionless and mistaken for their statues, as the Goths sacked the house around them.

And then a miracle happened. Raoul rose from the bed as if on a spring, or an invisible wave, and used his arms to thrust us apart, with superhuman force. The effort may indeed have cost him his remaining energies, but it was not a second too soon. We were flung apart as Betty fired.

I felt a searing burn as the gases blazed against my forehead. In fact, the bullet barely grazed me, travelling up to smash a hole in the adobe brickwork above the window. Both Betty and I crashed into opposite walls. I shook my head, wondering if I had a hole in it, and started to stand upright. Betty was taking aim again, this time a little lower down, at my throat. The newspaper was forgotten. This was a killing in the making, pure and simple: delicious in its way, as it demonstrated the founts of Betty's cuntish being. I was not moved to save myself. As if in a dream, I saw that the framed wedding photograph of Raoul and Betty had fallen to the floor and the glass had smashed. Betty's aim was rock steady, at my heart.

I was saved by my Scarlet Woman. Leah came in, grasped what was happening in a moment and threw herself on top of me, a human shield.

'Shoot me first. I'm pregnant' she said, unanswerably, to Betty. Betty put down the gun, and started to sob.

'I won't shoot you. In fact I won't shoot anyone' Betty said.

Then, like a tree whose trunk has been sawn through, Raoul started to sway. His eyes were closed and his face was a deathly white. But instead of falling like felled tree, he slowly crumpled to the ground, as if he weighed no more than a feather. He had given his all to save me.

We laid him out on the bed, Betty and I together. His pupils had rolled up into his head, and his pulse was weak and erratic. I never saw his eyes again, till after he died.

Betty's response, of course was to do what she did under stress. She tried to bolt again. She left, Ninette told me at dawn the next morning, dressed in her best finery. But this time, she actually found the British Consulate in Palermo.

It does not require much inventive skill to picture the scene, in the high-ceilinged, marbled consulate hall, on the morning of the sixteenth day of the month I had predicted her sick husband - against all our prayers and wishes - would embrace his Will to die.

Betty, dressed dramatically in black, already a widow, in the shadows of her mind, is waiting on the sofa, half-listening to a conversation wind up between a junior official, let us call him Buggins, and the local Fascisti bigwigs. They are talking about recent, new, strong, legal innovations from Rome curbing all associations, masonic clubs and secret societies. There is to be no structure for plotting in dark corners. Mussolini has made Freemasonry illegal, in the new, no-nonsense Italy. The strictures naturally extend to foreigners without any exception.

The Magickal current saw to it that it was Il Duce's paranoia about the effectiveness of the Masonic Brethren, which I had achieved a very high order in, that became my final undoing, rather than the sleazy scurrilousness of the English gutter press. From Masonic membership lists, seized in Rome, the word has now gone out to round up and expel all Masonic foreigners.

Finally, pinstriped young Buggins finishes his diplomatic *conversazione*, and saunters over to Betty, whose trim ankle he has been admiring from afar, over the past ten minutes. The time is two minutes to noon.

'I'm sorry, the consulate is closing until four. Unless you've been robbed' adds Buggins, to show he has a gallant heart in his bosom. Four o'clock naturally sticks a dagger in her heart. The Mystic has said that is when Raoul will die.

Buggins gazes down at the seam on Betty's best, nay her only pair of black silk stockings. Betty looks up at him, her eyes brimming with tears.

'My name's Betty May. I have reason to believe that my husband will die at four o'clock today.'

'That's when we reopen.' says Buggins.

'But he's been bewitched. Can you do anything?' Buggins is floundering. The meaning of what he is being asked to do eludes him. The gilt lists of former ambassadors behind Betty's head start to undulate, alarmingly.

'It depends. Is your husband a British citizen?'

'He is British. He got a history first at Cambridge. Can't you do anything to save him?' Buggins brain once more tries and fails to expand to take in the nature of the threat.

'.....Do you mean he has been kidnapped?'

'Yes. I mean no. ' The incantatory magic of the past illustrious names behind her head spreads round the pair, weaving a web of confusion and misunderstanding.

K.G.B.
K.C.
O.B.E.
M.B.E.
C.B.E.

Buggins starts to turn away. He feels the aura of a migraine coming on.

'Look! I'm not just anyone' Betty says. 'I have been painted by Augustus John...' Aye, and rogered too, unless you were sober, which was unlikely in those days, Betty. But the famous name means nothing. Buggins, who took a first in classics, is blind to the visual arts of the present day.

'How do you know he's going to die at four o'clock?' he manages to gasp out finally. The room is going round. The floor is curling, the heavy yellow curtains are shimmying, and Buggins needs very badly to sit down. As soon as he does so, he sees the back view of Betty, walking out of the consulate front door, drying her tears.

Betty now realises, obscurely, that there will be no eleventh hour rescue of Raoul and she will shortly be a widow. For lo, Raoul is the Abramic ram, caught in the thicket by his horns. In the magickal looking glass, there is no escape. Moira, who governs Fate, will nod to her other sisters, and Raoul will have his cord snipped proving his love: his last exertions mean he died to save me, and thereby Thelema, for all of us. He has proved amply that he is the Son who sacrifices himself: he is indeed, through his death, my Magickal Son.

XIX The Sun

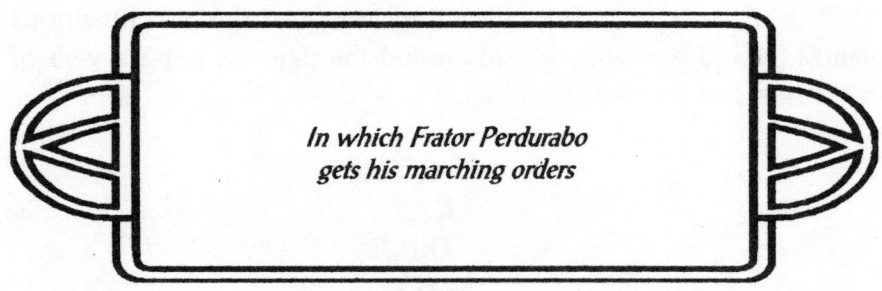

In which Frator Perdurabo gets his marching orders

At the same time as a jittery Betty was trying to denounce me in terms understood by modern diplomacy, I was making my way down the hill to reply to an urgent summons from the Cefalù police station. But first, ignorant of the shadow looming over the Abbey's future, I sent a telegram off to Raoul's parents. I did not know it, but I was visiting the post office for the last time.

Inside the Cefalù police station, it was too dark at first to take in the posters of Mussolini which survived undamaged, unlike the ones on the walls of the square. Behind the main desk, I saw sacks of mail being steamed open, in my view, by illshaven, potato-faced oaves in uniform.[128] As the largest of them went by to replenish the kettle, I pointed at the posters of Il Duce and said politely, in Italian,

'Good to see that the Boss is keeping you all so busy!', a piece of impudence that no doubt caused my police chief to delay his appearance and order another bottle of sweet wine, and a further quarter-kilo of marzipan disguised as miniature bananas, in the café next door.

Finally the barrel of lard in uniform appeared, with fat, half closed lids to deal with the dull business of expelling foreigners. In his hand, he had the manuscript which Giles had stolen. It was now well thumbed, to my amusement.

---

128 *All of them to a man, with an afflicted Mercury. A.C.*

'Is this yours?' he asked, in Italian. No doubt he was flushed with his recent success at the New Regime's extorting protection money from the local whorehouses.

'Yes, that's mine. Thank you.'

'You must go, all of you.' the police chief announced.

'May I ask if there is a link between what you are saying and your possession of the book?'

'Yes, it is because of the book.' I smiled. There had to be some ridiculous mixup.

'Why? Is it not a good read?' The Chief of Police blew out through the thickets of his nostril hair.

'We are obliged to deal with the new orders banning secret societies. You are aware of them?'

I confessed that with the kind of life we led at the Abbey, the outside world impinged very little.

'Your journal has been examined by the relevant authorities. Our experts say there are passages in it which clearly indicate Masonic practices.'

'It is the manuscript of a novel freely available in England. There must have been a mistake. Could I see the deportation order, please?' The police chief reached into a drawer, and pulled out a fat folder. Finally he located the deportation order, one of many. I looked it over.

'It only refers to me' I said. He took it back and stared at it.

'Yes. Aleister Crowley.'

'What about everyone else then? Can they stay?' The police chief shrugged. There was a historical obligation to dilute the orders from Rome. So in addition, I was allowed a week to collect my effects. At the end of the meeting, he bade me farewell, and extended his hand. I am not sure if he was hampered by the number and size of rings I was wearing, but I suspect that he gave me the Masonic greeting before he gravely showed me to the door.

Outside, the caribineri were gone from the café, running breathless, no doubt, to another remote spot to deliver a testing summons. The clock in the square said ten to four. I remember being pleased that

Raoul's parents, thanks to my vigilance, had notice of his illness before his time of extremest danger, when an old wrinkled man with a waistcoat and moustaches came and made a speech to me in Sicilian. The cafe owner whispered a running commentary in Italian, as he refilled my brandy glass - '*We've been invaded before and we survived that too. One day, you will know how much we hate those bastards from the North. We Sicilians have to hide what we feel. But you are respected here because you have no truck with Mussolini. You should stay and mock the fascist swine, the world needs people like you.*' The man was a natural Thelemite. I shook his hand. He took a double handful of small change from his pocket, and thrust it into the apron of the cafe owner. '*Tell him to drink this - as much as he likes.*'

The café owner waved the waiters away and served me personally. He wrapped the brandy bottle in a grubby linen napkin, and never allowed my glass to empty, making me feel like a king.

I went to sit outside, when I could see the clock. It read just after ten to four. I was becoming so mellow, indeed, silly-drunk, that it was increasingly hard for me to remember that my dreams were in tatters and Raoul was in his moment of greatest peril. I concentrated all my attention on the clock, in order to suck the greatest meaning I could out of the moments approaching.

The clock now said six minutes to four.

The yellow afternoon bus from Palermo rolled into the square and stopped under the clock, The chicken crates on its roof were empty. A figure got off which I recognised as Betty. The clock read one minute to four. Three peasants were waiting to board the bus. One of them was the old man who had been my sponsor of brandy. I fell into a trancelike state in which I understood from an inner prompting that Raoul was dying, and yet it was a death which he welcomed, because it brought together so many of my old friends. I did not understand what this meant till I looked away from the frozen time of the clock.

Betty had vanished. In her place, walking towards me was PAVOZ, in a floral summer dress to her ankles, and a straw hat that Vita Sackville West would have coveted.

This time I was not going to let her - PAVOZ, Mme Poitier or what you will, out of my eyesight for a moment. It was difficult, because behind her, the three peasants waiting for the bus had metamorphosed at exactly the same time.

There was Frank Harris in his white suit, and standing behind him, Raoul, arm in arm with Anubis. Raoul had a grey suit[129] on and Anubis was wearing a dinner jacket. Frank Harris was the first to board the bus. As soon as he was on, Anubis reached up with a plaid parcel he was carrying. By the way he passed it to Frank, I knew it was little Poupée.

I was watching my friends embark on the next leg of the Great Journey. I am ashamed to say that my powers of observation failed me completely at this stage. My eyes filled with tears. While I was dashing them away, I heard PAVOS, née Madame Poitier say her final sentence to me: at any rate, I have not heard her, since.

'Alastor, wanderer, weep not. Rejoice, for shortly you too shall join your loved ones, in the Journey across the Wasteland!'

The café owner stepped forward with his only linen napkin, and I dried my tears. The whole vision can only have taken a few seconds. I saw Betty coming closer, walking towards me across the square, with the yellow bus, shorn of its chicken coops, now driving off empty. I felt nothing but warmth and kindness towards Betty, even though she had just tried to betray me.

'What's the matter Mr Crowley?'

'It's nothing. I've just been given my marching orders, that's all.'

We went past the great bulk of the cathedral and began the long

---

[129] *The colour of the astral body immediately after death. A.C.*

ascent up to the Abbey for the last time.

༺༻༺༻༺༻༺༻༺༻༺༻༺༻༺༻༺༻༺༻༺༻༺༻

My tale is almost done. My asthma is bad, bad, bad. The winter storms, they say, will bury the Dutchman on the foreshore for ever, this year. Huge swathes of shale will smotherkiss the ribs and the treasure inside them, thrusting the treasure deep into the earth. The body of the ship, its golden booty and dionysiac secrets will be lost to rogue scavengers and honest treasure hunters alike.

I lack the strength to go down tonight, one last time and fuck mud in an Op. VIII° for the success of this vessel, my own Ship of death, that I am writing, to launch into the time after my death. The only truly Magick I can do any more, is that weak kind, writing magic.

I paid an ugly old bag to type this out by licking her cunt. The reason the chapters are getting shorter is that she is getting more and more voracious. Yesterday, for instance, (you will remember my lean and slippered pantaloon-like state, *sans* teeth) - I practically had to *gum* her bottom off, to get her to do the previous night's 2,666 words. Her husband stays up all night with his short wave radio, listening to the world, and won't come near her any more. I'll have to frig her all through the daylight hours, now, and then write all night. Strange how everything turns into work, in the end.

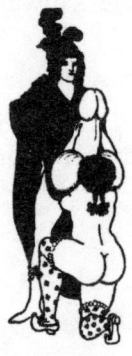

XX The Last Judgement

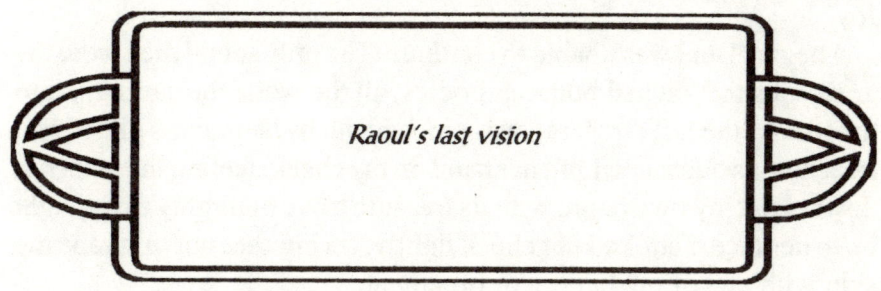

Raoul's last vision

I walked back towards the Abbey accompanied by Betty, with a tremor in my heart. Everything seemed over; my Magus-hood, the very core of my religious being, my ability to love, even my ability to have offspring, actual or magical.

Leah's typing exercise against Ninette had born fruit: twentyfour hours after their scrap, Ninette had spontaneously aborted. She screamed in her room and I had given her an eighth of a gram of heroin, with some misgiving - how much is 'enough' for a disciple of excess? The doctor, in an alcoholic blackout caused by Raki, had failed to come.

I knew in my soul, that the Black Current would later pluck the fruit of Leah's own womb and circumstances bore me out. But for the time being, however, Leah's vessel of reproduction had triumphed. Accordingly, Ninette's banishment was effectively suspended.

It was another evening of Sicilian visual ravishment as the sun set. Betty walked slower and slower, in companionable silence with The Beast. Finally the burning circle of golden sunlight touched its own long reflection in water.

'Would you excuse me? I should take Adoration, now.' I said. Betty bowed her assent. 'Perhaps you'd like to join me.' I said.

I assumed the Position of Adoration, and was not surprised to find Betty's hands raised up to the sun beside mine, in the direction of the setting sun.

'Hail unto to thee who travels over the heavens in they Barque of Joy'

I began. But I was unable to continue. The only sound then were the great sobs that racked both our bodies, all the while the sun sank into the sea. As the last direct ray was pinched out by Neptune's gilded and treacherous outriders, I felt her hand on my cheek, feeling the tears run down. I put my own hand, with its treasure trove of mighty rings, right up to her face. I stroked her cheek lightly, taking care not to scrape the skin with any of my battery of ornament.

'You think I don't care' I said.

'No I don't' said Betty.

'I'd *like* not to care. It would be so much less hard. But I do, I do.'

'I know you care' said Betty.

Betty and I were as close to a fuck as we had ever been. I idly wondered if she was packing the gun, in her handbag. It would have been absolutely stupendous if we could have done it with the gun pushed right in my face.

But then Leah came down the path with a face of death. Paint her as a dead soul, indeed. One needed no precognition to know four o'clock had brought the Angel of Death to the Abbey.

All the quivering life which I'd felt flowing between Betty and I went still and dark again. Normally death can thrust me into a dionysiac mode, as my Spark struggles against the engulfing Dust:- That has always been the motive for making love to the unlovely and grotesque, for me. But now, the moment of Raoul's death arrived, and I was unmanned by that unmanly emotion, pathos.

'Is Raoul worse?' asked Betty, always direct.

'You two had better come up to the house. He's dead.'

Betty fainted at the news. Leah patted her temples. Then she smoothed out Betty's posture on the ground, and did some of the other actions which are what happens, in the category of Popular Fiction, (my publishers advise me,) when a plucky and clean-limbed character is temporarily overwhelmed with grief, among caring friends.[130] This however is not fiction, indeed. You'd better believe every word, reader, or EPRAVI will take your lotus blossom of consciousness, tear off the leaves one by one, and thrust it, petals and all up your fundament.

I turned from Leah's ministrations of Betty, and watched the sunset fade from the sky, as if it were Raoul's life blood itself ebbing away. An asthma attack was 45% certain, in the next half hour, and 100% in the next twelve.[131]

Raoul's coffin was laid out on trestles in the covered way at the back of the house which connected the kitchen with Hermes' lair. His body had a completely waxen look, as if he had been instantly and expertly embalmed. The Sicilian carpenters who brought the coffin up were appalled at the idea of the corpse spending the night in the open, and with Betty's encouragement, kept trying to put the lid on. She would add a lily to the bunches which lay either side of them, and then tell the carpenters that they could nail down the lid because it was 'over'. *Basta*. As soon as their backs were turned, I opened it up again.

Raoul had died in exactly the same position that the ghostly plasmic horizontal figure appeared in, over his head, in their wedding photograph. The god-fearing carpenters left, crossing themselves after I assured them that I would personally be keeping an all-night vigil, to prevent the body being prematurely degraded by ghouls disguised as

---

130   *The faint is attested to, in Tiger Woman's autobiography, as the second time she passed out that day. A touching picture is painted by her of my attentions to her the first time, but surely, once is enough? [Father of Lies writes] . A.C.*

131   *There is a direct link with emotion. At my bankruptcy, it was only the onset of asthma in the dock that prevented me from exposing the conspiracies of the scoundrels and morally bankrupt imbeciles who had so cretinously forced my hand over so many years. A.C.*

242 Snoo Wilson

foxes, or ants and snails feasting in pagan rapture on the jelly of his unseeing eyes. We were going to save Raoul for the worms.

The fact was, that with all the ranks of Adepthood to prepare me, I still could not believe Raoul was dead. My mind utterly refused the concept. So much for being the reincarnations of John Kelly and Eliphas Levi.

I could hear Betty packing up in Raoul's room. She had completely readjusted after her faint, or faints, and was now getting ready for the return. She had found a dustpan and brush, (an achievement of a kind, in itself, at the Abbey) and the tinkle of broken glass could be heard as she cleared up the smashed frame of the wedding photograph. Then later a thump as the gun was dropped in the case; and finally the brassy snap as the case was closed. All full of my dead darling's clothes.

I had spent some time studying both the Tibetan and Egyptian Book of the Dead, and so was perfectly well prepared to act as guide to Raoul's soul leaving the body. It was a clear night and if I stood away from the house I could see the Pole star low in the north. I had a number of esoteric chants, which I alternated with a rhythmic tapping on the coffin, to remind the departed that they must indeed leave this life, in order to be born again. I must have dozed off because I remember the Dipper moving through several degrees about the pole, without my noticing it.

It was in one of these trances that I experienced a coda of the dream revelations of PAVOZ.[132] (I think it will be easier for the general

---

132 *PAVOZ can be considered as the female aspect of the deity who revealed himself to me as Aiwaz. PAVOZ as far as I am aware, is exclusive to this narrative. However I have not plumbed Her mysteries, and furthermore I had a nasty shock once when the O.T.O. turned up on my doorstep accusing me of stealing their deepest secrets; so if in your opinion the Name should not be Revealed, I offer to change the spelling to the anodyne and entirely harmless PAVUS, at the next edition - if there is one! A.C.*

reader if the sequence of events with PAVOZ is confined to dreams. There is not time, and certainly not space in a book of this scope, to go into the significance of the confusion, more apparent than real, of the other incarnation of my divine anaglyptic muse, my Eros, as the earthly Madame Poitier.)

PAVOZ had first revealed herself to me as a mighty angel swooping down over a ziggurat. In the second appearance, she revealed herself as the source of ultimate wisdom in Diana's temple in Cefalù. Written on her body were the Ultimate Mysteries.

The final revelation of PAVOZ took place outside the same ziggurat that she had first flown with me towards. I became aware that the bolts had been drawn back and the top door of the ziggurat was open, and I was outside, looking in at the square of light. Stretching away from the little buildings clustered at the feet of the mighty, seven-storied structure, the desert slept as before, the moon-silvered rivers in the distance.

I was puzzled that I could not have any sight of her, but then I realised as I drew away from the lighted square of the doorway, that the shaven headed, forbidding and archaic figure in its robes, framed in the doorway was me. For a few moments, I *was* PAVOZ, and PAVOZ was me.

This must have been in order to prevent my looking, and remembering, the symbols that covered her body. Looking through her eyes I tried to make her look down, but PAVOZ continued stubbornly looking at 'me'.

The figure in the ziggurat waved goodbye, and abruptly, the viewpoint ascended. The open door which had been as bright as the Dog star, was soon as hard to make out as one of the dimmer Pleiades, and then the little town in the desert was a dot, which then was erased, as Sin will be in the New Aeon.

I blinked, as PAVOZ rose faster than a meteor. The earth's curve could be seen, and then behind the earth, but close to it, almost jostling it, were the other planets of the solar system.[133] I heard most majestic music.[134] Then the vision faded.

I awoke just in time to squash a fat moth which had settled on the lapel of Raoul's double breasted graduation suit, intending to feast. There would be time enough for the worms, and all that, on the morrow.

What I had experienced in my vision was uniquely anagogic, and I came to my senses by Raoul's coffin with the most profound and comforting belief in the reality of astrology.

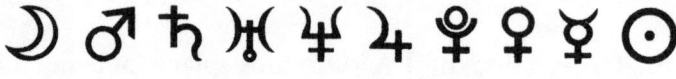

I also woke to find that Betty had come up undetected, and put her own shawl over my shoulders, to keep me from the early morning chill. But only when Sol had once again touched the eaves of the Abbey, did I stiffly give up my place, and go and dress, for Raoul's internment.

---

133   The planets were sized similarly so that Jupiter was not overwhelmingly vast. I believe that I was being shown through PAVOZ's eyes, a simple catalogue of the solar deities. A.C.

134   I confess I have difficulty recalling the musical theme at this instant, as a salesman lying in the next room as I write has just broken wind again, in his sleep, with a loud, and anachromatic areopagitica. Let Asterisks everywhere, Speak! A.C.

XXI The Universe

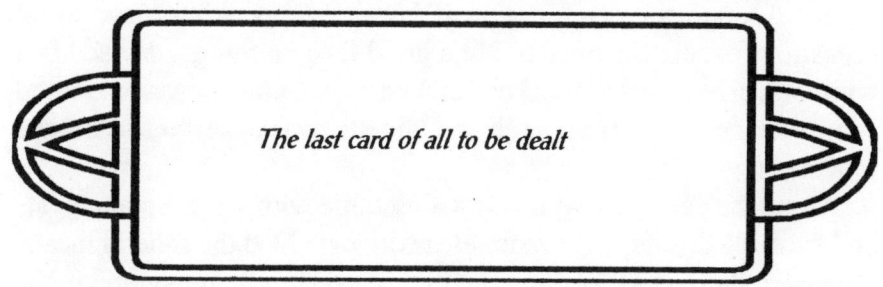

The last card of all to be dealt

Leah had opted to go into exile with me, thus, she believed checkmating Ninette's plans to become Scarlet Woman #1. In order to demolish Ninette's little intimacies for ever, Leah proposed leaving with me immediately after the funeral. We could take the train to Palermo the same day and from thence a steamer to Tunis, where I could commence dictating to her my autohagiography proper.[135]

I had mutely nodded my assent to everything that she proposed. If Leah had suggested a swim to Constantinople via Cape Town I would have meekly agreed. I simply had no steerage left and all the stuffing had been well and truly whacked out of me.

We buried Raoul outside the walled churchyard, which lay above the town. There was a small plateau outside it, and the grave was dug ready to receive the rude coffin that held his body. We followed it down from the house on a donkey cart, which Leah had reserved the use of afterwards for our own transport to the station. The Beast and his pregnant Scarlet Woman were going to leave on an ass, in true Biblical style.

---

135 *Not to be confused under any circumstances with this farrago of nonsense.* A.C.

Of the local population, Leah claimed two thousand turned up that day to watch the 'Purple Priest' put one of his acolytes underground. I went through the ceremony as if I was sleepwalking, dead to all sensations except the need to put a good face on things, dressed in a white silk priest's gown that I had picked up in China. Betty, who stood some distance away from Leah and Ninette, was nevertheless moved to tears.

Along the cemetery wall was a long table with wine, bread, meats and fruit. To this day, I have no idea who provided the funeral meats. However there was nothing in the Beaverbrook press about the miracle of the feeding of the two thousand.

I poured a libation of good red wine into the grave, and as the dry brown earth was shovelled back in, I recited my *Hymn to Pan*, to considerable applause from the crowd. It is a measure of success of my performance that while so few of the multitude gathered there spoke English, yet they instinctively understood the underlying feelings, and the yearning, above all for Rapture.

> ....*I am he that lifteth up*
> *Life, and flingeth it afar*
> *I have filled the crystal cup*
> *I have sealed the silver star*
> *I the wingless god that flieth*
> *Through my firmamental fane*
> *I am he that daily dieth*
> *And is daily born again*

It was so affecting that I am considering having it read at my own funeral, as well.

The donkey cart was next loaded with my manuscripts and possessions, and we set off again, down the little narrow track, with Leah and myself seated where Raoul's coffin had so recently been. We passed the cemetery where there were still a handful of people, as well as Betty, who had been standing in the same place, as still as a cypress.

But she broke away from her vigil, when she saw the cart with the suitcases in, and came over to say a formal farewell.

As we came into the town, Leah was trying to get the donkey-driver to hurry up. The Sicilians have no feeling for animals but in this case it was almost impossible, the little starved creature was so wretched it could barely pull the cart on the level ground with us in it. I got off to walk, just as we were about to enter the main square. There were numbers of people going in the same direction. I assumed they were leaving the funeral.

As the little donkey turned the corner, I saw the backs of ten caribineri, and beyond them, the square was packed with dark-clad peasants. Beyond them, a speaker on a podium declared the benefits of Fascism through a bad amplifying system, to a sea of stubbled, gnarled and sceptical faces.

In a matter of seconds, the donkey cart was trapped. The driver got into an incomprehensible argument with the caribineri. By this time it was too late to turn the cart around and try to get to the railway station by another route.

At this stage, there seemed to be little to do but sit back and enjoy the show. Ignoring the fracas between the caribineri and the donkey driver, I stood on the cart, the better to hear the usual false promises of '*Il Progresso!*' from a serious young man in spectacles declaiming in front of a microphone the size of a biscuit tin. A woman in the crowd passed me a basket of figs, and I amused myself by biting them open, then throwing them to a peasant girl with a mouth like a vast wound. Leah noticed the size of her rival's lips and tipped the rest of the figs to the floor. Out of the corner of my eye I caught a glimpse of Giles, one of life's taller Judases, standing listening near the corner of the cart. I pointedly ignored him. He had served his function, like Judas and now would be heard of no more.

I was suddenly accosted in English by a hysterical red-bearded figure wearing khaki shorts and sandals, with a small rucksack. For a moment I thought it might be D.H. Lawrence, returning to collect yet more calico from the post office. The speaker was from the north of

England and I remembered now, he had written to me asking if he could visit and find his True Will. He had no money, but I had agreed to let him come.

'Mr Crowley - name's Paul Simkins - I wrote to you from Barnsley, remember? I heard that there'd been a death, and that you're leaving?'

I held up my hand, with its impressive Akhnaten jewel, in benison.

'My goodness, is that a real diamond?' said Simkins.

'Of course it is. Don't worry, Paul, everything's going like clockwork. It's true I've had to leave, but the business of the Abbey continues. Its destiny is unstoppable. If you take the path up the hill, you will find Ninette Shumway, whose magickal name is Sister Cypris. She is remaining, and she will skilfully instruct you in *all* the rituals.' I winked at him, ' I shall return, though I have to pawn every precious stone I own.' The conversation ended as he was swept aside by the mob.

At the side of the cart, a fight now broke out between two gypsies, and the crowd, which felt so tightly packed, had immediately expanded to create a circle nine or ten feet wide, in which the combatants now circled, each one holding a knife. Excited warnings and encouragements came from all the men watching. At the same time, the speaker system in the square failed and all the attention of the sections of the crowd who could see them, was centred on the circling men.

The gypsy in his ragged headscarf and his knife on the one side, and on the other, a mirror image of himself. They circled each other as if they were in some sort of lethal dance, going round and round, with the left hand out, the right holding the weapon. I was quite indifferent to their fate but it seemed to me that if they could be persuaded to give up their quarrel, we might be able to win our way over to the other side of the square and to the approaching train.

While none of my readers will be under any illusion as to the constitution of the Akhnaten Diamond (originally rented from a forerunner of Berman's theatrical costumiers) the great ruby had the merit of being very noticeable, even at twelve feet. I leapt between the two contestants, and holding up my ring so it glinted in the sun, I recited the formula in Arabic for The Great Word About to become Mad And Go About Naked two or three times.[136] It seemed about as close to my state of mind as any ready made statement could be -

'Subhana Allahu Walhamdu lilahli walailaha illa allahu'

And then it was a question of eye contact - reader if you were here with me, I could show you. The power in these situations comes from exploiting the unexpected, and they certainly weren't expecting me, when they stopped their diabolical tango, to touch their knives, sanctifying the blades in Arabic with my magnificent Berman's Best. Subhana Allahu, indeed.

So when I touched their sacred weapons, whispering the formula for the third time, one of them dropped his knife in astonishment. From astonishment to mastery is a shallow step, provided it taken at speed. It was easy for me to snap my fingers: I knew I had hypnotised them both. They were alike as two peas in a pod and what one did, the other could not help but follow. I finally put my arms round them both, and reconciled them.

Everyone was staring at me. There was a gasp from the crowd, not so much one of shock, but an exhalation of admiration. I heard that sound once before in Africa, when a scorpion dancer cut his own jugular, so that his companions could dance in the pool of his life's blood:-

The crowd had recognised a Moment of Power.

The little pool of space around the two ex-fighters now broadened, and without a word being uttered there was a thoroughfare stretching right across the square, with edges as geometrically straight and

---

136 *Close the curtains [if you have them], before practising this at home. A.C.*

sharply delineated as if both sides had been lined by caribineri. A royal road. I looked to Leah to make sure she understood what had happened. She nodded at me smiling. She understood.

I took her hand. There was no point in delaying. All the faces in the crowd turned towards us. Hands stretched out to touch us.

With the little donkey dragging our luggage behind, staggering under the weight of its own sores under the harness,[137] we set out across what had been, a minute before, a packed fascist rally. It had now turned into a touching homage from an oppressed people to a monarch sent into banishment. They acknowledged his worth, and were paying homage in the only way they knew how, at his going into exile.

With Leah at my side, I turned the corner of the street. The same regimented crowds still lined each side of the further streets, with a rapt, religious air. Someone pressed a crown of laurel leaves, traditional for the victor in poetry and prophecy into my hands. I crowned myself as we walked. At the same time bouquets of white lilies were given to Leah by a smiling child. They may have indeed been the same lilies thrown onto Raoul's grave by Betty two hours back, recently robbed, but the past had been performed, and this was a new opera.

The procession turned again. I wanted to turn my head, to check that the little donkey was keeping up on the cobblestones. It looked on its last legs, but it seemed impious to question the arrangements when so much trouble had been taken.

'You see?' said Leah, out of the corner of her mouth. 'They love us.'

We turned the last corner before the station, and there was a threadbare but uniformed brass band from the fire brigade, waiting to play. The bony conductor, as soon as he saw us coming, rapped the top of his music stand with his wooden baton, and the band struck up a tune

---

[137] It was also responsible for transporting copies of several of the editions of Liber Legis, the bell, book and candles of the business of evocation, not to mention my Baphometwear - so perhaps it could be forgiven for staggering under its unquestionably weighty destiny! A.C.

from Verdi's Nabucco, a tune that was for many years the touchstone of Italian unity. Hearing it, the donkey brayed, and finally collapsed between the shafts. My unshaved scalp prickled, and the iceblock that had lain on my heart all day began to melt.

It is impossible to imagine a more graceful compliment, than to be feted by a whole town, then serenaded to the train with that most plangent of all the songs of exile, the Lament of the Hebrew Slaves.

In the distance, the hoots of the approaching steam train began to grow and mingle with the untongued lament of the Cefalù Fire Brigade's chief flugelhorn, which only ceased as the carriage doors opened for us.

Standing on the carriage steps I kissed Leah full on the lips, to applause, as faithful hands passed our luggage onto the train. Reluctantly, we both stepped inside, our passion roused by the crowd's warm sympathy.

As the locomotive drew the train out of the station, the whole platform was alive with other cheering wellwishers who clearly still wished to see us embrace. On the carriage door, beneath the open window I noticed it said, presciently -

É PERICOLOSO SPORGERSI[136]

I held Leah out of the window and she blew kisses to the cheering crowds, excitedly pulling the top of the sleeveless blue silk dress down to show her miniscule breasts. Really she had not much more on top than a boy. The train gathered speed. Under the dress, I began to frig her. My fingers in her mouth of Isis, my thumb's second joint secure in the Eye of Horus. *Do what thou wilt shall be the whole of the Law.*

Once more, the Master Therion and the Contessa de Kerval plunged recklessly into the Abyss of the unknown.

---

136 *'It is dangerous to lean out of the window'*

My tale ends here. And yet, I continue to live. I can hear Aiwass' resonant basso voice, in the velvet darkness, speaking in verses yet unscripted, urgent, imperious, with expressions that with all my scholarship I am still at a loss to understand -

......*'He is closer. He is ready. (Pause).....He waits.'*.....

What does it mean? What does *any of it* mean?

END

Other Mandrake Titles of Interest

Ramsey Dules, *What I Did In My Holidays - essays on black magic, satanism and devil worship*
420pp, 1869928-520 £18 pbk

Jan Fries, *Living Midnight, three movements of the Tao*
220pp, 1869928-504 £10.99, pbk

Kamil Zvelebil, *The Siddha Quest For Immortality*
Sexual, alchemical and medical secrets of the Tamil Siddhas, the *poets of the powers*.
192pp isbn 1869928-431 £9.99/$20 pbk illustrated

Nadia Choucha's *Surrealism and the Occult*
140pp 1869928-164, £8.99 pbk 16 Plates
'Highly readable...seminal...fascinating...'
Francis King writing in *Nuit Isis* II,i

Pan's Daughter - the magical world of Rosaleen Norton
by Nevill Drury
168pp, 48 illus, 1869928318 pbk, £7.99/$14.95

Shadow Matter and Psychic Phenomena
A scientific investigation into psychic phenomena and possible life after death
by Gerhard D Wassermann Ph.D, FIMA
200pp 1869928326 £7.95 /$15

Jean Overton Fuller's *Sickert and the Ripper Crimes*
1990, 260pp, 1869928-156 £14.95 hbk (and soon in paperback)
The author draws on the new evidence of Florence Pash, and with her artist's eye discovers clues in Sickert's pictures, pointing conclusively to

the true identity of the Ripper...
'new and important evidence..' Colin Wilson in *Hampstead & Highgate Express*

The Flying Sorcerer: Francis Barrett
by Francis King
Including Barrett's unpublished manuscript on Crystal Vision
80pp 1869928202 £6.99 /$9.99

Timothy d'Arch Smith's *The Books of the Beast*
1992 128pp, 1869928-172 £6.99/$14.99 pbk
The indispensable and authoritative guide to Aleister Crowley's magical first editions. Plus essays on Montague Summers; R A Caton and his Fortune Press; Ralph Chubb; Florence Farr; The British Library Private Case; and the Author himself.

Jean Overton-Fuller's *The Magical Dilemma of Victor Neuburg*
1990 270pp 1869928-121, 11 plates, £9.99,
A biography of Victor Neuburg, poet, magician and lover of Aleister Crowley.

**Available worldwide (ask your bookseller to order from New Leaf or Weisers). For information about other distributors, direct sales or details about future projects contact:
Mandrake of Oxford,
PO Box 250,
Oxford, OX1 1AP (UK)
tel +44 1865 243671, fax +44 1865 432929.
If you are connected to the internet you can email us on mandrake@mandrake.cix.co.uk.**